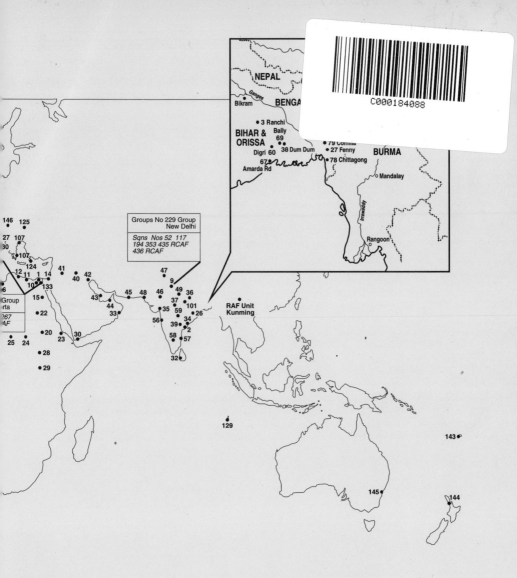

GROUPS & SQUADRONS

85	BOUCHERVILLE		
86	REYKJAVIK		
88	NASSAU		
89	JAMAICA		
90	ASCENSION IS		
91	EINDHOVEN		
92	CARPIQUET		
93	RENNES		
95	PIARCO (TRINIDAD)		
96	BORINQUEN		
97	MIAMI		
98	NATAL (BRAZIL)		
99	BELEM		
100	DORVAL		
101	SATNA		
102	IMPHAL		
103	ISTRES/MARIGNANE		
104	NIVELLES		
105	BRUSSELS		
107	ATHENS/HASSANI/SALONIKA		
120	PERRANPORTH		
121	LE BOURGET		
122	PERRANPORTH		
123	PERRANPORTH		
124	RHODES		
125	BANEASA (BUCHAREST)		
126	LYONS/PERRANPORTH		
127	BARI		
129	COCOS IS		
130	POMIGLIANO		
133	ALMAZA		
137	BORDEAUX		
138	TOULOUSE		
140	LOS ANGELES (HAMILTON FIELD)		
141	HONOLULU (HICKHAM FIELD)		
142	CANTON IS		
143	FIJI (NANDI)		
144	AUCKLAND (WHENUAPI)		
145	SYDNEY (MASCOT)		
146	BELGRADE		

HQ No 44	GROUP	GLOUCESTER
HQ No 45	GROUP	DORVAL
HQ No 216	GROUP	HELIOPOLIS/CASERTA
HQ No 46	GROUP	HARROW WEALD
HQ No 47	GROUP	HENDON
HQ No 229	GROUP	NEW DELHI
No 24	SQN	HENDON
No 48	SQN	DOWN AMPNEY
No 96	SQN	LECONFIELD
No 147	SQN	CROYDON/NORTHOLT
No 167	SQN	HOLMSLEY SOUTH
No 232	SQN	STONEY CROSS
No 233	SQN	BLAKEHILL FARM
No 238	SQN	MERRYFIELD
No 242	SQN	STONEY CROSS
No 243	SQN	MERRYFIELD
No 246	SQN	HOLMSLEY SOUTH
No 437	SQN	RCAF BLAKEHILL FARM
No 511	SQN	LYNEHAM
No 512	SQN	BROADWELL
No 525	SQN	LYNEHAM
No 575	SQN	BROADWELL
ADLS	SQN	NORTHOLT
MET COMM	SQN	HENDON/NORTHOLT
No 28	SQN	SAAF MAISON BLANCHE/BARI
No 44	SQN	SAAF CAIRO WEST/BARI
No 52	SQN	DUM DUM
No 117	SQN	BIKRAM
No 194	SQN	BASAL
No 216	SQN	CAIRO WEST/BARI etal
No 231	SQN	DORVAL
No 267	SQN	BARI
No 353	SQN	PALAM/DUM DUM
No 435 & 436	SQNS	RCAF GUJRAT

Forged in War

Approved

George R.I.

TRANSPORT COMMAND

ROYAL AIR FORCE

FERIO FERENDO

J.D. Heaton-Armstrong

Chester Herald
and Inspector of Royal
Air Force Badges.

College of Arms,
April, 1943.

Ministry of Defence
Air Historical Branch

Forged in War

A History of
RAF Transport Command
1943–1967

by
Humphrey Wynn

Air Historical Branch (RAF)
Ministry of Defence

1996

London: The Stationery Office

*Dedicated to the aircrew and
groundcrew who flew and serviced
transport and reinforcement aircraft
in the 1939–45 War and to
their successors in the post-war
Transport Command*

© Humphrey Wynn 1996

Applications for reproduction should be addressed to The Stationery Office,
St Crispins, Duke Street, Norwich NR3 1PD.

Crown copyright material used by kind permission of the Controller of HMSO.

First published 1996

ISBN 0 11 772756 3

Cataloguing in Publication Data
A CIP catalogue record for this book is available from the British Library

Contents

Foreword

by Air Chief Marshal Sir Thomas Prickett KCB DSO DFC
AOC-in-C Transport Command, January–August 1967

A HISTORY of RAF Transport Command is long overdue, and as its last Commander-in-Chief I am glad to welcome this one, written by Humphrey Wynn who has had many years' experience of research in the Air Historical Branch and was himself a pilot on wartime ferry and transport operations.

His title, *Forged in War*, is I think an apt one. The formation of Transport Command in 1943 gave organisational recognition to existing worldwide transport and reinforcement operations by the RAF – across the Atlantic (which had hitherto never been flown over with such frequency and regularity), to the Mediterranean theatre, across Africa and on to India. Soon after its formation the new Command was involved peripherally in Operation Husky (the invasion of Sicily), then in 1944–45 made direct contributions to the great airborne operations on D-day, over Arnhem and at the crossing of the Rhine.

During the Cold War crisis, the Command's Dakota, York and Hastings squadrons played a major part in sustaining the Berlin Airlift of 1948–49. Its Hastings and heavy-lift Beverleys supported the Suez operation of 1956. Its Comet 2s pioneered military jet transport services and its Britannias shared the long-range role with them. Tactical transports like the Argosy and Andover, plus helicopters and ground-attack Hunters, armed its revived No 38 Group from 1960 to enable Army/RAF air mobility forces to operate anywhere in the world. The Belfast 'heavy lifter' and VC10 jet transport came into service during 1966, the year before Air Support Command was formed.

In the 1950s and '60s, Transport Command consistently supported Bomber and Fighter Commands in their exercises, dispersals and overseas deployments, and its aircraft were constantly called upon for relief and emergency operations worldwide.

All in all, the 24 years' existence of Transport Command have amounted to a distinguished contribution to the annals of the Royal Air Force, and I am proud to have been its last C-in-C. The Command's achievements and operations have been worthily put on record for posterity in this valuable history.

Acknowledgements

TO my late colleague, Paul Wood, for the posthumous assistance of the many years' research he did into the history of RAF air transport operations. To the Head of the Air Historical Branch (RAF) of the Ministry of Defence, Group Captain Ian Madelin, RAF (Ret), for authorising my research into the records of Transport Command and making available to me the facilities of the AHB. To Group Captain Tony Stephens, RAF (Ret) (a former Transport navigator), for commenting on the text and compiling the Glossary. To Squadron Leader Joe Davies, RAF (Ret), for his dedicated skill in producing charts of the Command's formations, squadrons and aircraft, drawing maps of its routes and staging posts and for his help in selecting photographs. To Sqn Ldr Peter Singleton, RAF (Ret), for his invaluable liaison with HMSO. To Donna Walsh and her successor Leslie Morrison for their endless patience in ordering copies of Operations Record Books for Joe Davies and myself from the Public Record Office. To other members of the AHB staff at 3–5 Great Scotland Yard for the cheerful assistance given to me: S H Clarke of PCB (Air); Graham Day and Richard King of AHB5 and Don Blevin, Eileen Hill and Shirley Spooner of AHB4 for their assistance in producing RAF records; Mike Hatch of AHB3 and the late Betty Morley of the AHB Registry for her unfailing knowledge and help in administrative matters.

No one who works in the Air Historical Branch for any length of time, as I have done (both in full-time and consultancy employment), can fail to absorb its unique atmosphere of RAF information and dedicated research by its staff to find answers to historical questions – whether these come from Ministers, from the Air Staff, from MPs, from RAF or aviation industry public relations, from historians and authors or from members of the public asking about relatives or friends: all receive the same courteous and conscientious attention, from which I myself have benefited over many years.

Finally, thanks are due to Stuart McLaren, HMSO publishing manager, and his staff (particularly naming Lynda Turner, Emily Bates and Jennifer Hannaford) for their experience and technology which have transformed words, diagrams and photographs into a book, and to Dave Barlow of CS (Graphics) and his colleagues (Patricia Beauchamp and Patricia Carpenter) who so skilfully and so patiently printed the charts and maps. For any shortcomings, inherent or perceived, the author alone is responsible.

Humphrey Wynn

A note on Rank abbreviations

When the RAF was formed in 1918 from the air elements of the Army and the Royal Navy it created new ranks, which were longer than those of its parent Services: e.g. a Lieutenant became a Flying Officer, a Major a Squadron Leader. To use these ranks in full would be ponderous, so commonly accepted abbreviations have been employed. These are explained in the Glossary, as are those for decorations and medal awards.

Chapter I

Introduction

Everything must have a beginning

16th century proverb

THE CREATION OF RAF Transport Command in March 1943 did not signal the beginning of a new role for the Royal Air Force: it gave organisational recognition to transport and aircraft delivery operations which had been going on since the start of the Second World War, intensified by the supply of American machines flown across the Atlantic since 1940, by worldwide ferry flying and by an increasing number of transport squadrons. Like the self-sown oak tree, the reinforcement and air transport business had become big and widespread, fertilised by ever-increasing wartime demands. So, as the Secretary of State for Air (Sir Archibald Sinclair) put it in the House of Commons on 11 March 1943: 'I have, therefore, decided to establish a Royal Air Force Transport Command'.

Why was such a Command not created sooner? The answer was, quite simply, a shortage of transport aircraft. The emphasis pre-war in RAF Operational Requirements, and hence in design and production, had been on bombers and fighters and on maritime reconnaissance types. The only indigenous British bomber/transport aircraft were the high-wing, fixed-undercarriage Bombays and Harrow transports known as Sparrows. As the Minister put it:

'To create such a Command sooner would have been to put the cart before the horse. It has not been commanders and staff that we have been short of, but aircraft. Now the Command will come naturally into being through the process of bringing supply and organisation into focus'.

The new Command, formed on 25 March 1943, was made up of three existing Groups and a Wing: No 44 Group in the UK; No 45 (Atlantic Transport) Group (formerly RAF Ferry Command) in Montreal; No 216 Group in Cairo and No 179 (Ferry) Wing in Karachi. The AOC No 45 Group, Air Chief Marshal Sir Frederick Bowhill, was appointed Air Officer Commanding-in-Chief. With its component formations in the UK, Canada, Egypt and India, Transport Command had an international status and outlook from the start. Its purpose was 'to undertake the responsibility for the organisation and operation of all Service Air Lines, Service Air Movements of freight and personnel, and Overseas and

Inter-continental delivery of aircraft by operational and ferry air routes'. This official description of its roles said nothing about the military operations in which the new Command was soon to become involved.

Transport Command went into battle five times during the Second World War: supporting the invasion of Sicily in 1943 (Operation Husky) and the abortive Dodecanese Islands operations later that year (Operation Accolade), spearheading the Allied invasion of Europe in 1944 (Operation Overlord), transporting the airborne forces in the ill-fated attempt to capture the Arnhem bridges in September of that year (Operation Market), and carrying troops across the Rhine in March 1945 for the final onslaught on Nazi Germany (Operation Varsity). Care has been taken in this work to describe only operations by Groups and squadrons under Transport Command control, difficult though it has been to resist the temptation to describe heroic transport support operations – for example in Burma – by squadrons in other Commands.

When the war in Europe had been won, Transport Command squadrons were employed in a massive trooping operation – to take reinforcements out to the Far East for a final onslaught against the Japanese and to bring home repatriated Servicemen. After Japan's unconditional surrender on 14 August 1945 this airlift continued – bringing troops home and flying out replacements.

At the end of the Second World War the Transport Command organisation spanned the globe. At 1 May 1945 it had seven Groups, 19 Wings, 47 stations, 36 squadrons and 161 staging posts (all but three of them overseas), not to speak of a host of miscellaneous units. On 7 May it took over No 4 (Bomber) Group – 12 stations and 14 squadrons – and three Liberator squadrons from Coastal Command. These acquisitions gave it an additional long-range capability.

What was to be done with this large wartime-created Command, once the hostilities it had supported were over?

There was no question of it being disbanded. 'Experience has shown', said an Air Staff paper of 28 May 1945, 'that Air Transport has a lasting place in the RAF which cannot be filled by other forms of transport or by the Merchant Air Fleet'. However, organisational changes had to be made: the overseas Commands were to be given autonomy in matters of air transport. On 3 February 1946 the Air Council decided that Nos 216, 229 and 232 Groups were to become MEDME (Mediterranean and Middle East), BAFSEA (British Air Forces South East Asia – later AHQ India) and ACSEA (Air Command South East Asia) Groups respectively instead of being Transport Command Groups.

Thus one of the Groups from which Transport Command was originally formed, No 216, reverted to its original local status. On 5 March an Air Ministry Directive delegated the Command's responsibilities to individual overseas Commands.

The Command also suffered post-war, as did the RAF as a whole, from the loss of experienced aircrew and groundcrew through demobilisation[1];

---

1 As will be seen, Releases from the RAF in 1946 created acute manpower problems.

and the supply of American aircraft like Dakotas and Liberators was going to dry up with the ending of Lease-Lend arrangements. The Air Ministry would have to produce new types from British industry to replace them. Only one machine, the four-engined Handley Page Hastings, was already in the pipeline: its maiden flight was in 1946.

The Command's post-war policy had been defined in mid-1947, with the tasks which its squadrons would be required to carry out in war set down as transport support and route transport operations – those tasks which, in addition to the ferrying of aircraft, it had successfully fulfilled during the 1939–45 conflict.

Within three years the Command had to face a major crisis in Operation Plainfare, the RAF/USAF Berlin airlift of 1948–49, when its aircraft were Dakotas (still), Yorks (which had made their debut in 1943), Valettas and the Hastings (the first post-war British transport aircraft, in service only since 1948, succeeding Yorks on long-range routes).

The Command was also peripherally involved in the Korean War (June 1950–July 1953) with the airlift of British troops to Japan – flights made in the earliest days (October 1950) of the United Nations operation – and with the evacuation of casualties.

A regular weekly service began in February 1951 and continued until 1953. No 47 Squadron, based at Topcliffe, positioned a single Hastings in Singapore at Changi, with a crew. Four lifts were made each month to Iwakuni, Japan, taking British forces in support of operations in Korea and flying out casualties – British, Turkish, Greek, Dutch, Belgian, Indian and French. Each crew was relieved after four weeks' duty.

During the mid-1950s Transport Command was involved in the Suez Operation of October–November 1956 and received into service two highly different types of aircraft – the Blackburn Beverley and de Havilland Comet. The Beverley, specially designed for Army/RAF air support operations, was commodious but slow. The Comet had put Britain into the vanguard of jet airliner services until three tragic accidents to BOAC Comets in 1953 and 1954 put paid to the type's civil success until it could be modified to withstand the airframe stresses imposed on its pressurised cabin at high altitudes.

The Comets operated by Transport Command from mid-1956 onwards were the Mk 2 versions, modified for service with the RAF, which No 216 Sqn – that famous old squadron from Middle East days – flew and maintained with conspicuous success.

During 1957 the Command achieved three distinctions with its Comets – in September making the first direct Atlantic crossing by an aircraft of this type, in October starting a weekly service to Christmas Island in support of the nuclear tests there and in November–December conveying the AOC-in-C (Air Marshal Sir Andrew McKee) on a round-the-world flight of 32,000 miles in 72 hours' flying time.

Side by side with the Comets in the 1960s but with much greater freight-carrying capacity were the turboprop Bristol Britannias, which went into service in mid-1959 as carriers for the Army's strategic reserve, supplementing the Beverley's voluminous cargo capability with greater speed and range. These were Britannia 253s and they were joined in the

Command during 1961 by a tactical freighter, the Hawker Siddeley Argosy (Armstrong Whitworth AW660).

At another extreme there was intensified Army/RAF co-operation, with the Beverleys and Whirlwind helicopters of No 38 Group (revived in 1960) practising for deployment to any overseas area where British forces might be called upon to act in a peace-keeping role.

The Command's helicopter force was also increased, with Sycamores (1959), Whirlwinds (1960), the twin-rotor Belvedere (1961) and the Wessex (1964). In November 1962 the Air Minister (Mr Hugh Fraser) was able to list the Command's full complement of aircraft as 23 Britannias, 11 Comets, 48 Hastings, 28 Beverleys, 27 Twin Pioneers, four Pembrokes, 26 Whirlwinds, ten Sycamores and 18 Belvederes – a varied and very comprehensive range of types.

Three new types of aircraft were delivered to Transport Command in 1966 – the Short Belfast in January, the British Aircraft Corporation VC10 in July and the Hawker Siddeley Andover in December, respectively a heavy-lift long-range freighter (Shorts' 'Big Lifter', as it was called), a strategic transport which could fly 150 men and their kit to Singapore with only one stop, and a medium-range passenger/freight aircraft with short take-off and landing capability.

These were types whose origins went back to 1957–59 and 1960 respectively when the Operational Requirements for them were first drawn up.

Transport Command was to have had a STOL (short take-off and landing) transport, the Armstrong Whitworth AW681, which would have replaced the Hastings and the Beverley. But this project (to OR3510) was cancelled by the Labour Government in February 1965 as part of its sweeping review of the Defence programme. Instead, Lockheed C-130s were ordered and entered service in April 1967. This was the first American type to be flown in Transport Command since its wartime Dakotas, Hudsons and Liberators.

With this new equipment came a change of name. When the first Hercules C.1 was delivered to No 36 Squadron on 1 August 1967, Transport Command ceased to exist, becoming Air Support Command – though its historic roles, performed for 24 years in support of UK defence policy, continued against the background of an ever-changing scenario.

Chapter II

Prologue: A Command is Formed

'. . . happy prologues to the swelling act
Of the imperial theme . . .'

Shakespeare, Macbeth, *I iii*

WHEN RAF Transport Command was called into existence by Parliamentary proclamation on 25 March 1943 its component parts had already been on active service for three-and-a-half years. Like a great tree with many branches, it had widespread roots. Its chief functions of ferrying and transport had grown under the demands of a world war. A network of reinforcement routes crossed the Atlantic and Africa; UK-based transport squadrons had played an active supporting role in the Battles of France and Britain and had carried supplies to beleaguered Malta; and the Middle East Air Force transport wing had operated in co-operation with the Eighth Army – a first use of integrated tactical air power, setting a precedent – with the addition of airborne forces – for the Italian and European campaigns of 1943–45.

Middle East transport squadrons

Air transport had been an integral part of RAF operations in the Middle East since the 1920s, because of the huge distances between stations – principally between Cairo and Baghdad – and the importance of maintaining communications, particularly by the mail service. In the United Kingdom, air transport took fourth place in the RAF to the demands of the bomber, fighter and maritime squadrons in the rearmament programme of the 1930s. The only military transports which went into service before the war were dual-purpose bomber/transport aircraft, the Bristol Bombay and Handley Page Harrow, neither of which was used as a bomber because they were superseded by more up-to-date designs like the Hampden, Wellington and Whitley. This lack of transport aircraft was one reason – as will be seen – for the delay in forming Transport Command.

The Middle East air transport role had been created and sustained by two squadrons, Nos 70 and 216, initially with First World War twin-engined bombers – Handley Page 0/400s and Vickers Vimys. (Although the latter type had not been used on operations it had proved itself as a long-range aircraft by making the first non-stop Atlantic crossing in 1919, piloted by Capt John Alcock with Lt Arthur Whitten Brown as navigator). The squadrons' geographical scenario – great stretches of featureless desert – made air transport an operational necessity, and their aircraft could revert to the bomber role when an emergency occurred. In the 1920s they formed part of the 'colonial policing' role performed by Britain in the Middle East, in which air power – as advocated by Sir Hugh Trenchard and supported by Winston Churchill – was a crucial element.

When stationed at Hinaidi, Iraq, in 1922 (before the great base at Habbaniyah was built) No 70 Sqn with its Vickers Vernons – successors to the Vimys – transported urgent stores to Kirkuk during operations on the Turkish frontier; and in September of that year two of its aircraft were involved in evacuating the garrison at Sulaimania when it was besieged by tribesmen. These were very early examples of airlifts by the RAF. Then in 1923 the Vernons began carrying the Cairo–Baghdad air mail[1].

Both Middle East transport squadrons subsequently re-equipped with Vickers Valentias, No 70 operating from Habbaniyah and No 216 from Heliopolis near Cairo, and continued in this role until Italy entered the Second World War. No 70 then became a bomber squadron with Wellingtons and No 216 – of which much more will be heard in this history – received Bristol Bombays in November 1939.

There was thus a natural tradition of air transport in the Middle East, and No 216 became one of the four squadrons in the transport group (No 216) of the Desert Air Force, supporting the Eighth Army in its advances, retreats and final victorious push westwards to Tunis. The other squadrons were Nos 267, 117 and 173 and between them they operated Bombays, Lodestars, Hudsons, DC-2s and Dakotas (DC-3s)[2]. In late 1941 a detachment of No 31 Sqn came from India in support, flying ageing DC-2s.

UK air transport

In the UK the air transport situation was quite different, not only in geographical but also in organisational terms, and it was quite clear that this role was a Cinderella to bomber, fighter and maritime squadrons. At the beginning of the Second World War there was just a squadron at Hendon (No 24) and a flight at Doncaster (No 1680), both controlled by Fighter Command.

No 24 (Communications) Sqn spent the first day of the Second World War moving into new premises just vacated by two Auxiliary Air Force fighter squadrons – No 601 which had gone to Biggin Hill and No 604 which had gone to North Weald. No 24's role was the transport of VIPs and the carriage of mail for the Services. While its administrative and flying control was vested in Fighter Command, it also had two other bosses: 'The control of ADLS [Air Despatch Letter Service] will be

---

1 See *The Baghdad Air Mail*, by Wg Cdr Roderic Hill (Edward Arnold & Co, 1929), who became AOC-in-C Air Defence of Great Britain in 1944.

2 One of the most dramatic operations was by Hudsons of No 117 Sqn, which on 13 November 1942 moved No 243 Wing from Amiriya to LG 125 – well behind enemy lines – from which its Hurricanes strafed retreating Afrika Korps units, taking them totally by surprise. See *In the Midst of Things* (Hodder and Stoughton, 1986), the autobiography of Marshal of the Royal Air Force Lord Cameron who led the Hurricanes.

exercised by Director of Signals', noted the Operations Record Book[3], 'and for all other Communications purposes the unit will be controlled by the Director of Staff Duties'. The squadron had a motley collection of aircraft, some of which came from internal airlines.

The squadron's Operations Record Book (ORB) for September 1939 records a diversity of types, some of them impressed for war service, like a Lockheed 10A (Electra) of British Airways which arrived at Hendon for affiliation to the unit for Communications work and two DH 89As of Isle of Man Air Services which came to No 24 Sqn on similar terms. Its other aircraft at the start of the war were a Vega Gull, a DH 86B (four-engined civil airliner, an enlarged version of the Rapide), a Q6 twin-engined Percival monoplane and a DH95 Flamingo, a high-wing monoplane civil airliner, the first mention of which in the squadron records occurs on 26 October 1939.

The chief function of the other air transport unit in the UK at the start of the Second World War, No 1680 Flight at Doncaster, was the movement of fighter squadrons – a crucially important role during the Battle of Britain, for while the fighters themselves and their pilots could move swiftly from one airfield to another the squadron groundcrew and equipment had to be air-transported with equal swiftness, into or out of the front line. This accounted for No 1680 Flight's location at Doncaster, midway between RAF stations in the north of England and Scotland and those in the southern counties.

But during the desperate days of the Battle of France and the evacuation of British forces No 271 Sqn – to which No 1680 Flight was upgraded in 1940 – operated mainly from Manston. Indeed, two of its pilots (Fg Off Williamson and Plt Off Hawley) who arrived there late in the day on 16 May 1940 'gathered the impression that all the transport and communications aircraft of the RAF were there'.

No 271 Sqn achieved its squadron status in March 1940: a pencilled note in the Operations Record Book says that it was formed on 28 March in 12 Group, Fighter Command, and later (on 27 April) transferred to Bomber Command. Its aircraft in May 1940 were a Ford TriMotor, four Savoia Marchettis (one of which was shot down over France on the 22nd), two Harrows and three Bombays – although the ratio of the two last-named types was changed as more Harrows (or 'Sparrows' as they were known after conversion from the bomber role) arrived on the squadron, Bombays being far more numerous in the Middle East on No 216 Sqn. Indeed, No 271's ORB records that the OC No 70 Sqn, Acting Sqn Ldr Wells, had arrived in the UK and gone to Doncaster on attachment on 24 May to ferry a Bombay back to Egypt. He was still with No 271 in June, for on the 19th he made what seems to have been the squadron's last flight from France – in a Handley Page Type 42 from Nantes to Jersey and from there to Hendon. No 24 Sqn had been instructed by the Air Ministry on

3 There will be frequent references in this history to the 'Operations Record Books', often abbreviated to 'ORB'. These are the unit diaries, compiled month-by-month by every squadron and established formation in the Royal Air Force. All are eventually lodged in the Public Record Office.

the 17th that routine flights to France were to cease.

Both UK-based transport squadrons played heroic and hard-pressed parts in the Battles of France and Britain. No 24 Sqn had set up an AASF (Advanced Air Striking Force) detachment near Rheims on 18 January 1940 to supersede the civilian-run ADLS (Air Despatch Letter Service), and this continued to operate until the evacuation from France, the squadron ORB proudly stating: 'During the whole of the evacuation mail went to AASF HQ every day'. From 19 May the mail run was continued to Paris's Le Bourget instead of Amiens and from the 23rd to Villacoublay instead of Le Bourget.

It was No 24 Sqn which carried Prime Minister Winston Churchill to France on 11 June 1940 to find out 'what the French were going to do', as he recalled in Volume II of *The Second World War*[4]:

'I ordered the Flamingo to be ready at Hendon after luncheon, and, having obtained the approval of my colleagues at the morning Cabinet, we started about two o'clock'.

Flamingo R2764 of No 24 Sqn, piloted by the squadron commander, Wg Cdr H K Goode, with Flt Lt Blennerhassett and Plt Off Bisley, took off from Hendon at 15 15hr for Paris, conveying the Prime Minister on the fourth of his many momentous air journeys during the Second World War. It was followed by a second Flamingo, R2765, piloted by Fg Off Oldroyd, with Flt Lt H B Collins (who three days earlier had been awarded the DFC) and Flt Lt B Romanoff carrying Secretary for War Anthony Eden to the same destination.

Winston Churchill's account of this journey continued:

'... since military conditions evidently predominated, I asked the Secretary of State for War, Mr Eden, to come with me, as well as General Dill, now CIGS, and of course Ismay[5]. The German aircraft were now reaching far down into the Channel, and we had to make a still wider sweep. As before, the Flamingo had an escort of twelve Hurricanes. After a couple of hours we alighted at a small landing-ground. ...'

In its record of this flight, the ORB of No 24 Sqn simply says 'Hendon – Paris', and makes no mention of the return. Churchill refers to 'our departure from Tours at about half-past five' and says: 'I slept sound on our swift and uneventful journey home'.

Clearly, Nos 24 and 271 Sqns made their mark early in the Second World War and their work set the standards by which Transport Command was later to become famous, for the reliability and undramatic work of its squadrons.

---

4 Cassell & Co, 1949.
5 Churchill's Chief of Staff.

But Transport Command's origins were not based only on these operations from the UK. There were also the great reinforcement routes established across Africa and across the Atlantic. These came into being because of the wartime need for Lease-Lend aircraft to be delivered quickly and in large numbers from North American factories to theatres of war in Europe and the Middle East.

The West African (Takoradi to Cairo) Reinforcement Route had its origins in the 1920s and '30s. In 1925 the then Sqn Ldr Andrew ('Mary') Coningham of No 216 Sqn, who was to become AOC the Desert Air Force in 1941, made one of the pioneering survey flights in a Fairey IIID to Kano in Nigeria (the route to the Cape was also surveyed). Four years later Flt Lt O R Gayford, who became famous in 1933 for a non-stop UK–South Africa flight, 'visited Takoradi and examined site for landing ground' (to quote from the AHB Narrative)[6]. His visit was followed-up by one from Mr W A Campbell of the Air Ministry and in due course (1936) landing-grounds were created at both Takoradi, where a port had been operating since 1930, and Accra – midway to Lagos, which was to be the first servicing stop on the reinforcement route.

The decision to designate Takoradi–Khartoum (in the Anglo–Egyptian Sudan) via Kano in Nigeria as the reinforcement route was taken by the Air Ministry on 20 June 1940. In July two senior officers arrived at Takoradi to look into the practical implications of shipping-in aircraft there and flying them up to the Middle East. Gp Capt H K Thorold got there on the 14th with an Advance Party aboard SS *Durban Castle* and Air Cdre L H Slatter flew in by BOAC aircraft from Khartoum. As a result of consultations and reports by their officers they decided that the scheme for RAF Takoradi and the en-route staging posts was feasible, and on the 22nd signalled the Air Ministry to that effect.

With remarkable speed, from the end of July 1940, RAF Station Takoradi was planned and constructed, and on the 30th the Officer i/c Flying (Actg Sqn Ldr A W Sweeney) and the Chief Signals Officer (Sqn Ldr Shepperd Smith) went up the route by chartered BOAC aircraft to make a second survey – following that from Khartoum by Air Cdre Slatter. It was to be a long haul for the ferry pilots who were to fly along it to Egypt in convoys from September 1940 onwards, originally a flight of Hurricanes led by a Blenheim.

Their first stage (378 st mi) from Takoradi to Lagos was flown just out to sea, keeping the West African coastline in sight; the second (525 st mi) from Lagos to Kano was mainly over forests; the third and fourth – Kano to Maiduguri (325 st mi) and Maiduguri to El Geneina (689 st mi) – led out of Nigeria into the Sudan, across scrubland, sandy wastes and marshes; the fifth, from El Geneina to Khartoum, mainly across deserts (754 st mi), took the aircrew to the confluence of the White and Blue Niles, one of the great sights of the world; then they followed the Nile via Wadi Halfa, the length of this final leg to their destination in Egypt, if it was Abu Sueir, being 1,026 st mi. The total length of the West African Reinforce-

---

6 'The West African Reinforcement Route'. AHB Narrative. PRO AIR 41/38.

THE WEST AFRICAN
REINFORCEMENT ROUTE

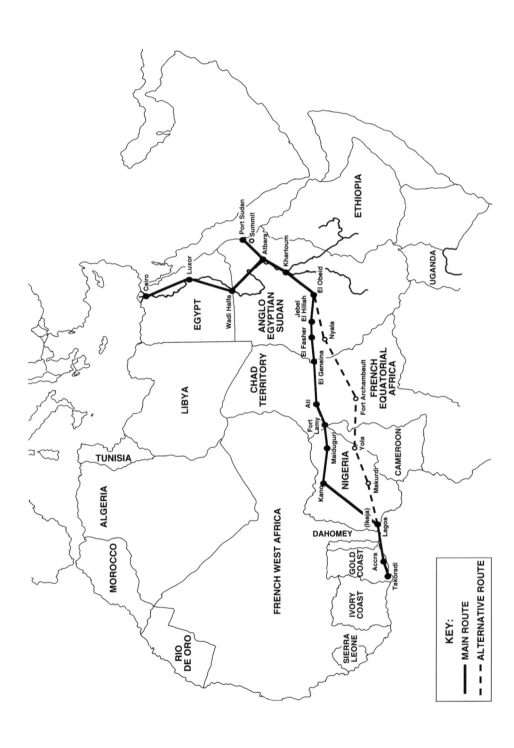

KEY:
—— MAIN ROUTE
– – – ALTERNATIVE ROUTE

ment Route was thus about 3,697 st mi, and each convoy took some four days (with night stops – there was no night flying). Each of the five main staging posts had to provide servicing, refuelling and accommodation and were staffed accordingly.

On 21 August 1940 the main RAF party reached Takoradi aboard MT *Aska* and five days later those of them who were to staff the staging posts were sent up the route. A Ferry Pilots' Pool was formed from aircrew who had arrived with the main party. It was originally decided that pilots should be based at Takoradi and flown back there by BOAC charter, but in the event they were based in Cairo. This was a wise decision, because route flying in single-engined aircraft under the unaltering glare of a tropical sun for stage lengths of up to 3hr 40min was an intensive experience and Egypt offered better recreational facilities than West Africa. Convoys were to consist of one Blenheim (with pilot, navigator and wireless operator) leading six Hurricanes.

RAF Takoradi was placed under the command of a newly formed Group, No 203, at Khartoum, with Air Cdre Slatter as AOC, and the Egyptian section of the route became the responsibility of No 202 Group at Heliopolis.

By September 1940 the West African Reinforcement Route was in business: on the 5th and 6th two consignments of aircraft arrived, six Blenheims and six Hurricanes in crates aboard SS *Berreby* and 30 Hurricanes, complete except for mainplanes and long-range tanks, in the carrier HMS *Argus*. On the 19th the first convoys took off, Flt Lt Blackwood with 1st Off Rendell of BOAC in a Blenheim leading six Hurricanes. Eight days later, on the 27th, they arrived at No 102 MU, Abu Sueir. One of the great air supply lines of the Second World War had been successfully opened up.

In December 1940 the Air Ministry decided that the output of aircraft from Takoradi should be 120–150 a month and other types started to follow the Blenheims and Hurricanes up the route, including Curtiss Mohawks and Glenn Martin Marylands, the first of the latter to be assembled making a successful test flight on the 12th. On 27 November fifteen Hurricanes and three Fairey Fulmars had flown off from HMS *Furious*. The Hurricanes were a first instalment of 36 of No 73 Sqn being sent to the Middle East in Operation Stripe, and during four days from 29 November they left in convoys of six aircraft led by Blenheims for their desert destination.

When on 2 December Air Marshal A W Tedder arrived at Takoradi on his way to take up the appointment of Deputy AOC-in-C Middle East he said he was 'very impressed by what Thorold and his people have done'. A year later, as AOC-in-C, he was to tell a group of West African Reinforcement Route ferry pilots in Cairo, among them the author: 'You are our lifeline'.

The other main reinforcement route – across the Atlantic – opened up a couple of months after that from Takoradi to Cairo; on 11 November 1940 seven Lockheed Hudson Mk IIIs arrived at RAF Aldergrove in Northern Ireland having flown non-stop from Gander in Newfoundland in 10½ hours. This historic flight not only marked the breaking of the 'Atlantic barrier' and the initiation of regular west–east and east–west flights across that broad ocean (though the Return Ferry Service did not begin until May 1941) but also the further establishment of worldwide air routes which were to become the arteries of RAF Transport Command.

The impetus for Atlantic deliveries stemmed from the British Purchasing Commission's order in June 1938 for 200 Hudsons to bolster the medium-range reconnaissance force of Avro Ansons in Coastal Command. The first of these Hudsons were delivered by sea, arriving in Liverpool on 15 February 1939. But when war came, a swifter and safer means of delivery was required – by air.

As in the case of the West African Reinforcement Route, much planning had gone on before the first aircraft were delivered. In July 1940 at the initiative of the Minister of Aircraft Production, Lord Beaverbrook, the first steps were taken to form a unit – which came to be known as ATFERO (Atlantic Ferrying Organisation) – for the air supply of military aircraft (50 Hudsons initially) to Britain. Following a request from Mr Morris Wilson of the British Embassy and the Air Section of the British Purchasing Commission (BPC), Mr G E Woods Humphery, who had formerly been managing director of Imperial Airways, undertook to build up this organisation quickly, and the BPC said that the Hudsons would be delivered to ATFERO in August and September 1940[7].

Mr Woods Humphery started the organisation with a nucleus of people from British Overseas Airways Corporation who had served under him in Imperial Airways, and engaged additional pilots from the USA and radio operators from Canada.

Unlike the Takoradi route which was flown by Service pilots – RAF, Fleet Air Arm or Polish Air Force – the North Atlantic ferry crews came initially from widely differing aviation backgrounds: US or Canadian airlines, or bush flying (as epitomised in the film *Captains of the Clouds* where ex-bush pilot James Cagney delivers a Hudson to the UK), or the RAF. One of the original members of ATFERO was Capt D C T Bennett who was made Flying Superintendent at Dorval, the Montreal Airport which was the departure point for wartime transatlantic flights, and led the first Hudsons to make the crossing to Northern Ireland. Subsequently he rejoined the RAF and became AOC No 8 (Pathfinder) Group in Bomber Command[8].

Many other types of aircraft followed the pioneering Hudsons across the Atlantic. Between November 1940 and November 1944 RAF deliveries totalled 4,321 – 819 Hudsons, 672 Liberators, 558 B-25 Mitchells, 541 Catalinas, 516 Dakotas, 195 Canadian-built Mosquitos (one of which, piloted by Capt Gill, made the fastest direct crossing – 6hr 8min on 29 November 1944), 149 B-17s and 142 Canadian-built Lancasters.

USAAC/F (the Army Air Corps became 'Army Air Forces' in June

---

7 These details are derived from the ORB of RAF Ferry Command. See also *Ocean Bridge The History of RAF Ferry Command*, by Carl A Christie, University of Toronto Press/Midland Publishing Ltd, 1995.

8 See *Master Airman A Biography of Air Vice-Marshal D C T Bennett CB CBE DSO* by Alan Bramson; Airlife, 1985.

1941) deliveries via the Northern route were more than twice as great, at 10,468, reflecting the build-up of strategic and tactical air forces and the demands of Operation Overlord: 6,628 B-17s, 2,254 B-24s, 632 C-47s, 194 P-38s and 111 B-25s. A southern route from Natal in Brazil to Accra in West Africa had been opened in 1942.

At the Eastern end of the North Atlantic route, handling incoming deliveries as well as those going out to the Middle East, was the OAMCU (Overseas Air Movements Control Unit) which had been set up at Gloucester in October 1940 and was like a Clapham Junction of the air. So busy and responsible were its functions that in August 1941 it was raised in status to become No 44 Group. Its equivalent in Montreal had become Ferry Command a month earlier, with Air Chief Marshal Sir Frederick Bowhill as C-in-C.

No 44 Group organised the British receiving end for all aircraft coming across the Atlantic and for those going out to the Mediterranean and Far East theatres. It was based at Gloucester because the Air Ministry W/T receiving station (keying high-power/high-frequency transmitters for point-to-point communications between the UK and Newfoundland, and for the ground-to-air radio channel) was near there at Birdlip. Not only was it concerned with American aircraft being delivered to the RAF and with RAF overseas reinforcements; it also had to handle USAAF aircraft coming to Britain under Operation Bolero, the build-up of American air forces in the UK to support a projected Allied invasion of Europe. This build-up was on an enormous scale, especially during 1943. Entries in the Group's ORB reflect the number of aircraft movements, both westwards or eastwards. Thus on 6 March, 'SASO (Senior Air Staff Officer) notifies that 70 USAAF aircraft are to land in Cornwall during the afternoon. 18 will go to Portreath. In addition, 18 P-38s will land at Portreath.' Then on 24 April: 'Prestwick TAC (Transit Atlantic Control) inform us that they expect 65 B-17s "Bolero", 12 already airborne and diversions may be necessary. We inform them that diversion stations, Nutts Corner and Langford Lodge, still hold good'.

The logistics of receiving such large numbers of aircraft and their crews were formidable, and the responsibility of briefing RAF crews for their outward flights to overseas theatres was a heavy one. The crews were trained at No 44 Group Ferry Units.

The Group had also had a transport function, providing a passenger and freight service between the UK and overseas theatres. But as its responsibilities for reception, training and reinforcement increased this function was relinquished and taken over by a separate formation, No 116 Wing at Hendon, which by the end of 1944 controlled six squadrons: Nos 24 at Hendon, 511, 246 and 525 at Lyneham, and 232 and 242 at Stoney Cross.

To the Middle East via Gibraltar

In addition to the main reinforcement routes across the North and South Atlantic and across Africa there was a route to the Middle East via Gibraltar controlled by OAMCU (No 44 Group). At the ends of the main routes there were the units whose pilots flew the aircraft to squadrons (or, in the Western Desert, to RSUs – Repair and Salvage Units). In the UK these comprised men and women members of the ATA (Air Transport Auxiliary); in the Middle East, RAF pilots of the ADUs (Aircraft Delivery Units).

Aircraft sent out to the Middle East – Blenheims, Beauforts, Wellingtons or Beaufighters – were flown by their own crews, taking off from Portreath in Cornwall for a perilous transit of the Bay of Biscay en route to Gibraltar and then to Malta. The route was perilous in two senses – the long sea crossing and the threat posed by the Luftwaffe Ju 88s or Condors.

In a biography of Air Marshal Sir Ivor Broom[9] the author describes how the then Sgt I G Broom and his crew of No 114 Sqn, posted to the Middle East in September 1941 after doing 12 operations from West Raynham, were chosen to lead a convoy of six Blenheims from Portreath because they were the most experienced crew. They got their charges safely to Luqa with one exception, an aircraft which sheered off and force-landed in Sicily. But there were many losses, owing to bad weather, enemy action, faulty navigation or shortage of fuel. Gp Capt Patrick Foss who in April 1942 became Assistant Director of ADO(F) (Assistant Directorate of Organisation (Ferrying)) at the Air Ministry was concerned that one aircraft in four flying to Malta was being lost.

OAMCU's output was initially small: by the end of 1940 fewer than 30 aircraft had gone down the route, but from the beginning of 1941 there was a steadily increasing upward trend; by June of that year some 250 aircraft a month were being controlled, compared with an average of nine a month in 1940. This increase showed the need for a large-scale organisation, not only to maintain the flow of aircraft, but to keep up with the rapidly accelerating pace. It was, therefore, decided to place the whole organisation under the control of the RAF by the creation in July 1941 of Ferry Command, with its headquarters first in Montreal – later at Dorval Airport – with, as mentioned, Air Chief Marshal Sir Frederick Bowhill as C-in-C[10]. He was later to become the first Commander-in-Chief of Transport Command.

After Ferry Command had been set up, signifying the transfer of control of Atlantic Ferrying from the Ministry of Aircraft Production to the Air Ministry, OAMCU was elevated in status, becoming No 44 Group in August 1941, and during the following year it was involved in two significant operations – air support of Malta and the Allied landings in North Africa.

The 'Malta shuttles' (via Gibraltar) were flown by Hudsons of No 24 Sqn, the first on 31 May 1942 with 2,000lb of freight, from Hendon via Lyneham and Portreath. After the third on 7 June the squadron received a message of congratulations from the Air Ministry:

---

9 *Clean Sweep The Life of Air Marshal Sir Ivor Broom KCB CBE DSO DFC[xx] AFC* by Tony Spooner DSO DFC (Crécy Books, 1994).

10 History and Development of 44 Group (Oct 1940–Nov 1944): HQ 44 Gp Intelligence – IIR/56/9/36.

DAY & NIGHT ROUTES UK - GIBRALTAR - NORTH AFRICA - SEPTEMBER 1943

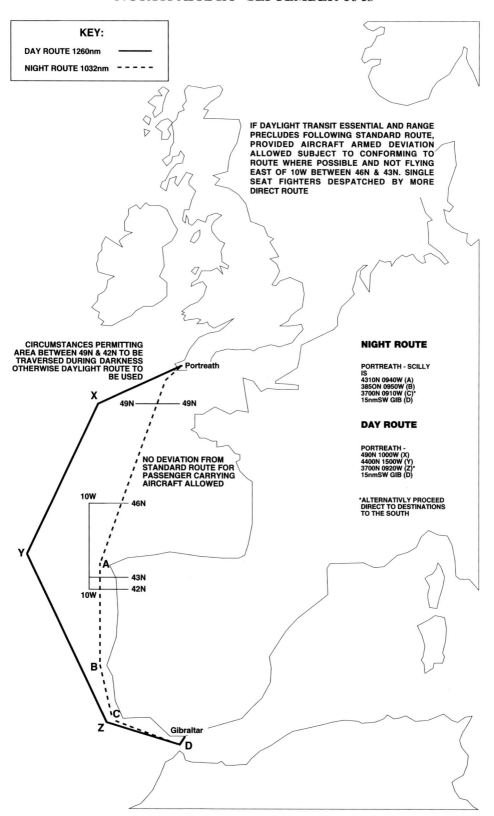

KEY:

| DAY ROUTE 1260nm | ——— |
| NIGHT ROUTE 1032nm | - - - - - |

IF DAYLIGHT TRANSIT ESSENTIAL AND RANGE PRECLUDES FOLLOWING STANDARD ROUTE, PROVIDED AIRCRAFT ARMED DEVIATION ALLOWED SUBJECT TO CONFORMING TO ROUTE WHERE POSSIBLE AND NOT FLYING EAST OF 10W BETWEEN 46N & 43N. SINGLE SEAT FIGHTERS DESPATCHED BY MORE DIRECT ROUTE

CIRCUMSTANCES PERMITTING AREA BETWEEN 49N & 42N TO BE TRAVERSED DURING DARKNESS OTHERWISE DAYLIGHT ROUTE TO BE USED

Portreath

X

49N ——— 49N

NIGHT ROUTE

PORTREATH - SCILLY IS
4310N 0940W (A)
385ON 0950W (B)
3700N 0910W (C)*
15nmSW GIB (D)

DAY ROUTE

PORTREATH -
490N 1000W (X)
4400N 1500W (Y)
3700N 0920W (Z)*
15nmSW GIB (D)

*ALTERNATIVLY PROCEED DIRECT TO DESTINATIONS TO THE SOUTH

NO DEVIATION FROM STANDARD ROUTE FOR PASSENGER CARRYING AIRCRAFT ALLOWED

10W

46N

Y

A

43N
42N

10W

B

C

Z

Gibraltar

D

'Have been watching the progress of the Gibraltar–Malta shuttle service on Hudsons. I much appreciate results achieved to date. Please convey my congratulations to the CO[11] and all concerned on the valuable assistance they are giving Malta in their hard fight'.

These Malta shuttles continued to the end of February 1943, many captains doing two at a time and Fg Off P Dixon achieving five between 17 February 1943 and the end of that month. It is interesting to note that after doing two between 18 and 25 July 1942 Fg Off J F P Matthews brought back to Hendon three famous fighter pilots – Sqn Ldr Whitney Straight (soon to be AOC No 216 Group), Sqn Ldr 'Laddie' Lucas and Flt Lt W R Daddo-Langlois.

These shuttle services to Malta involved the carriage of spares and stores to the island, and the evacuation of women and children at a time when conditions were desperate there. Hudsons of No 216 Group squadrons also flew in supplies from Egypt.

The other significant operation in which No 44 Group was involved in 1942 was Torch, the Allied landings in North Africa in November. When these were being planned the Group was charged by the Air Ministry with arrangements for the airborne operations and a Combined Anglo–American Control and Operations Room was set up by the RAF and USAAF at No 44 Group Headquarters.

The Anglo–American landings in Algeria and Morocco on 8 November 1942 were successfully achieved, being virtually unopposed, and there was a plentiful supply of aircraft via Gibraltar – chiefly fighters and medium bombers – for the advance eastwards to Tunis.

Getting these RAF and USAAF aircraft out there was one of the roles of No 44 Group; it had had two years' experience of those kinds of overseas air movements. The fact that, once this tactical air power had been deployed to north-west Africa, things there did not at first go well was not the Group's fault: a divided command structure, difficult mountainous terrain and bad weather were all factors which played a part in initial failures to achieve a quick and triumphant link-up with the Eighth Army enclosing the Afrika Korps and its supporting Luftwaffe in a pincer movement around Tunis. But that is another story, not part of Transport Command's history[12].

Aircraft delivered to the UK by Ferry Command initially went to Maintenance Units and then, as has been said, were flown to their operational destinations by ATA pilots. A former member of No 115 Sqn at Marham has recalled[13] seeing in July 1942 a brand new Wellington

---

11 Gp Capt P W M Wright, later to become OC No 179 Wing.

12 For a vivid description of some of the initial calamities in north-west Africa after Operation Torch, see John Terraine's *The Right of the Line The Royal Air Force in the European War 1939–1945* (Hodder and Stoughton, 1985).

13 *One of the Many on the Move*, by Jim Burtt-Smith (Merlin Books Ltd, 1992). The 'little girl' was Joan Hughes who was one of the eight original women pilots who signed contracts with the ATA in 1940. Initially she qualified to fly Hurricanes and Spitfires. See *The Forgotten Pilots*, by Lettice Curtis; Nelson & Saunders, 1985.

'make a perfect landing and out of it stepped a little girl. . . . A full-blown member of the ATA, a super force of peacetime flyers from all walks of life who kept the RAF stocked up with replacements'.

The reinforcement aircraft which came up the Takoradi route to Egypt were likewise flown to MUs to be prepared for operational service and then taken to squadrons in the Delta area or to RSUs in the Western Desert – wherever these might be, according to the fluctuations of the war – by ADU pilots.

The original Aircraft Delivery Unit (Middle East) had been formed in Cairo on 15 December 1941 with HQ on a houseboat on the River Nile and it was responsible for ferry flying on the West African Reinforcement Route, from Port Sudan (into which aircraft were shipped) and into the Western Desert. By December 1942 the ADU had grown to five times its original size and its different roles had been organisationally clarified: No 1 ADU, based in Cairo, was responsible for Takoradi route ferrying; No 2 ADU, with headquarters originally at Abu Sueir, did all the flying in the Delta area and into the Western Desert: its (unofficial) motto was 'Omnia ubique volamus' – 'We fly everything anywhere'.

This elaborate ferrying organisation – all part of the repair and reinforcement policy of a newly formed Maintenance Group, No 206, with Air Vice-Marshal Graham Dawson as Chief Maintenance and Supply Officer[14] – not only covered a vast area, from the West African to the North African seaboard, but also handled every type of aircraft used in the Mediterranean theatre, from single-engined Fairchild Argus to four-engined Consolidated B-24 and Handley Page Halifax.

In April 1942 the Air Ministry received a request from RAF Headquarters Middle East to set up a Ferry Group, 'in view of the increasing ferry commitments of reinforcing aircraft on the West African, Port Sudan and Mediterranean Reinforcement routes'.

Air Ministry approval was given in May: it authorised the formation of No 216 Ferry Group at Heliopolis under the command of the Air Reinforcement Controller (Gp Capt B H C Russell). One of its main functions was to be the supervision of ferry routes in Africa, and with its staging posts and transport squadrons it was in many ways a role model for Transport Command, as one of the officers who served in it has recalled[15]:

'The "Ferry and Transport" Headquarters that Group Captain Bunny Russell designed and created, known as No 216 Group, was tiny. It had its being in a medium-sized rented apartment of about half-a-dozen rooms, not too far from Heliopolis airfield and about seven miles from the centre of Cairo. There were only a couple of staff officers from each of

---

14 See *The End of the Beginning*, the RAF Historical Society Symposium on the Mediterranean war, for the author's paper on this subject. (20 March 1992). Dawson operated directly under Tedder as AOC-in-C Middle East Command: he operated through No 206 Group, which was commanded by Gp Capt C B Cooke.

15 In a lively autobiographical book *Wings Over North Africa* (Airlife Publishing Ltd, 1987), by Air Vice-Marshal Tony Dudgeon, who as Wg Cdr A G Dudgeon headed the Air Staff of No 216 Group from 21 May 1942. Gp Capt Russell became AOC on the 29th of that month.

the disciplines – Operations, Equipment, Engineers and Signals – plus one accountant, a few clerks, some radio operators and one car with a driver. Bunny turned out to be a fabulous organiser and his men soon learned that his battle-cry was "Why have more? You are paid to get things done. Don't ask me what to do. Find an answer – and *do* it. . . ."

'Everybody helped each other to do anything that was necessary, went flat out all the time and prided themselves that it worked very effectively. Bunny made it work so well that the mighty Headquarters Transport Command was formed in March the following year, using Bunny's 216 Group as a model – but bigger and on a worldwide basis'.

The Group's transport squadrons were Nos 216, 267, 117 and 173. It also had the two Aircraft Delivery Units already mentioned, Nos 1 and 2. In 1943 two more were to be formed – No 3 at Fez, Morocco, to ferry aircraft from Casablanca to Cairo; and No 4 at Azizia, south of Tripoli, to reinforce the squadrons in Sicily and Italy.

India reinforcement; the South Atlantic Bridge

Two other pieces in the giant jigsaw puzzle that was completed in 1943 to become RAF Transport Command fell into place during the latter months of 1942. One was No 179 (Ferry) Wing, established at Karachi in October 1942; the other was the inauguration of the South Atlantic 'Bridge' – southern span of the 'Atlantic Bridge', the ocean ferry route from Canada – in December 1942.

No 179 Wing was set up because, to quote from its ORB, 'Owing to the expansion of the Air Forces in India and the consequent growth of ferrying of reinforcement aircraft' (this was at a time when there were three operational Groups to support in the Burma counter-offensive) 'the supervision of ferry control routes had got beyond the capacity of No 226 Maintenance Unit to undertake, in addition to its India-wide responsibilities.'

The new Wing, with Gp Capt P W M Wright DFC in command, was responsible for reinforcement flying organisation and the Ferry Pilots' Pool at Karachi, for organising and supervising Staging Posts in India and for co-ordinating flying control on reinforcement routes with Air Headquarters. Later it came to control a Pilots' Pool at Bombay.

The South Atlantic ferry route, from Natal in Brazil to Accra in West Africa, resulted from arrangements which had been made more than a year earlier for the use by the Americans of the RAF reinforcement route to the Middle East. According to the AHB Narrative (quoted earlier), on 12 August 1941 contracts had been entered into between the US War Department, Pan American Airways and its subsidiaries which 'provided for the operation by these companies of ferrying services across the South Atlantic and the trans-African route'. PAA were contracted to ferry up to 200 (subsequently amended to 125) bombers a month to Khartoum and later to ferry British and American aircraft erected by the RAF at Takoradi. US bombers would be flown from Natal to Bathurst (a landfall

THE ATLANTIC BRIDGES

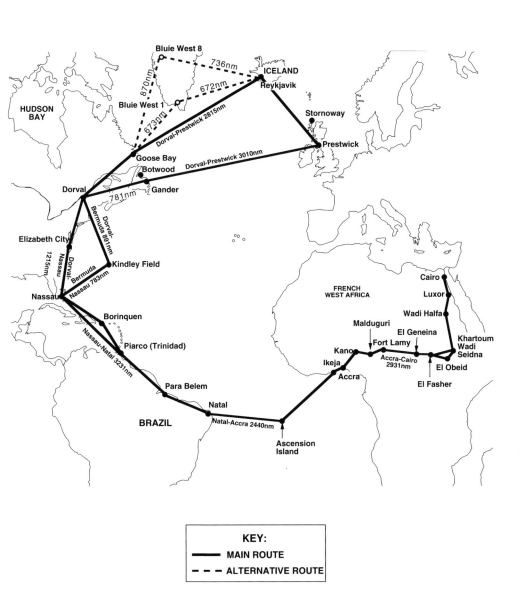

later amended to Accra which was on the existing West African Reinforcement Route).

On 28 October 1941 the first American crews for the new route arrived at Lagos, and thereafter American aircraft were ferried across the South Atlantic to West Africa. Then in the following months there was a change in operational demands. As the official account, *Atlantic Bridge*[16], puts it:

'During 1941 and 1942 the pressure of air warfare shifted to the Mediterranean, where the conflicts of the desert absorbed great quantities of air power. The chief need in Africa was for such bombers as Marylands, Hudsons, Bostons and . . . Mitchells. . . . Many aircraft had been sent out from Britain to the Middle East; but the logical method of ferrying new aircraft from American workshops to the African desert was by way of the South Atlantic. So another pattern was added to the Atlantic maps, and another important commitment to the ferrying enterprise – the Bridge of the South Atlantic from South America to Africa.

'This Bridge was initiated by the United States over territory which was partly British, partly American and partly Brazilian. In December 1942, agreement was reached between the RAF and the US Army Air Force that the responsibility for delivery of RAF aircraft from US production plants across the South Atlantic should fall upon Ferry Command. . . .'

There was now a double-spanned air bridge over the Atlantic Ocean.

The success and regularity of transatlantic flying throughout the Second World War – converting what had been something pioneering and daring in the 1920s and '30s into something unremarkable and routine – spelled the beginning of the end for the great ocean liner services which for so many years had been the main passenger link between Europe and America.

ME Ferry and Transport Group; formation of Transport Command

Increased activity on the West African Reinforcement Route from late 1942 onwards had its organisational repercussions in Cairo:

'By December (1942) the flow of aircraft from the United Kingdom and the United States was still increasing, and in view of this and of the provision of additional air transport aircraft in the Middle East Command it was found necessary to concentrate ferry and transport operations under a single authority. For this reason it was decided to expand No 216 Group, which was now to be known as No 216 (Air

---

16 Subtitled 'The Official Account of RAF Transport Command's Ocean Ferry prepared for the Air Ministry by the Ministry of Information'; HMSO, 1945.

Transport and Ferry) Group, and was placed under command of Air Commodore W W Straight' [17].

This new and enlarged No 216 Group superseded No 216 Ferry Group, and its establishment under the command of a relatively junior officer from the United Kingdom caused some resentment among long-serving senior air rank officers in the Middle East, especially as the new chief was an American who had never before held command of a Group, nor even a Wing. But Whitney Straight's varied and adventurous career well qualified him to deal with the unusual situations which might confront him in his new appointment, particularly in his dealings with the Americans who were taking an increasing part in Middle East air operations.

He had been born in New York but became a British citizen and went to Trinity College, Cambridge. Pre-war he had been a motor-racing driver and also participated in air races, both as pilot and aircraft designer. He joined the Auxiliary Air Force and in March 1940 was sent to Norway as Liaison Officer to the Norwegian High Command, submitting reports to the Air Ministry on which of two frozen lakes (Vangsmjösa or Lesjeskogen) could be used by the fighter squadrons to be flown off HMS *Glorious*. Although his advice on the suitability of the former was ignored and the latter was chosen for the Gladiators of No 263 Sqn to land on, Sqn Ldr Straight organised the clearance – by 200 civilians – of two feet of snow covering the ice, to make a usable surface.

For his service in Norway Whitney Straight was awarded the Military Cross; then having got back into airborne operations with command of a Spitfire squadron (No 242) in 1941 he won the DFC; but on 31 August 1941 he was shot down over France, being subsequently 'absent without leave' – as his Record of Service dryly described his successful escape and evasion – until 20 August 1942 when he arrived back in the UK (as previously related).

There was much logic, therefore, in posting him to a different theatre of war and in less than three weeks he was given a new appointment. When on 10 September 1942 he was posted to command the expanded No 216 Group, he was promoted to Air Commodore although his substantive rank was only that of Flight Lieutenant. His wartime record, his pre-war reputation and his charismatic personality were to prove invaluable assets in commanding a Group whose operations ranged over a vast area of Africa, throughout the Mediterranean theatre and out to India with transport and reinforcement services.

As the RAF Narrative described the wide functions of the reorganised Group, its ferry element 'comprised ferry controls, staging posts and aircraft delivery units' and its other roles included 'operational and administrative control of all transport, ferry and communication aircraft, flights and squadrons as might be allotted by Headquarters, RAF Middle East'. It had similar powers over Ferry Controls in the Middle East, which included No 2 Ferry Control at Wadi Seidna (Khartoum) and No 5, then

---

17 AHB Narrative: 'The West African Reinforcement Route'. PRO AIR 41/38.

in process of formation at Ikeja, Lagos, in West Africa Command. In other words, No 216 Group supervised, and was responsible for, every transport and ferry aircraft moving in the African/Mediterranean theatres and en route from the Middle East to India.

With Ferry Command in operation in Canada from July 1941 and its associated No 44 Group (created in August of that year by the absorption of OAMCU) both receiving aircraft from overseas and despatching reinforcements to war zones, with the greatly expanded No 216 Group, and with No 179 Wing established in Karachi a month later for the control of reinforcement routes in India, the stage was set for the curtain to be rung up – by the Secretary of State for Air – on the first appearance of Royal Air Force Transport Command on 25 March 1943, co-ordinating the operations of these far-flung, worldwide air transport and ferry organisations.

It was not until early in 1943 that the Air Staff considered the formation of a Transport Command to control and co-ordinate all these activities. The basis of their discussions, begun in February of that year, was a Memorandum by the Chief of the Air Staff and PUS, Air Ministry[18], which recommended the formation of a new Command.

This paper, 'Organisation for Air Transport', which the Air Council considered at its meeting on 3 March 1943[19], looked first at the situation which existed and the main features of the current organisation: Ferry Command, responsible for delivering aircraft across the North Atlantic to the United Kingdom and across the South Atlantic to Africa; No 44 Group, a subordinate formation of Ferry Command and responsible for the despatch of aircraft from the UK; No 216 (Ferry and Transport) Group, responsible for all ferrying, reinforcement and air transport operations in the Middle East (also operating three air transport and one communication squadron – Nos 216, 117, 267 and 173 respectively) and No 179 Ferry Wing in India.

In referring to No 44 Group, the Memorandum said that it had three major responsibilities: wireless control of all non-operational aircraft operating between 61° North and 40° North approaching or leaving the United Kingdom; the reception, preparation, training and despatch of all ferry and reinforcement aircraft from the UK; and the operation and administration of home-based transport aircraft – Nos 24, 271, 511 and 510 Sqns. [The first three of these squadrons have already been referred to in this history; No 510 had been formed at Hendon in October 1942 from a nucleus of No 24 Sqn and it had a miscellaneous assortment of aircraft – Lysander, Hornet Moth, Tiger Moth, Proctor, Hart and Anson – for communications purposes.]

The Memorandum also noted the position of BOAC: in addition to the air transport and ferry operations by RAF formations in the Middle East, India and North-West Africa, 'the British Overseas Airways Corporation with a restricted fleet of aircraft is running services over a wide field,

---

18 AC 20 (43).

19 Conclusions 4(43). CAS was Air Chief Marshal Sir Charles Portal and PUS (Permanent Under Secretary) was Sir Arthur Street.

including those to Canada, Portugal, Sweden, West Africa, Russia, South Africa and India. It also operates various air routes in Africa. The lift of the BOAC Fleet is exclusively at the disposal of Government Departments'.

In making reference to four distinct aspects of the existing organisation the Memorandum referred to 'regular strategic services – for example that run by 511 Sqn to the Middle East or by BOAC to Stockholm' [20] – and to air reinforcement (the movement of operational aircraft and their crews between Commands), ferrying (the movement of aircraft – like that from the USA to the UK) and air transport (the movement of stores, personnel, etc from bases to the front line, or for the training of airborne forces).

All these aspects and their implications had been considered at a representative meeting held in the Air Ministry on 19 February.

Referring to the current situation, the Memorandum questioned the divided responsibility for air transport organisation between two departments in the Air Ministry, those of the Air Member for Supply and Organisation, and of the Permanent Under-Secretary. Whereas, 'running through the problem as a whole', it said, 'is the common factor of air routes and air facilities, control of which . . . should be centralised as far as possible'.

Although much detailed work had to be done before the new organisation could take shape, it was recommended that the Air Council should approve the formation of the new Command.

Why had a Transport Command not been formed before? According to the Memorandum the reason was the acute shortage of aircraft and the need to concentrate all available productive capacity on meeting the requirements of the first-line air force. As a result, the development of British air transport over the previous 3½ years had been largely a matter of progressive improvisation.

But the situation had changed: some 90 Yorks would be delivered during 1943 and a further 100 during the first half of 1944 (predictions not in fact fulfilled), and there was to be a modest but still most welcome allocation of American transport types. With such resources now in sight, 'a considerable development of our air transport system becomes possible, and the problem must now be tackled of setting up an organisation, under strong central control, to ensure that the development proceeds on profitable and economical lines'.

There were three further meetings to thrash out these problems, including one on 8 March 1943 to discuss relations between a Transport Command and BOAC, and on the 11th the Secretary of State for Air (Sir

---

20 No 511 Sqn, to which later reference will be made, operated long-range services – Albemarles to Gibraltar and Liberators to Cairo. BOAC operated a Mosquito service to Stockholm which kept up an essential supply of ball bearings and also brought to the UK the nuclear physicist Professor Niels Bohr. The passengers on this service, including VIPs, travelled in acute discomfort, crouched in the icy darkness of the bomb bay. In his book about the Mosquito, *The Wooden Wonder* (Airlife, 1980), Edward Bishop relates how, 'delivered in Scotland or Sweden as breathing parcels wrapped up in two flying suits, Mae West and parachute harness, the passengers were unpacked and revealed as diplomats, industrialists, bishops, musicians, professors and cloak-and-dagger experts. Out of one parcel stepped Sir Malcolm Sargent; from another, Dr Bell, Bishop of Chichester'.

Archibald Sinclair) announced in the House of Commons[21] that he had decided to establish a Royal Air Force Transport Command. To create one sooner would have been 'to put the cart before the horse. It has not been commanders and staff that we have been short of, but aircraft'.

The Secretary of State defined the roles of the new Command: 'In addition to controlling the operations of Royal Air Force transport squadrons at home [it] will be responsible for the organisation and control of strategic air routes, for all overseas ferrying and for the reinforcement moves of squadrons to and between overseas theatres. The Royal Air Force Ferry Command at Montreal will become a subordinate formation'.

As for relations with BOAC, 'the guiding principle will be that the . . . Command and the Corporation will work in the closest collaboration, freely exchanging information and experience, avoiding duplication wherever possible and helping each other to the best of their ability to carry out the respective tasks allotted to them'.

Ferry Command in Montreal did indeed become a subordinate formation in Transport Command as No 45 Group, but its C-in-C, Air Chief Marshal Sir Frederick Bowhill, moved across the Atlantic to become the first AOC-in-C Transport Command, formed on 25 March 1943, with Headquarters first at Bush House in London and then at Harrow in Middlesex. No RAF Command had previously been created with such immediate worldwide commitments and with subordinate formations in North America, Africa and India.

The Commander-in-Chief, 'Ginger' Bowhill, red-haired and with 'very direct blue eyes under bushy eyebrows that made him look fiercer than he was'[22], had the distinction of being one of the 'sea dog' air marshals of the RAF, having served in the Naval Wing of the Royal Flying Corps in 1913. In that year (after being in the Royal Navy since 1904) he had gained his Royal Aero Club Flying Certificate, then joined the Royal Naval Air Service. No wonder that a distinguished contemporary wrote that he had sea water in his veins[23]. In 1916 he had taken part in the very first air supply operation in military history, flying a Short Type 184 floatplane. This was a joint RFC/RNAS attempt to relieve the beleaguered British garrison in Kut-el-Amara on the River Tigris, in what was then Mesopotamia.

Sir Frederick had been C-in-C Coastal Command at the outbreak of the Second World War, then in 1941 – when he was 61 – was sent to Montreal to head Ferry Command. By the time of his appointment as C-in-C Transport Command in March 1943 he was 63 and one of the most senior officers in the Royal Air Force.

The new Command was inaugurated on 25 March and its first Headquarters appointments (from the 24th) were of Air Commodore H G

21 Hansard, Cols 892–3, 11 March 43.
22 *Ferry Command*, by Don McVicar; Airlife, 1981.
23 Sir Maurice Dean, in *The RAF and Two World Wars*; Cassell, 1979.

Brackley CBE DSO DSC as Senior Air Staff Officer[24] and Air Commodore A Fletcher CMG CBE MC as Air Officer Administration. It initially had three Groups – Nos 44 at Barnwood, Gloucester; No 45 (the former Ferry Command) at Dorval, Montreal; and No 216 in Cairo. By December 1943 it had four Groups, for from the 16th of that month No 179 (Ferry) Wing at Karachi was upgraded in status to No 229 Transport Group.

Thus from its inception Transport Command was an international – and internationally minded – organisation. Its aircrew daily flew thousands of miles over land and sea; its supporting personnel were positioned on staging posts threaded through deserts, jungles and the tropics to sustain transit aircraft – of whatever type might appear out of the sky. At its Headquarters exotic names like Takoradi, Gander, Ras-el-Ma, Nassau, Rabat Sale, Masira, Dum Dum, Poona, Natal and Reykjavik became common currency in Memoranda, signals and corridor conversations.

Its contribution to the Second World War, albeit perhaps not as dramatic as that of Bomber, Fighter and Coastal Commands, needs now to be recorded and assessed. Within a few months of its formation it was involved in supporting a major new Mediterranean campaign, the invasion of Sicily. It took part in the abortive attempt to capture the Dodecanese Islands; it sent squadrons to Burma; and its airborne forces component contributed to the 1944–45 European operations – the Normandy landings, the Arnhem disaster and the final Rhine crossing.

---

24 In a reference to Royal flights during the war, *The Queen's Flight Fifty Years of Royal Flying*, edited by Michael Burns (Blandford Press, 1986), says that 'planning was the same as for the PM's flights and we were fortunate that in our relationship with No 10 we dealt through the SASO of Transport Command, Air Vice-Marshal H G Brackley, formerly of Imperial Airways and widely experienced over the Atlantic and Empire routes. As the intermediary between the requirements of the Palace and No 10 . . . his knowledge and judgement saved us from a lot of petty interference by well-meaning but often ignorant staff officers. . . .'

Chapter III

A Command at War

'. . . when the blast of war blows in our ears,
Then imitate the action of the tiger. . . .'

Shakespeare, Henry V, *III, i*

ON 2 April 1943 the newly formed Command transferred its Headquarters to Harrow, and on 7 May decided that its official title should be Transport Command. On 1 June its badge and motto were approved by King George VI. The badge depicted a globe surmounted by a lion, with the motto 'Ferio feriendo' – 'I strike by carrying', and this badge and motto were reproduced on the nose of the Command's aircraft. By the end of June its No 216 Group squadrons were fulfilling the motto – supporting the Allied invasion of Sicily (Operation Husky), mounted on 9/10 July 1943.

This operation marked the first use by the Allies of airborne forces in the Second World War, but those of the British contribution were not provided by Transport Command: No 38 Wing of the Airborne Division, Army Co-operation Command – whose airborne forces' role Transport Command was gradually to assume, provided Halifaxes of No 295 Sqn which towed Horsa gliders from the UK to North Africa and Albemarles of No 296 Sqn which flew out to the same destination. These flights, collectively known as Exercise Beggar, were in support of Operation Husky.

In the 3–29 June period 23 Horsas were delivered by No 295 Sqn in what was a particularly dogged and daring operation, considering the long stretch of hostile waters to be crossed at low speed and the duration of the flight (9hr 20min) from Portreath in Cornwall. During the 26-day period when 23 Horsas were delivered, two Halifax-Horsa combinations were lost: one was shot down on 14 June and another was assumed missing on the 27th, no message being received from it. On the 11th Halifax DG391 took off from Holmsley South on a positioning flight to Portreath but crashed into a hill near Porlock in Somerset.

The Transport Command contribution to Operation Husky, through No 216 Group, was a logistic one. Seven of the Group's squadrons were involved: No 17 with Ju 52s and No 28 with Ansons, both of the South African Air Force (SAAF); Nos 117 and 267 with Hudsons; No 173 with Lodestars; No 216 with Dakotas and No 230 with Sunderlands. A new aircraft delivery unit, No 4 ADU, was formed in May at Azizia, south of Tripoli, to deliver reinforcement aircraft to Sicily.

The involvement of these squadrons and the ferry unit can best be described by quoting the Group's Operations Record Book, datelined from La Marsa, Tunis, on 25 July 1943:–

'The main feature of transport work during July has been the participation of our transport aircraft in the Sicilian campaign. Advanced 216 Group was formed at the end of June to co-ordinate all air transport lifts in the operational area under the direction of NATAF [North African Tactical Air Force, formed on 18 February 1943, combining No 242 Group, RAF, and the US XII Air Supply Command], and for the first fortnight of the invasion Air Cdre Whitney W Straight commanded personally.

'He had in the Tunis area a detachment of Dakotas from 267 Sqn, the Australian Air Ambulance Unit, a detachment of flying-boats from 230 Sqn, and call on certain units of the US Troop Carrier Command. Besides this force, he controlled 249 Wing, located at Castel Benito [south of Tripoli], which consisted of 117 Sqn with a mixed strength of Hudsons and Dakotas, and 28 (SAAF) Sqn (which however was still in its embryonic stage so did not participate to any extent).

'The transport work consisted in the main of ferrying personnel and stores to the Air Forces and the Army in Sicily from the mainland, and evacuating casualties. . . .' (In this latter role the Dakotas, with newly modified stretcher racks, played an important part.)

More detail on these operations was given in a later ORB entry which said:

'Aircraft at the disposal of the AOC comprised a detachment of ten Dakota aircraft of 267 Sqn based at El Aouina together with ten Dakota and 20 Hudson aircraft of 117 Sqn of 249 Wing based at Castel Benito. Against the possibility of aerodromes at Malta being so congested as to be unable to receive land-based transport aircraft a flight of six Sunderland flying-boats of 230 Sqn was allocated and based at Sidi Ahmed (Bizerta).

'To supplement these resources it was arranged that immediately the US Troop Carrier Command had fulfilled airborne troop commitments its aircraft would come under the operational control of Advanced HQ 216 Group for transport purposes. Such control was exercised from 14 to 24 July inclusive.

'During the operation No 1 Australian Air Ambulance Unit (two DH 86s – a four-engined version of the Dragon Rapide – and four Bombays) was placed under the control of HQ Advanced 216 Group and was employed in clearing casualties from Tunis to Base Hospitals, e.g. Algiers, and in ferrying casualties from the forward areas to evacuation centres in Sicily'.

The ending of the Tunisian campaign and the invasion of Sicily had opened-up the Mediterranean reinforcement route for aircraft coming from the UK to the Middle East and on to India for the build-up of squadrons in the Burma campaign. On 20 March 1943 No 3 ADU was designated by No 216 Group for formation at Fez, Morocco, to ferry aircraft from Casablanca to Cairo (later, in October, it was re-located at Oujda). But the Bay of Biscay still presented a huge danger for transit aircrew. In June 1943 one of the Group's most experienced transport squadron COs, Wg Cdr R G Yaxley DSO MC DFC who had commanded No 117 Sqn throughout the desert campaign, was lost with all those aboard his aircraft when en route to the Middle East.

He had gone back to England to collect a refurbished Hudson (FK386) and its departure was delayed by unserviceability. Wg Cdr Yaxley told Air Cdre 'Bing' Cross, who was hoping for a passage back with him, that take-off had been put back for 24 hours. Then he said that there was a further postponement and that the aircraft might need an engine change. As 'Bing' Cross was in a hurry to get to Algiers to take up a new command he instead got a lift from Prestwick in a USAAF C-54[1].

Wg Cdr Yaxley eventually took off from Portreath on 3 June at 0737hr. Nothing further was heard from the Hudson, aboard which, among its ten occupants, were four Wing Commanders and two Squadron Leaders. As the flight was being made in daylight it is presumed, in view of the lack of any distress signal, that the aircraft was shot down.

Accidents such as this one were a personal loss to Transport Command and to the families and friends of the aircrew involved. But another one which occurred at Gibraltar only a month later received widespread publicity and aroused much controversy because of its political repercussions.

This was the loss on take-off of a Liberator II (AL523) of No 511 Sqn on 4 July 1943. The aircraft came down in the sea about a mile from the eastern end of the runway and there was only one survivor – the captain, Flt Lt E M Prchal, who was seriously injured. This disaster would not have been noteworthy in the middle of a world war when lives were being lost every day had it not been that the aircraft was carrying the Polish leader General Vladislav Sikorski, his daughter Mme Lezniowska and several members of his staff.

Flt Lt Prchal was an experienced and reliable pilot of No 511 Sqn, the long-range squadron of Transport Command. He had flown out from Gibraltar to Cairo on 28 June. On 3 July he took off from there at 0406hr with his 12 VIP passengers and landed at Gibraltar at 1437hr. After a night stop Flt Lt Prchal and the same crew[2] took off at 2107hr GMT. The intention was to make a night crossing of the Bay of Biscay. Instead, a few minutes after take-off, the Liberator fell into the sea[3].

---

1 See Air Chief Marshal Sir Kenneth Cross's autobiographical book *Straight and Level* (Grub Street, 1993) for his own account of this episode.

2 Co-pilot Sqn Ldr W S Herring DSO DFM, WO L Zalsberg DFM navigator, Sgt F S Keely flight engineer and two W Op/AGs, Flt Sgt G B R Gerrie DFM and Flt Sgt D Hunter.

3 This accident gave rise to a great deal of speculation and was seized upon by both German and Russian propaganda. A book, *The Death of General Sikorski Accident*, was written about it by David Irving (published by William Kimber in 1967). He quoted the Report of the Air Ministry Court of Inquiry, which said that it was '. . . apparent that the accident was due to

Operations Accolade and Microbe

No 216 Group had played a supporting role in Operation Husky, but in Operation Accolade in September–November 1943 in the Eastern Mediterranean it was called upon to take a much more active part. This was another Allied invasion – of three Dodecanese Islands, Cos, Leros and Samos. It was hoped that this operation would discomfit the German forces in the Aegean Sea area, take some of the pressure off the Allied Armies in Southern Italy, and perhaps even bring Turkey into the war against the Axis powers.

As things turned out Accolade was a disaster for the Allies. There is a sad brevity in the index references to one of the islands in *Grand Strategy Vol V* by John Ehrman[4]: 'Cos: 88; occupied, 93; lost, 94'. This island venture proved, strategically, a sideshow and a tragic one for the many sailors, soldiers and airmen who lost their lives because nothing was gained as a result of their sacrifices.

In its ORB for September 1943, Rear HQ No 216 Group (at Heliopolis, Cairo) reported that 'the outstanding event of the month . . . was the use of our transport aircraft in the abortive attempt to gain some control in the Dodecanese Islands. . . . Briefly, . . . 22 Dakotas and a few Hudsons from Ramat David (Palestine) and Nicosia (Cyprus) were landing by day and night and supply-dropping by night from September 11 to the end of the month'.

But the cost was high: 'Six Dakotas were lost, five being burnt out by low-flying enemy attacks on the landing-ground at Cos [Antimachia – initially the only airfield], and the sixth presumed shot down over the sea. It is believed that the crew and passengers of this latter aircraft were picked up by the Turks and interned. The only other casualty was one Wireless Operator killed during the strafing attacks'.

No 216 Sqn played a prominent part in these operations, which were a major feature of Operation Accolade, whose first objective was the island of Rhodes. The plan was to capture and hold the airfield at Maritza.

From 6 to 14 August 1943 eight of the squadron's Dakotas were detached to No 4 Middle East Training School at Ramat David to train for parachute operations[5]; then at the end of that month the Dakota force was

---

jamming of the elevator controls shortly after take-off. It has not been possible to determine how the jamming . . . occurred but it has been established that there was no sabotage'. A theory has been advanced by Mr J Bartelski (in an article in *Aeroplane Monthly* for October 1993) that one of the side hatches came open during the take-off run and a mailbag was sucked out, and it was this which jammed the elevators.

4 HMSO, 1956.

5 In a letter to *RAF News* for 17 June 1994 (Issue No 850), ex-Cpl Dolman of Ipswich recalled, in describing his Service days in the Middle East: 'Eventually we all moved to 103 [MU] Aboukir and settled in. By now, Alamein had come and gone and the war had moved along North Africa and across to Sicily. Enter the RAF Regiment unit, who among other things took us on a 'backers up' course for aerodrome defence. After a while, when we had all had a bash at it, a notice appeared looking for volunteers for special duties. My oppo and I were a bit cheesed off with the humdrum lifestyle we had got into and were in two minds to put ourselves forward, when we remembered the old criterion of Service life, "Never volunteer". Just as well we didn't as this unit and the volunteers were dropped over Cos and were wiped out'.

AREA OF OPERATIONS 13 SEPTEMBER - 22 NOVEMBER 1943
OPERATIONS ACCOLADE & MICROBE

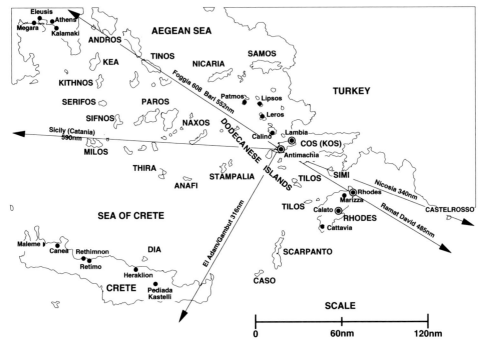

increased by 12 (later 14) aircraft, to be allocated to the Air Commander, AHQ, Air Defence, Eastern Mediterranean (Air Vice-Marshal R E Saul).

By 10 September 120 paratroops and aircrew had been trained at Ramat David, but on the 12th – when the German garrison overpowered the Italians across the whole length of Rhodes – Operation Accolade was abandoned and a new plan adopted, to seize and hold the smaller island to the north-west of Rhodes, Kos. But, as the ORB of No 216 Group[6] pointed out:

> 'Because of the sudden decision to reinforce Cos[7] there was no plan made for the use of transport aircraft prior to the initial landings. The wholesale application of the 'Accolade' plan to the Cos operation (code-named 'Microbe'), was hardly feasible, because both operations in strength and purpose were quite unrelated. Planning for the use of transport aircraft developed as the operation proceeded. . . .'

Nevertheless, on 14 September transport support operations began, from both Ramat David and Nicosia, with paratroops from the former and supplies from the latter to the Spitfire Flight at Antimachia. As the No 216 Group ORB for September recorded:–

---

6 Air 25/872.

7 The wartime spelling (now Kos).

30   *A Command at War*

'On the night of September 14/15 six Dakotas under the leadership of Sqn Ldr Forsyth . . . executed a most successful paratroop operation on Cos: 122 troops were dropped with only one minor injury, and the great precision and accurate timing with which the operation was carried out has received the praise of a great many people, including the C-in-C'[8].

Sqn Ldr C R A Forsyth and his navigator Flt Sgt J McP Whitelaw received the DSO and DFM respectively for their gallantry. The citation said that Sqn Ldr Forsyth and Flt Sgt Whitelaw

'. . . were pilot and navigator of the leading aircraft of a formation detailed to drop parachute troops on the island of Cos in September 1943. The operation demanded a high degree of skill, precise timing being essential to success. Nevertheless, Sqn Ldr Forsyth, brilliantly supported by Flt Sgt Whitelaw, whose navigation over a difficult route was faultless, unerringly led his formation to the target, where, with amazing precision, the troops were dropped in the selected zones. The success achieved reflects the greatest credit on the efforts of this officer and airman'.

Leros and Samos operations

In its ORB account of Operation Microbe, No 216 Sqn records that on 18 September five of its aircraft were destroyed on the ground by enemy strafing, and Sgt G E Newall was killed. On the 21st a new landing-strip was completed as an alternative to Antimachia, where stocks of petrol, oil and ammunition had been built up by aircraft operating from Nicosia. This was used until closed by bombing on the 29th. From 20 September operations had had to be limited to night only, to avoid interference by the enemy. On the night of the 22nd four aircraft dropped supplies, the squadron ORB commenting that 'although this commitment had not been foreseen, pilots were easily able to develop the required technique'.

From 19 to 28 September there was intensive supply-dropping of stores on Cos by No 216 Sqn aircraft – seven operating on the 19th, four on the 20th, 22nd and 23rd and one on the 28th; and on the 21st the first landing on the newly completed airstrip had been made by the Squadron CO, Wg Cdr E M Morris, at night.

Then on 3 October the last transport aircraft landed on Cos: five aircraft successfully landed supplies at night on the badly cratered airfield near Cos town and left just before an attack by the enemy which soon after resulted in the capture of the island.

Cos operations had gone on from 14 September to 3 October and during that time 121 landings had been made – 82 by day and 39 at night[9].

Two more of the Dodecanese Islands were to be the objectives of British

---

8 Air Chief Marshal Sir Sholto Douglas.
9 HQ No 216 Group ORB Appendices.

(or, in particular, Prime Minister Winston Churchill's)[10] hopes for a foothold in the Aegean – Leros and Samos, names famous in classical history. In its ORB for October 1943 No 216 Sqn recorded that

'The supply-dropping on Leros Island became a most interesting operation. After the fall of Cos the situation became most precarious for the occupants of Leros. On the south, separated by only five miles of sea, is the isle of Kelino, upon which was an enemy force. Still further south on Cos, and within fighter range of Leros, were two reasonable airfields. Also within fighter range were enemy-based aircraft on the Greek mainland. While the ground position was strong, no air cover could be given, and it was for this reason that the island eventually fell. Leros has no airfields and there is no area on which one could be constructed.

'At first a more or less regular flight was made from Cairo West[11] carrying routine equipment and stores. The policy was however laid down that, in common with other air transport commitments, only priority loads were to be carried by air as Naval units were still able to reach the island. As the operation proceeded, and just before the enemy attack, loads which had previously been classified as routine became priority and the intensity of the operation was stepped up until finally 12 aircraft were employed plus eight Halifaxes of No 178 Sqn attached to No 216 Sqn to assist.

'When the enemy attacked with paratroops and landing craft, the island garrison was split and only the southern positions could be used for supply dropping. Operations were carried out entirely at night in moonless conditions without lights or signals from the dropping zone. Our aircraft were engaged from the ground by both friend and foe, the former being Italian gunners – who, however, had every excuse, as frequently, while our aircraft were dropping, enemy aircraft were at the same time bombing from a higher altitude.

'No 216 Sqn aircraft were briefed to fly almost at sea level, or at minimum dropping height while over the land. The fact that only one aircraft was lost through flying into water reflects upon the great skill of the pilots, especially in view of the hilly terrain of Leros'.

At the end of the month, operations turned to Samos:

'An outstanding event was the paratroop operation involving the dropping of 200 officers and men of the Greek Sacred Squadron on the isle of Samos on two consecutive nights, 31 October/1 November. On

---

10 On 10 October he 'telegraphed to [General Sir Henry Maitland] Wilson, on hearing that he intended to fight for Leros: "... Cling on if you possibly can. It will be a splendid achievement" ' (*Grand Strategy, Vol V* – see previous reference).

11 Which at the insistence of No 216 Group had become the operational base.

both nights five Dakotas carrying 100 troops, followed by a sixth carrying their equipment, set off at 15-minute intervals. Both nights were moonless and the dropping zone lay in a valley with a high hill on each side, broken hills on the third and with the sea at the other end of the valley. Altogether, the dropping zone from the pilots' point of view was most difficult, being both short and narrow. However the DZ lights were excellent and all troops were successfully dropped with only a few minor injuries to the men'.

What was the result of all these operations in the Dodecanese Islands in which Army and Naval forces, fighter, bomber and reconnaissance aircraft were also involved, and which went on until late in November? The AHB Narrative *Operations in the Dodecanese Islands September–November 1943* says:[12]

'As soon as resistance ceased on Leros [after intensive Luftwaffe attacks up to 16 November], the [German] bomber effort was switched to Samos, and on 17 November about 75 sorties were made against the island. . . . However, no further attacks were made, and the only other bomber activity until 22 November, when Samos was occupied by the Germans (the British forces having already been evacuated), consisted of an attack on an Allied Naval force south of Castelrosso harbour the same day. German air forces in the Aegean area were then withdrawn to the main bases in Greece. . . .'

These operations, in which Dakota crews of No 216 Sqn played such a gallant part, rate little more than a footnote in the history of the Second World War because they were unsuccessful. Had they been successful – had the islands been captured and held, German forces withdrawn from the West, Turkey brought into the war, the Balkans 'set ablaze' (the term used by Field Marshal Sir Alan Brooke, Chief of the Imperial General Staff) and peace brought nearer – they would have been hailed as a daring and triumphant strategic stroke, as Churchill intended them to be.

'What I ask for', he wrote to President Roosevelt on 7 October 1943, 'is the capture of Rhodes and the other islands of the Dodecanese, and the movement northward of our Middle Eastern Air Forces and their establishment in these islands and possibly on the Turkish shore[13].

But the root cause of failure was the virtual isolation of the Middle East Naval, Air and Army Commanders – Cunningham, Douglas and Wilson – from the main centres of power because of the indifference of Eisenhower (reflecting American policy towards the Balkans) and the coolness of Tedder; so no support was forthcoming from the Mediterranean Commanders, who were intent on the Italian campaign and the forthcoming invasion of Europe. Consequently the Accolade/Microbe planners in Cairo were starved of moral and materiel support, as Sholto Douglas described in his autobiography *Years of Command*[14].

---

12 PRO AIR 41, Items 53 and 61.
13 *The Second World War Vol V*; Cassell & Co, 1952.   14 Collins, 1966.

Shipping and assault craft had been despatched to India for an operation against the Arakan, which never came off;[15] troops who had done exercises for landings on the islands were instead sent to the central Mediterranean; the heavy bomber support which Douglas requested was never forthcoming; and – in practical terms – there was never a Combined Operations HQ to plan and control the Dodecanese campaign.

Yet at its outset Operation Accolade – the objective of which was to capture Rhodes, the biggest of the Italian-controlled Dodecanese Islands – was very nearly successful. In *Years of Command* Sholto Douglas cites the official Naval historian Capt S W Roskill, who quoted the War Diary of the German Naval Group Command, South, for 12 September 1943: 'If the enemy had made full use of the moment of weakness [following the Italian armistice] he could easily have taken Rhodes'.

Operations to capture the island (which had two airfields) had been abandoned on that day; the alternative plan was to bypass it and go on to Cos. On the 9th the Prime Minister had signalled the Commanders-in-Chief: 'This is the time to play high. Improvise and dare'. Improvise they did – with what resources they had available. The daring was up to the airmen, sailors and soldiers. Some account as far as the transport squadrons were concerned has already been given of these operations, which extended the range by air from Cyprus to nearly 400 miles, whereas the Germans could mount counter-attacks from nearby Rhodes, Crete and the Greek mainland. As Sholto Douglas recalled: 'The Germans were pouring bombers and fighters into the Aegean; and not having to make the long flights with which our pilots were faced before even getting to Cos, they were able to operate much more effectively'. Cos fell on 3rd October; Leros on 12th November. Sholto Douglas quotes Churchill as writing that 'once Rhodes was denied to us our gains throughout the Aegean became more precarious' – and so it proved. He recalled that the situation in the Aegean was by then chaotic. Cunningham (who had become First Sea Lord) in his Despatch on Aegean operations gives as the reason for the British failure the enemy's command of the air through lack of airfields from which the RAF could operate, and the lack of heavy bomber support through American official indifference. According to Sholto Douglas the RAF lost 115 aircraft in the Dodecanese operations, in which Wellingtons, Baltimores, Hudsons, Spitfires, Hurricanes and Beaufighters were involved in addition to the Dakotas. (The part played by the Beaufighter squadrons in the operations has been vividly documented by Roy C Nesbit in his book *The Armed Rovers*, published by Airlife in 1995).

So the daring strategic stroke which Churchill envisaged failed completely, with considerable losses and with nothing gained. There was perhaps another reason for failure – a certain war ennui. Operations had long since moved away from Egypt to the West, leaving HQ staffs in Cairo and Alexandria with a well-regulated 'peacetime' routine. This attitude

---

15 In *The Second World War Vol V* Winston Churchill refers to 'the Quebec decision to send four landing ships with the craft they carry from the Eastern Mediterranean to the Bay of Bengal . . . for training purposes'.

was reflected in some rather smug entries in the No 216 Group ORB for November and December 1943, compiled at its HQ in Heliopolis, Cairo, the former entry saying that

'. . . the final chapter of the Aegean affair was written during the first twenty days of November. . . . The cessation of activity in these islands provided a great deal of relief to all concerned with Transport Operations in this theatre, and it is hoped that normal work will be renewed during December'.

For the latter month the compiler recorded:

'Consequent upon the final curtain on the Dodecanese affair the efforts of Transport Operations were once more directed to the organising of Routine and Special Flights. As a result the report for this month cannot provide such interesting details as have the previous few months. Nevertheless it is felt that the proper function of Transport Operations was carried out and the normal loads, which may not appear as so "operational" as paratroops, were the main concern'.

Chapter IV

Transport Command's Groups and their Roles

'From east to west, from shore to shore. . . .'

Hymn *by Sedulius, tr by J Ellerton*

WHILE the operational transport support roles of the new Command had been established and tested in its Husky and Accolade/Microbe contributions, and its routine transport services were consolidated with a reliability that came to be taken for granted, its ferrying role was continuing as reinforcement aircraft were needed in the European, Mediterranean and Far East theatres.

At the very end of 1943 No 113 (South Atlantic) Wing despatched its 1,000th aircraft. These were the American types which equipped units in the Mediterranean area or in India Command for the offensive in Burma. No 113 complemented No 112 (North Atlantic) Wing which ferried US machines to the UK for service in the European theatre. Both Wings were component parts of No 45 (Atlantic Transport) Group.

This pattern was repeated with No 216 Group in the Middle East. The geographical spread of the Group's authorities had become too wide to be administered conveniently from the one headquarters in Cairo. From 1 September 1943 two subordinate Wings were formed, No 282 in Cairo and No 284 in Algiers. The former was responsible for routes east of Cairo as far as Karachi, and the other would control the routes and Staging Posts west of Cairo and north of 30°N.

With the hard-won opening-up of the Mediterranean to the Allies in 1943 the main ferry route for aircraft into the theatre could now go via Casablanca. In October of that year the last aircraft was assembled at Takoradi and the West African reinforcement route was closed down. During the three years of its operation, from September 1940 to October 1943, it had handled 5,203 aircraft, among them 2,272 Hurricanes, 1,114 Blenheims and 736 Spitfires. This highly successful operation had sustained the Desert Air Force and played an indispensable part in its eventual victory.

Four No 216 Group Aircraft Delivery Units were responsible for getting newly produced machines to Maintenance Units, Repair and Salvage Units and squadrons: No 1 ADU, based in Cairo, did the West African Reinforcement Route ferrying; No 2 ADU, based from February 1943 at LG (Landing Ground) 237 on the Cairo–Alexandria road and with forward detachments at Benghazi and Tripoli, was responsible for all Western Desert and North African ferrying (in 1943 it delivered 11,939 aircraft); No 3 ADU, formed at Fez in March 1943 and in October

THE NORTH AFRICAN
REINFORCEMENT ROUTE

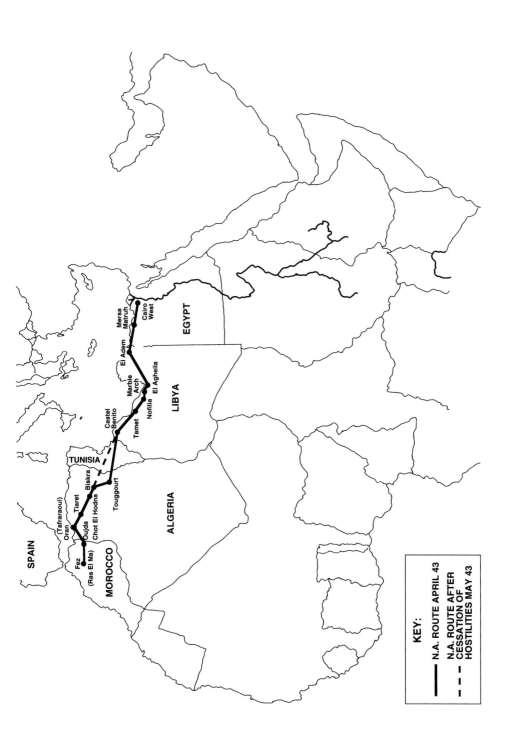

re-located at Oujda, was responsible for delivering machines from Casablanca to Cairo; and No 4 ADU, supporting the invasion of Sicily with reinforcement aircraft, was formed in June 1943 and based at Azizia south of Tripoli.

The history of Transport Command's contribution to the RAF during the Second World War can best be summarised by recounting the achievements of its component Groups – Nos 44, 45, 46, 47, 216 and 229. All facets of transport and ferrying operations in all theatres were covered by these Groups' activities.

Nos 44 and 45 Groups were at either ends of the great ferry organisation already described, set up from 1940 onwards to get aircraft across the Atlantic to Britain from the 'arsenal of democracy' in the United States.

No 44 Group organised the British receiving end for all aircraft coming across the Atlantic and the despatch of machines going out to the Mediterranean theatre or on to India. To give some idea of the volume of its ferry operations – worth reiterating for the sheer magnitude of reinforcement statistics, in the four-year period from October 1940 to 19 November 1944, 4,231 aircraft were delivered to the UK from North America. In the last weeks of 1940 following the pioneer Hudson deliveries on 10–11 November there were 26 arrivals; in 1941 there were 722; in 1942 1,163; and in 1943 1,450[1].

In the same period the Group processed 10,468 USAAF operational deliveries – the largest number of them B-17s (6,628) and the next largest B-24s (2,254), all destined for the daylight strategic bombing offensive. These were Northern route deliveries; during the same period, 4,486 American aircraft were delivered over the Southern route, from Natal in Brazil to West Africa and from there to St Mawgan, Valley or Prestwick via Marrakesh in Morocco. The greatest number of these were B-24s (1,788), followed by Dakotas (1,208).

No 45 Group had been RAF Ferry Command until it was taken over by Transport Command in April 1943: on the 11th, it was re-named No 45 (Transport) Group. It then assumed overall Ferry Command responsibilities in the North and South Atlantic and British West Indies areas. It also had a Training Wing and a Communications Squadron at Dorval. At its head was Air Vice-Marshal R L G (Reggie) Marix CB DSO, who had been second-in-command to Bowhill at Dorval.

In addition to its ferrying role, the Group was also responsible for VIP transport. All the wartime conferences of Allied leaders involved airlifts on a considerable scale. Thus after the Trident conference in Washington in May 1943 Prime Minister Winston Churchill and his immediate party were passengers to the UK in the BOAC flying-boat *Bristol*. It took five Liberators to transport the other conference delegates across the Atlantic. When the Quebec conference was held in August 1943, two Liberators of the Return Ferry Service departed from Dorval on the 26th with 25

1 These figures are given in *Atlantic Bridge The Official Account of RAF Transport Command's Ocean Ferry*, prepared for the Air Ministry by the Ministry of Information and published by HMSO in 1945.

delegates, and on the 28th the Foreign Secretary, Chief of the Air Staff and other VIPs embarked in the BOAC Clipper *Bangor* for their return flight to the UK.

The salient features of No 45 Group's transatlantic contribution during the war were, first, the actual supply of aircraft from US and Canadian factories to Europe and Africa to reinforce squadrons in the European, Mediterranean and Far East theatres; secondly, making air transit of the Atlantic a routine business.

Before the war, flights across the Atlantic were made by heroic record-breakers like Alcock and Brown, Lindbergh and the Mollisons. Under the demands of wartime supply-lines transatlantic flying became commonplace and records were broken in the course of ferrying duties. For example, on 10 April 1944 Capt Douglas in a Dakota made the first direct flight by twin-engined aircraft from Newfoundland to North Africa – Gander to Rabat Sale, Morocco, in 13hr 18min.

Not only by its reinforcement flights with new aircraft, but also by its return passenger-carrying flights in Liberators, No 45 Group made transatlantic flying an everyday occurrence. Until then, the way to go to America from Britain was by liner from Southampton or Liverpool to New York. All that was to change after 1945 and the regular services for ferry crews from Prestwick to Dorval helped to alter the pattern of inter-continental travel.

By the end of 1943 No 113 (South Atlantic) Wing had despatched its 1,000th aircraft since the first delivery from Nassau on 6 March; but not all flights by its crews or those of No 112 Wing were successfully accomplished. Engine or systems failures or weather hazards over the ocean wastes could – and did – take their toll. A Hampden (AF309) which had been built in Canada by Fairchild Aircraft Co was missing on 14 October 1943. On the 25th the three-man crew were found alive, though suffering from frost-bitten feet, on an island off the east coast of Greenland. They were picked up and taken by sea to Bluie West 1[2], from where they were flown back to Dorval. On 7 May 1944 a Canadian-built Mosquito was reported missing between Bluie West 1 and Reykjavik, Iceland, and this time there was no rescue operation. On the 13th a Marauder crashed into the sea a mile west of Windsor Field[3], Nassau, Bahamas, with the loss of its two-man crew. Ferry flying, especially over hundreds of miles of empty, hungry oceans, was no sinecure for wartime aircrew.

One very unusual flight was made, when between 24 June and 1 July 1943 a Waco glider carrying one-and-a-half tons of freight was towed across to the UK by a Dakota (with a Catalina for company) via Goose Bay, Bluie West 1 and Reykjavik to Prestwick; and there is an extraordinary entry in the Transport Command HQ ORB for 18 October 1943, describing the delivery of a B-25 by a medical officer:

---

2 One of the emergency landing-grounds in Greenland for aircraft flying from Goose Bay, Labrador, to Reykjavik, Iceland. The others were Bluie West 8 (also on the west coast) and Bluie East 2 on the east coast.

3 Named after the Duke of Windsor, then Governor of the Bahamas.

'Wg Cdr C C Barker, Senior Medical Officer of No 45 (Air Transport) Group, Dorval, reported at this HQ having arrived the previous day in a Mitchell reinforcement aircraft of which he had been Captain. This was believed to be the first time a pilot with medical qualifications had brought an aircraft over the transatlantic route. He had been unable to attend the three-day preparation course and had had to familiarise himself with the aircraft from notes that others had taken. His flight was undertaken with the object of obtaining personal knowledge of the duties and strains experienced by pilots on this route.'

One of the more bizarre incidents in these transatlantic operations occurred in a Ventura – not involving the aircraft but its occupants. When AJ164 was en route from Gander, Newfoundland, to Goose, Labrador, on 8 May 1943 on a normal scheduled freight-carrying flight the cabin filled with smoke as a result of the failure of a heater fan. The Ventura was then about halfway between its departure and arrival points and at about 12,000ft, in cloud. The pilot put it into a shallow dive and switched off the heater, rectifying the trouble. However, during the descent four of the passengers became panic-stricken and baled out, although no order to do so had been given.

Extensive searches were made by aircraft on delivery flights and others from Gander, but without success. On the 10th the search was abandoned and the four were posted as missing. But that was not the end of the story.

On 26th June, more than seven weeks later, a message was received at Gander from Port Saunders on the north-west coast of Newfoundland that Newfoundland Ranger Hogan and Cpl E C Butt who had parachuted from Ventura AJ164 on 8 May had been found and were at Port Saunders. Hogan was reported as well and Butt suffered only from frost-bitten toes. 'It was obvious', said the ORB account, 'that were it not for Ranger Hogan's endurance and knowledge of woodcraft, Cpl Butt would have died. Efforts are now in hand to ascertain the whereabouts of the other two personnel who baled-out of the aircraft at the same time'. But there is no further record of them.

The Lockheed Ventura (or B-34 in USAAF nomenclature) did not apparently enjoy a good safety record. According to Don McVicar in his book *Ferry Command*[4] the type had a higher loss record per delivery than any other aircraft to date. He found it 'pretty tricky to hold on take-off and on single engine'.

Nevertheless, Venturas were the most numerous type, along with Martin Baltimores, to be flown across by the South Atlantic route during 1943. The Transport Command Unit at Belem, Brazil, had 55 arrivals of the latter type and 52 departures, and 51 Venturas with 49 departures. Dakotas were the next most numerous type, with 23 arrivals and 25 departures.

By contrast, for the North Atlantic route the month of January 1944 was the busiest one for the Transport Command Unit at Gander since July

---

4 Airlife, 1981. (Previously cited.)

1942: 89 delivery aircraft were despatched, comprising 21 Liberators, 35 Dakotas, 26 Mitchells, four Lancasters and three Venturas. The Unit also handled eight Return Ferry Service aircraft.

When Canadian-built Mosquitos started to come through from August 1943, it was inevitable that some record times would be achieved for Atlantic crossings. On 10 May 1944 two Mosquitos crossed to Ballykelly, Northern Ireland, and one of them – piloted by Wg Cdr John Wooldridge DSO DFC DFM – took 6hr 46min runway-to-runway, or only 5hr 39½min coast-to-coast. In October this time was beaten by a minute and by May 1945 the crossing time had been reduced to 5½hr; then on 23 October of that year a PR Mosquito of No 540 sqn, helped by a 70 mph tailwind, flew from Gander to St Mawgan in 5hr 10min.

These flights, of course, had the natural advantage of prevailing westerly winds. It was a different matter for the westbound Liberators, struggling back with returning ferry crews on board.

The Consolidated B-24 Liberator, that distinctive four-engined bomber/maritime/transport aircraft (as its wartime roles developed), made a notable contribution to USAAF and RAF operations. It did yeoman service in Ferry/Transport Command, which could hardly have managed without it on the North Atlantic route, as the 'airliner' equipping the Return Ferry Service between Prestwick, Gander and Montreal.

The swift genesis of the Liberator was one of its most remarkable features: it all came about in 1939, designed to a US Army specification for a heavy bomber issued early in that year and built to a contract dated 30 March. It was to supplement the Boeing B-17, whose origin went back to a requirement issued in 1934. Remarkably, the prototype Liberator (XB-24) made its maiden flight before the end of 1939 – on 29 December. Its notable characteristics were a high, very thin wing of 110ft span (known as the Davis Wing after its designer Mr David R Davis and conferring on the aircraft its remarkably long range); a deep, slab-sided fuselage; and a tricycle undercarriage – the first to be fitted to an American bomber.

RAF interest in the Liberator came about in 1940 when a French order for 120, nullified by the German invasion, was taken over by the RAF who then added contracts for 165 more. The first Liberator for the Royal Air Force (AM258) made its maiden flight on 17 January 1942. The first export models to come off the production line were flown across the Atlantic in March, but six of them were immediately diverted to transport duties for use on the recently instituted Trans-Atlantic Return Ferry Service between Prestwick, Newfoundland and Montreal. Operated at first by British Overseas Airways Corporation then by Ferry Command, this service flew ferry pilots to Canada to collect the increasing numbers of American aircraft for the RAF. The first westbound Liberator left Prestwick on 4 May 1941.

Not only did Liberators provide a staple, reliable transport service across the Atlantic; their very long range made them ideal maritime patrol aircraft in the war against the U-boats, and they operated as RAF strategic bombers in the Mediterranean and Far East theatres. In addition they equipped five squadrons in Transport Command (Nos 53, 59, 220, 232 and 246) and partially equipped three more (Nos 10, 102 and 511).

In the later stages of the war, RAF Transport Command took delivery of 24 Liberator C.VII aircraft, known in the USAAF as the C-87. 'This version . . . carried no armament, had a faired nose and tail, and [had] seats in the bomb-bay, with windows along the sides of the fuselage. The C.VII was used on Transport Command routes between England and the Far East. It was in service with No 46 Group of Transport Command in England and with No 229 Group in India.

'The final task of Liberators with the RAF, before their return to the USA after the war, was the massive operation of flying home British prisoners of war from all over the world. The total number of Liberators supplied to the RAF from Consolidated was 1,694'.[5]

Liberators of No 45 Group made many Atlantic crossings during the war years with VIPs, as well as with returning ferry crews, generally with reliability and safety though in conditions of acute discomfort for their hapless bomb-bay passengers; but there were some losses. One particularly sad one, late in the war, was that of a Liberator of No 45 Group Communications Sqn which disappeared on 27 March 1945 when en route to Canada. Among those on board were Air Marshal Sir Peter Drummond, the Air Member for Personnel, and H A Jones CMG MC, Director of Public Relations (RAF), one-time Head of the Air Historical Branch and author of all but the first volume of *The War in the Air*, the official history of the RFC/RAF in the First World War[6].

While Nos 44, 45 and 216 Groups had been taken over as going concerns by the newly formed Transport Command, No 46 – the European Transport Support Group – was the first new one to be formed. Given authority to do so at the beginning of 1944 when Allied landings in Europe were being planned, the Group came into being on 4 February with HQ at The Cedars, Hatch End, Middlesex – a very suburban address, with Air Cdre A L Fiddament DFC as AOC.

The new Group was allocated three airfields in the Cotswolds – Blakehill Farm, Broadwell and Down Ampney, and it was to have had five squadrons – Nos 271 and 512 from Transport Command, and Nos 569, 575 and 597. In the event Nos 569 and 597 were never formed. Its squadrons were to be equipped with Dakotas, with which transport–support experience had been gained in the Western Desert campaigns. Negotiations were opened under the Lend–Lease scheme and by the beginning of 1944 a total of 150 had been earmarked for No 46 Group.

The choice of airfields had been determined by their proximity to other stations from which the airborne assault spearheading Operation Overlord would be launched, and to be within range of north-west France for a Dakota with a Horsa glider in tow. But in the shorter term they were not without deficiencies. For a start they were unfinished; although the runways were complete and certain services had been installed, they needed considerable adaptation and improvisation to fit them for the

---

5 For all these details on the Liberator the author is indebted to Owen Thetford's invaluable reference book *Aircraft of the Royal Air Force since 1918* (Putnam, 1988).
6 *The War in the Air*. Raleigh and Jones; Clarendon Press, Oxford 1922–1937.

transport support role. So the new No 46 Group had a difficult beginning, with D-day and the first landings in Normandy only four months away.

The squadrons which moved into these bare airfields, originally intended for the USAAF 8th Air Force, were Nos 512 and 575 which went into Broadwell, Nos 233 and 48 which came straight from Coastal Command – the former going to Blakehill Farm and the latter to Down Ampney[7], and No 271 – the veteran UK-based squadron which had moved Fighter Command squadrons around during the Battles of France and Britain – which also went to Down Ampney. The new No 46 Group thus had its five squadrons.

One of the original officers on the Air Staff of No 46 (Transport) Group at Harrow Weald was Wg Cdr L A Strange DSO MC DFC, under whom the AOC, Air Cdre 'Fido' Fiddament, had served during the First World War. In 1940 while serving on No 24 Sqn he had flown to France in a DH Dragon and brought back a Hurricane, a type he had never flown before, evading Luftwaffe fighters and landing safely at Manston. For this feat he was awarded the DFC, being one of the few officers to be decorated in both World Wars. (When he rejoined the RAF in 1939 he was 49). From 1940 to 1941 he commanded the Parachute Training School at RAF Ringway, Manchester, so his knowledge of Airborne forces' techniques was very useful to the newly formed No 46 Group[8].

Louis Strange played an energetic part in getting the new Group's squadrons ready by the beginning of June 1944 for Overlord. After the landings in Normandy the AOC sent him a letter of appreciation for his work:

'I have been intending to write to you ever since D-day to thank you for all the sterling work you did for 46 Group in the Airborne Training. All of us here know quite well that, but for you, the Group would not have been ready on the day. I realise . . . the difficulties you had to contend with – not the least of which arose from the set-up of the two Groups [No 38 which was in the Allied Expeditionary Air Force, while No 46 was in Transport Command] and some of the personalities involved. . . .'

This letter is quoted in the biography by Gp Capt Hearn which notes that

'Strange's job as the first Ops officer of the new formation was to learn what he could from the staffs and stations of No 38 Group [which had previously been No 38 Wing in Army Co-operation Command], transpose it into a training programme and operational procedures for 46, and pass these on for immediate action to the new Dakota squadrons now forming on recently constructed airfields at Down Ampney, Broadwell and Blakehill Farm. He also began to beg, borrow and steal

---

7 A name which became famous for two different reasons – because of the hymn tune by Ralph Vaughan Williams and because it was the RAF base from which Flt Lt D S A Lord flew when he won the VC (as will be recounted).

8 See *Flying Rebel The Story of Louis Strange*, by Peter Hearn (HMSO, 1994).

as many of 38 Group's staff and as much of its equipment as he could without making too much of a nuisance of himself. For once he received heartening co-operation, particularly from within 38 Group under its energetic commander Air Vice-Marshal 'Holly' Hollinghurst. . . .'

The Air Ministry itself admitted the dearth of transport–support experience in the UK-based RAF in 1943, when plans for the airborne forces' contribution to Operation Overlord were being prepared. In a paper on the organisation and role of No 46 Group it stated:

'There was only one squadron in the UK then with any (and very limited) transport support experience, No 271 Sqn, which had given airlifts to fighter units during the Battle of Britain and had been engaged in deploying by air those fighter squadrons moved to the south of England for the raid on Dieppe in August 1942. It was equipped with modified Handley Page Harrows. . . .'[9]

No 271 began to receive Dakotas in August 1943, and all the squadrons in No 46 Group were similarly equipped. Its faithful Harrows continued in service until 1945.

The other newly formed Group in Transport Command was No 47, 'the trunk route Group', which had a modest inauguration at the beginning of 1945, when on 1 January the Headquarters of No 116 Wing at Hendon was disbanded and immediately re-formed as No 47 Group. The Group assumed the responsibilities and functions formerly exercised by HQ No 116 Wing, namely the organisation and control of long-range and VIP transport in the RAF.

At the end of February 1945 the Group had five squadrons and a flight – Nos 24 (the VIP squadron), 246, 511 and 525, the Metropolitan Communications Squadron and No 1680 (T) Flight. Nos 246, 511 and 525 were described as being engaged in 'the airline rôle'.

The VIP transport role for which No 47 Group held responsibility was illustrated by two journeys in early 1945. On 19 February, Skymaster EW990[10] arrived at Lyneham, having flown from Cairo non-stop in 13hr 42min carrying the Prime Minister home from the Three Power Conference at Yalta. Then on 23 March the Prime Minister and the Chief of the Imperial General Staff flew from Northolt to Y55[11] in a Dakota of No 24 Sqn. Their visit coincided with the opening of the 21st Army Group offensive and the crossing of the Rhine on the northern sector of the Western front. The Prime Minister and the CIGS returned to Northolt on the 26th March.

By the end of April the roll of squadrons in No 47 Group showed an additional entry, No 187, and it was with a Dakota of this squadron that

---

9 Air Ministry folder on the organisation and role of No 46 Group (IIS/76).

10 Developed version of the Douglas DC-4/C-54.

11 Venlo, Holland. Post-D-day airfields were all numbered, with an alphabetical prefix, e.g. A54 (Le Bourget), B56 (Brussels) etc.

the ST (Small-scale Trooping) service was inaugurated on 1 May 1945. As the Group's ORB explained in its entry for that day, datelined Merryfield: 'The ST Service was inaugurated today – Dakota KN415 of 187 Sqn which left Merryfield for Poona with 22 troops, to carry out the first Small Scale Trooping service to India'. In its entry for the last day of that month the ORB recorded that 'the commitment for the carriage of 1,000 troops to India has been met – 1,006 troops have actually been transported and there have been no accidents or serious delays en route'.

At the end of the last month of the Second World War, May 1945, the ORB of No 47 Group summarised the passengers, freight and mail it had carried and listed the following destinations:

> Aden and Iraq, Africa, Australia, the Azores, Belfast, Belgium, Ceylon, the Channel Islands, China, France, Germany, Greece, Holland, Iceland, India, Italy, Malta, the Middle East, Norway and the USSR.

There could not be a more graphic illustration of Transport Command's international arena of operations.

The other Group which Transport Command controlled, No 229 at Karachi, was formed on 16 December 1943 by upgrading No 179 (Ferry) Wing whose formation has already been mentioned.

Earlier in 1943 two No 179 Wing Officers, Wg Cdr Crawford and Sqn Ldr Thomas, had visited No 216 Group to see how its ferry controls and staging posts worked. Their report on their tour provides a useful description of reinforcement routes through the Middle East to India.

They left Karachi by flying-boat on 5 March and when they got to Cairo went to see the AOC No 216 Group, Air Cdre Whitney Straight, and his SOA (Senior Administration Officer), Gp Capt May, to plan a schedule of visits. This meeting was on the 7th and on the following two days they visited the two Aircraft Delivery Units – No 2 at Kilo 40, an airfield on the Cairo–Alexandria road which the unit shared with No 135 MU, and No 1, the HQ for aircrew flying the West African and Port Sudan Reinforcement Routes, then accommodated in three river steamers – *Delta*, *Arabia* and *Egypt* – anchored near Gezira Island in Cairo. These had been requisitioned from Thomas Cook; in pre-war days they had been used for tourist cruises up the Nile.

On 10 March the two No 179 Wing officers departed by Blenheim for a tour of Ferry Controls and RSPs on the North African coast, calling at El Adem (Tobruk), Benina (Benghazi) and night-stopping at Castel Benito (Tripoli), and inspected the operation of No 6 Ferry Control. They were following the route flown on hundreds of delivery flights by ferry pilots during the Western Desert campaigns. They then returned eastwards, visiting on 11 March RSP Marble Arch [the triumphal arch on the Tripoli–Benghazi road erected by Mussolini where – to quote Shelley – 'boundless and bare/The lone and level sands stretch far away'], night-stopping at El Adem RSP and returning to Cairo on the 12th.

The two officers experienced their only misadventure on their return flight to India (by the southern route, via Aden). They had not been provided with the most reliable form of Middle East air transport:

No 216 GROUP - FORTNIGHTLY SERVICE
CAIRO WEST - TAKORADI &
CAIRO WEST - KARACHI APRIL 1943

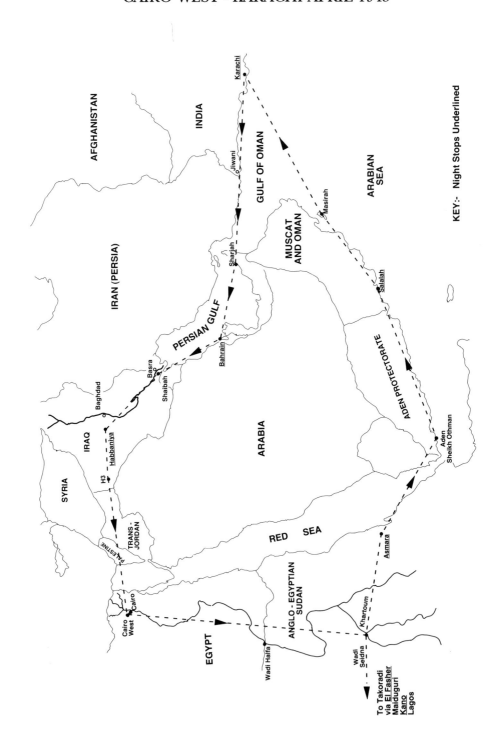

KEY:- Night Stops Underlined

Karachi

AFGHANISTAN

INDIA

GULF OF OMAN

Jiwani

ARABIAN SEA

Masirah

IRAN (PERSIA)

MUSCAT AND OMAN

Sharjah

PERSIAN GULF

Salalah

Basra

Baghdad

Bahrain

Shaibah

ADEN PROTECTORATE

IRAQ

Habbaniya

ARABIA

H3

Aden
Sheikh Othman

SYRIA

TRANS-
JORDAN

PALESTINE

RED   SEA

Asmara

Cairo

Cairo
West

ANGLO - EGYPTIAN
SUDAN

Khartoum

EGYPT

Wadi Haifa

Wadi
Seidna

To Takoradi
via El Fasher
Maiduguri
Kano
Lagos

'March 14th left by Bisley[12] from LG224 (No 1 Ferry Control) [Cairo West] for India, but with engine failure over the desert, forced-landed at Luxor (RSP). March 15th returned to LG224 by Beaufort.

'March 17th left LG224 for Khartoum by Hudson. March 18th departed from Khartoum by Bisley for India, visiting RSP Asmara en route and night-stopping at Sheikh Othman (Aden). March 19th left for Masirah, visiting the RSPs at Riyan and Salalah and night-stopping at Masirah. March 20th returned to Karachi. . . .'

The outcome of the officers' Odyssey was a report which was highly complimentary to No 216 Group and depicted how reinforcement aircraft and their pilots were looked after when en-route to the Middle East or India:

'The high standard of efficiency of the Ferry Controls (FC) and RSPs controlled by 216 Group is due to the flexibility of their organisation, which allows an OC Ferry Control to be a law unto himself with regard to the control of personnel and MT at his FC and at the RSPs under him, and this is in large measure due to the fact that the whole organisation has administrative as well as operational control.
'At all staging posts the outstanding feature was the manner in which aircraft are met, serviced and despatched. Pilots do not need to look for servicing parties or food; they are conducted to them.'

---

12 The final (Mk V) version of the Bristol Blenheim.

Chapter V

Bari to Burma; the Killer Monsoons; Heroism over Arnhem

'. . . of most disastrous chances,
Of moving accidents by flood and field'

Shakespeare, Othello, *I iii*

BY April 1945 there were 11 Dakota squadrons in No 229 Group under South East Asia Command, including No 31 which had taken part in intensive supply-dropping operations in support of General Orde Wingate's Chindits during 1943, and No 267 which had distinguished itself as a No 216 Group squadron.

No 267 made remarkable contributions to the air war both in the Mediterranean and in the Burma campaign. After the Western Desert battles it operated in Italy during 1944 as part of the Balkan Air Force, dropping and landing supplies in Yugoslavia and Albania and even operating into Poland to support the Resistance forces. Then in February 1945 it was abruptly transferred from Italy to Burma where as one of the No 229 Group squadrons it provided air support for the 14th Army's final offensive against the Japanese.

It had been based at Bari in southern Italy since mid-November 1943, having moved there from Cairo West, and its operations into Poland and Yugoslavia took place during 1944. The former, code-named Wildhorn, involved a Polish officer, Flt Lt Korporski, as 2nd pilot; in the latter, code-named Righthook and Cyanide, the AOC No 216 Group, Air Cdre Whitney Straight, flew one of the two Dakotas which landed at targets in Yugoslavia taking-in special equipment and evacuating Allied Army and Air Force personnel, some of whom had been PoW.

Then in a signal dated 29 January 1945 the squadron received orders to move to India with 25 aircraft and 30 crews. The first echelon of eight aircraft left Bari on 2 February, and the move was completed by 10 February when the third echelon of eight aircraft arrived safely at Bilaspur. The squadron ORB proudly recorded:

> 'It will be seen that, 13 days after receipt of the order to move, 25 aircraft with most of the squadron personnel and equipment had flown from Bari in Italy to Bilaspur in Central India, a distance of about 4,700 miles'.

The Dakotas staged through Basrah in the Persian Gulf, and there is an interesting note in the ORB which supports what has already been said in this narrative about the service that reinforcement crews and aircraft received at staging posts:

'It is apt to mention here the excellent organisation and hospitality accorded to all personnel at 42 Staging Post, commanded by Sqn Ldr J Hyde. Throughout the whole move arrangements at Staging Posts were good, but 42 SP was quite outstanding'.

One major problem when No 267 Sqn got the order to move was that many of its personnel were nearing the end of their tours of duty. One of them was the adjutant; his place was taken by Fg Off R Bramer[1] who made the following entry in his diary for 30 January 1945:

'Signal at breakfast. Squadron posted to India for eventual operations in Burma. After all, we are a mobile squadron but have been so long in Bari that we've come to regard ourselves as anything but mobile.

'Feverish activity and high feelings. We have to be in India by February 12th, which means an immediate start. . . .'

'It was decided that those personnel within six months of tour-expiry date would not go. The adjutant himself was within that category, so having stood in for him, I was ordered by the CO to continue that duty. I found myself, therefore, with all the organisation of the move of a complete squadron many thousands of miles. . . .'

During No 267's last three days at Bari it snowed, and on 5 February Fg Off Bramer recorded:

'We set off, shaking the snow of Italy off our flying boots (everybody in winter clothing), for the first stop – El Adem'.

Two months after receiving the signal at Bari that they were to move to Burma, No 267 Sqn had become operational in their new environment, exchanging the rain and mud and snow of Italy and supply drops into Yugoslavia for the humid jungles of Burma and air support for the 14th Army in its relentless push to drive the Japanese to Rangoon and out of the country altogether.

A few days after 267's Dakotas had all reached Bilaspur, orders came for a move forward to Tulihal between 21 and 25 February, and for operations to begin from there by 1 March. The ORB recorded that on that date 'the squadron commenced operations from Tulihal with 30 tactical flights, consisting of one landing at Sinthe, seven landings at Shwebo, nine landings at Thaburton, one landing at Sadaung, two landings at Allagappa and ten landings at Alon'. These names meant

---

1 On 29 January 1946 Flt Lt Ronald Bramer was awarded the DFC for 'supply dropping missions to the Partisan troops in Yugoslavia' and for 'supply dropping operations in Burma, flying through severe monsoon storms and landing supplies, often within five miles of the front line' – a distance he corrected in his diary to '500yd'.

No 267 SQUADRON SUPPLY OPERATIONS - MARCH 1945

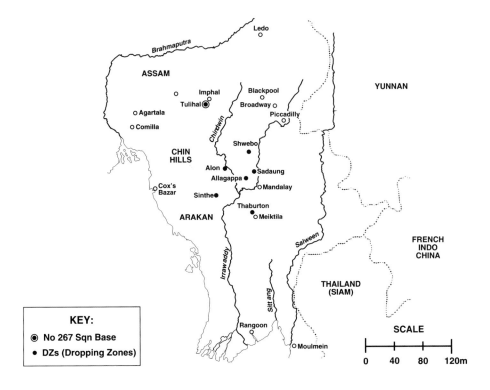

much to the aircrew involved but are meaningless to later generations: the map above shows their location. The ORB noted: '11 flights were successful and the total weight carried was 231,388lb'.

In his diary for 2 March, Fg Off Bramer is more specific about one of those landing-grounds:

'We are operating two sorties a day – fly to Sinthe, about 20 miles from the Japanese lines. Had a load of petrol in 40gal drums. [The] landing strip being used today had been taken only two nights earlier and the front [a wide one] had moved 13 miles in that time'.

More vivid detail of supply-dropping operations was provided in an entry for 19 March:

'Did the first detail with Blackie's [Fg Off Blackburn's] crew and did a drop just north of Mandalay, now held only lightly by the Japs. The 19th Division have apparently been making enormous strides and need equipment and stores urgently. Carried a multifarious load of about three tons. Tried to drop on any DZ in the area and found one clearly marked and obviously in use. . . . Began to drop and completed it in nine runs. It was terribly hot.

'Flew over DZ at about 100ft, if possible, and into wind, for free drops and [at] about 400ft for parachute drops. Quarter flap to reduce speed, ideal being 100 mph. . . .

'Finally, we did a "special drop", very low, alongside a truck in which troops were sitting, waiting to collect supplies – a small, home-made parachute containing 60 cigarettes with a note reading: "With the compliments of the boys of the Flying Horse Squadron, RAF Transport Command" ' [2].

Monsoons in India and Burma were a terrible natural hazard to aircrew, often proving fatal if their aircraft inadvertently flew into towering cumulo-nimbus clouds. The ORB of No 229 Group HQ recorded that a Dakota (FZ597) of No 353 Sqn, based at Palam and flying on the Delhi–Calcutta–Delhi service, crashed 120 miles north-east of Allahabad on 4 August 1944 in daylight after it encountered one of the worst monsoon storms ever recorded in this area. It had a crew of four and carried 14 passengers; there were no survivors.

The ORB said that 'evidence shows that the aircraft hit the ground in a vertical dive and a subsequent investigation indicates that the filet of the mainplane was torn away in a very bad bump and, thrown back, damaged the elevator and put the aircraft out of control. The rescue party encountered very great difficulties in reaching the [wreckage], as the whole countryside was flooded, but eventually succeeded'.

The CO of No 267 sqn, Wg Cdr W S Hillary DFC DFM, commented in his Remarks in the squadron ORB for July 1945:

'Due to the monsoon, and severe storms, flying this month in Central Burma was hazardous, one aircraft being thrown upside down three times within the space of ten minutes when the pilot, flying through heavy rain, inadvertently flew into a cu-nim. . . .

'One accident occurred when a captain broke cloud over the sea near base, the base of the cloud being 400–500ft, and severe monsoon rains and conditions existed. The aircraft flew level at about 50ft and then struck the sea and exploded, all occupants being killed. No plausible explanation is possible as the wreckage sank immediately, making investigation impossible'.

One of the most striking descriptions of flying conditions in Burma was provided by Sgt Simon Eden, son of the Foreign Secretary the Rt Hon Anthony Eden, who was a navigator on No 62 Sqn and fell victim – on 23 June 1945 – to the twin perils of mountains and monsoons he describes. In his diary, quoted in Robert Rhodes James' biography of his father[3], he wrote of an experience he had undergone in the previous month:

2 No 267's badge depicted the winged horse of Greek mythology, Pegasus.

3 Published by Wiedenfield and Nicolson in 1986: the extract is quoted with their permission. Simon Eden's commission came through just after his death.

'We flew along towering banks of cloud trying to find a gap. Those clouds, with savage up and down currents of air, meant destruction to any Dakota that tried to force its way through. Gently we nosed our way along till we saw a gap. We tried it, we go through the first barrier, and on to the next. This time the gaps were not so obliging. We descended to try our luck underneath. The mist and rain enveloped us in a blinding shroud; we flew by instruments and instinct, peering out through the windscreen wipers, trying inadequately to deal with the torrential water that hammered its ceaseless tattoo on the aircraft. The currents of air caused the plane to bump, pitch and jolt, and it was blown we could only guess where. The normal air navigation, as used over Europe, is useless over the hills and valleys of Asia. In squalls like these you guess and keep your fingers crossed.

'The time came when we judged ourselves over the Irrawaddy and its fertile valley. Slowly we went down; we must find the river to check up our position on the map. Eyes were really strained this time. The pilot opened the throttles time and time again as the shadow of a hill crept below our wings – dangerous, sombre, forbidding. Then again we would go down and once we saw a green hill half a mile off our port wing, and the summit was above us. We were in a valley. God alone knew what valley. We never stayed to find out; we went up again to try later. This game continued for ten minutes that seemed like an eternity; then the weather cleared and the Irrawaddy lay before us, glimmering in the sun, a friendly symbol of safety'.

Sadly on 23 June 1945 there was to be no clearance, no friendly symbol of safety, for Simon Eden and his crew – Fg Off Roe, Fg Off Loder and Sgt Hyne. Wreckage of their Dakota, KM455, was found in the vicinity of Sumsu village in the Arakan hills.

The No 62 Sqn ORB had noted on the 23rd that KM455 had failed to return from operations. From reports given by other aircraft it was believed the aircraft crashed on or near Mt Victoria. The ORB had previously recorded: 'The monsoon has become progressively worse during the month, though not with the violent electrical discharging storm clouds experienced earlier. Frequently in the second week aircraft had to climb through a heavy layer of cloud over the base area to 10,000ft, with the lurking danger of heavy cumulus. Later in the day base would clear, but it became necessary to climb to 14,000ft and sometimes more to clear the heavy cloud building up over the Arakan Yomas'.

Heroism over Arnhem

It is not the intention of this history to recount the contribution made by squadrons of No 46 Group of Transport Command to the major European airborne operations of 1944–45 in Operations Overlord, Market Garden and Varsity. These great airlifts have been fully documented in many accounts of the RAF and the airborne forces' part in the Second World War. But we should not pass on without highlighting an individual act of great heroism on 19 September 1944 over Arnhem in Operation Market (the air aspect of Market Garden), by Flt Lt David Lord DFC of No 271 Sqn which earned him a posthumous Victoria Cross. He was, it might well be said, the Guy Gibson of Transport Command, typifying all that was best in its aircrew, having shown outstanding courage over many years of operations.

Like Gibson, he joined the RAF before the war, but not as a pilot; he was an AC2 Armourer, serving on the North-West frontier of India 1937–39[4], and being recommended for training as an airman pilot in 1938. He qualified as a Sergeant Pilot on 5 April 1939 when he was 25, having already served in the RAF for three years.

He did his flying training in the UK at No 2 Flying Training School, and was then posted back to India, joining one of its long-serving squadrons, No 31 (described as 'First in the Indian skies') at Lahore in October 1939. He was to serve on this squadron for four years, operating over India, Burma, Iraq and the Western Desert. He was commissioned in 1942 and awarded the DFC in 1943, after having survived two near-fatal accidents.

In autumn 1941 the DC-2 flight of No 31 Sqn was sent to the Middle East where they operated from Bilbeis with a detachment of No 117 Sqn[5]. When on a sortie into the Western Desert on 8 December 1943 carrying supplies to LG134, Lord's aircraft was disabled by anti-aircraft fire, although he managed to make a successful forced landing. After their three months' detachment, No 31 Sqn was ordered eastwards, to Akyab in Burma.

By December 1941 David Lord had been promoted to Temporary Warrant Officer and on 1 June 1942 he was commissioned, a well-deserved recognition of his character, his flying skill and his contribution to transport operations.

His coolness and judgement were demonstrated again when on 12 January 1943 he lost an engine on a night sortie, making a successful belly landing after a single-engine approach through cloud and drizzle. Then on 16 April 1943 he was awarded the DFC, the citation saying that he had

'. . . completed a very large number of operational sorties in Iraq, the Western Desert and in Burma. His duties in Burma included the evacuation of casualties, women and children, often in the face of severe opposition. During the past two months he had done admirable work, dropping food supplies to troops in the field. His sorties have often taken him deep into enemy territory, frequently without fighter escort, and have called for courage and endurance of a high order. Flying Officer Lord's keenness and cheerful disregard of danger have set a fine example to the pilots of his squadron'.

---

4 He held the India General Service medal, with Clasp North-West Frontier 1937–39.
5 One of whose pilots, W F Higham, a friend of the author's, has recalled that when he first joined the squadron he flew as co-pilot with David Lord, who 'never failed to kneel down and say his prayers at night'. Another fellow pilot remembered him as 'a real gentleman'.

By May 1943 David Lord had been promoted to Flight Lieutenant, and in November of that year his long service with No 31 Sqn came to an end when he was repatriated and posted to No 271 Sqn at Doncaster, one of the No 46 Group squadrons tasked especially with airborne operations in support of Overlord. His long and varied experience of transport–support operations, his DFC (in a Command where such decorations were rarer than in the other operational Commands) and his integrity and steadiness of character were welcome contributions to his new squadron and its inexperienced crews, who were training with the Airborne Forces for their part in spearheading the invasion of Normandy in four months' time.

By the 17th February the squadron had built up a strength of 30 Dakotas at Doncaster, and this number increased after the move to its operational base at Down Ampney, with the addition of the Horsas its aircraft were to tow. On 13 March the squadron ORB recorded: '38 Dakotas . . . and now 19 gliders of 24 allotted, making aircraft dispersal a problem'.

With only some three months to go before D-day, No 271 was tasked with a minimum of 400hr per week training, involving glider towing and paratroop dropping. When the aircrew and the airborne soldiers had become accustomed to the techniques involved, exercises were held, like one on 24 March mounted from Errol on the Scottish east coast between Perth and Dundee, which had as its purpose the training of 240 men of an assault unit, and of aircrews in supply-dropping.

One of Lord's fellow Dakota captains on No 271 Sqn during the run-up to Operation Overlord was Maj P S Joubert, a South African Air Force officer who, aged 48, was said to have been the oldest captain of an operational aircraft in the Royal Air Force and was later awarded the AFC and the DSO, the latter for 'skill, courage and leadership' in taking part in three airborne operations. In January 1945 he became CO of the squadron[6]. Another No 271 Sqn pilot was Flt Lt K O Edwards, who like Lord was shot down over Arnhem but survived, becoming famous in post-war years as the comedian 'Jimmy' Edwards.

On the night before D-day, 5/6 June 1944, Lord was in the squadron's 'A' Flight detachment at Blakehill Farm, and took off at 2320 hr in Operation Tonga, dropping paratroops to protect the left flank of the British 2nd Army landing on the beaches.

He survived the Overlord operations, and three months later was involved in Operation Market, the ill-fated attempt to capture and hold the Dutch town of Arnhem, the 'bridge too far' as the doomed enterprise came to be called.

---

6 Details of the remarkable career of Lt-Col P S Joubert have been provided by his nephew Mr J W Rosenthal, who recounts from the Down Ampney ORB entry for 15 August 1945 the tragic accident which ended his life when the end of the Second World War was being marked with national and local festivities:

'VJ celebrations took place and a programme of dances etc was arranged. Lt-Col P S Joubert DSO AFC, while helping to light a VJ Day firework sustained injuries from its explosion which caused his death the following day. The tragic loss of this universally popular and respected officer was deeply felt by all at the station'.

It was on this operation that Lord lost his life and earned his VC. His last take-off from Down Ampney was on 19th September 1944 – Operation Market D+2.

The citation for his Victoria Cross described in slow motion the courage and steadfastness which won him this highest award for valour:

'He was pilot and captain of a Dakota aircraft detailed to drop supplies at Arnhem on the afternoon of the 19th September 1944. Our airborne troops had been surrounded and were being pressed into a small area defended by a large number of anti-aircraft guns. Aircrews were warned that intense opposition would be met over the dropping zone. To ensure accuracy they were ordered to fly at 900ft when dropping their containers.

'While flying at 1,500ft near Arnhem the starboard wing of Flight Lieutenant Lord's aircraft was twice hit by anti-aircraft fire. The starboard engine was set on fire. He would have been justified in leaving the main stream of supply aircraft and continuing at the same height or even abandoning his aircraft. But on learning that his crew were uninjured and that the dropping zone would be reached in three minutes he said he would complete his mission, as the troops were in dire need of supplies.

'By now the starboard engine was burning furiously. Flt Lt Lord came down to 900ft, where he was singled out for the concentrated fire of all the anti-aircraft guns. On reaching the dropping zone he kept the aircraft on a straight and level course while supplies were dropped. At the end of the run, he was told that two containers remained.

'Although he must have known that the collapse of the starboard wing could not be long delayed, Flt Lt Lord circled, rejoined the stream of aircraft and made a second run to drop the remaining supplies. These manoeuvres took eight minutes in all, the aircraft being continuously under heavy anti-aircraft fire.

'His task completed, Flt Lt Lord ordered his crew to abandon the Dakota, making no attempt himself to leave the aircraft, which was down to 500ft. A few seconds later, the starboard wing collapsed and the aircraft fell in flames. There was only one survivor, who was flung out while assisting other members of the crew to put on their parachutes.

'By continuing his mission in a damaged and burning aircraft, descending to drop the supplies accurately, returning to the dropping zone a second time and, finally, remaining at the controls to give his crew a chance of escape, Flt Lt Lord displayed supreme valour and self-sacrifice. There could be no finer example of sustained courage and determination by a transport pilot on air supply operations'.

There was to be a sad echo of David Lord's last operation nearly eight months later when the only survivor of his crew was repatriated. On 13 May 1945 the No 271 Sqn ORB recorded that

'Fg Off H A King returned to England today in a Fortress, after being a PoW in Germany since the Arnhem re-supply operation in September 1944. Fg Off King was flying in Flt Lt D S A Lord's crew and apparently the aircraft was badly hit before crossing the river by light ack-ack when flying at approximately 2,000ft.

'The Skipper enquired if any of the crew or despatchers were hurt and as everybody seemed to be all right, even though the aircraft had suffered badly, Flt Lt Lord pressed on and reached the DZ.

'Suddenly Flt Lt Lord gave orders for the crew to bale out, and after all the panniers had gone and the crew were ready to jump there was a terrific "whoof", and the next thing Fg Off King knew was that he had hit the ground.

'The starboard wing was shot off and the aircraft dived in from about 5–600ft. Fg Off King was the only survivor, the remaining members of the crew being killed'.

Chapter VI

The War Years: A Summary

'In ranks and squadrons and right form of war'

Shakespeare, Julius Caesar, *II, ii*

IN Volume 3 of the official history *Royal Air Force 1939–1945, The Fight is Won,* co-author (with Denis Richards) Hilary St George Saunders summed-up the wartime achievements of Transport Command with such comprehensiveness and elegance of style that the words deserve to be reproduced here as a summary of what has been said in the preceding chapters[1]:

'On 19th February, 1943, the Air Council reviewed the existing organisation of air transport and reached the decision that a radical change was necessary. Up till then Ferry Command had been responsible for bringing American aircraft across the Atlantic and to Africa. . . . The Command also took a hand in the delivery of aircraft to Australia and India, and bore supplies to bases in far-off Labrador, Greenland and Newfoundland. By February, 1943, it was flying some 66,000 hours a month and the pilots and crews were ferrying every kind of aircraft. One of the Groups – No 44 – controlled in flight all non-operational aircraft approaching or leaving the United Kingdom to the south and west for approximately 1,000 miles. The Group received, prepared and despatched aircraft reinforcements from the United Kingdom, trained crews for air transport duties, and also operated Nos 24, 271 and 511 (Transport) Squadrons, based in Britain. No 216 (Transport and Ferry) Group performed similar duties in the Middle East and Africa, as did No 179 Wing in India. In addition to these Royal Air Force organisations, there was the British Overseas Airways Corporation, which maintained, with a somewhat motley fleet of aircraft, services to Canada, Portugal, Sweden, West Africa, South Africa, the USSR and India. The policy governing its operations was laid down by the Air Minister on the advice of the Director-General of Civil Aviation.

'For the first three-and-a-half years of the war, British air transport was, it is true to say, conducted by a variety of bodies, acutely short of

---

1 *Royal Air Force 1939–1945,* by Denis Richards and Hilary St G Saunders; HMSO, 1974. Extract by kind permission of the publishers.

aircraft, and maintaining themselves by a system of more or less successful improvisation. Not until a larger number of suitable aircraft were produced could matters be placed on a more rational basis. The opportunity came early in 1943, when about 90 York aircraft, a transport version of the Lancaster bomber, became available[2].

'Accordingly, on 25th March of that year, Transport Command came into being and was placed in the capable hands of Air Chief Marshal Sir Frederick Bowhill, who set up his headquarters at Harrow. The new Command was made up of No 44 Group in the United Kingdom, No 45 Group (up till then Ferry Command) in Canada, with two Wings – one, No 112, operating over the North Atlantic, the other, No 113, over the South, No 216 Group in the Middle East and No 179 Wing in India. Its relations with the British Overseas Airways Corporation, with which it was to work in close co-operation, were settled by the end of March.

'Expansion of the activities of the Command began at once, and by the beginning of 1944, Nos 46 and 47 Groups had been added to those in Britain, and No 229 in India[3] to fulfil the requirements of the South East Asia Command. Transport Command stations were by then dotted all over the Allied world. They numbered 36, and the aircraft of the squadrons and flights using them flew along between staging posts, of which the number rose to 100. They were the beads on the long string of communications running in every direction.

'Nor were passengers neglected. The standard of comfort was not, perhaps, that of the British Overseas Airways Corporation, but the travellers were for the most part members of one or other of the Services and were glad enough to exchange the amenities of a troopship for the comparative luxury of a York or a Liberator.

'Ground staff formed the backbone of the new receiving organisations. Their first problem was to familiarise themselves with American-built aircraft which they were called upon to overhaul after an ocean crossing prior to a continental crossing [i.e. Natal to Accra, Accra to Cairo]. "I arrived in Accra", writes a Flight Sergeant, "with 23 men in February 1943. We came from the place known as the land of sweat and toil, so we thought we were in for fourteen days' good rest, but we were not long in finding our mistake. . . .

' "On arrival we were told that we had to do 54hr inspections on Baltimores – planes we had heard of but never seen – and that was our first fix. Our next fix was that we had English tool kits which were no good on American planes, and on asking for American tool kits we were

---

2 It was not until 1945, however, that Avro Yorks entered Transport Command service in significant numbers: those that did so in 1943 were for VIP duties.
3 To which No 179 Wing was upgraded in December 1943.

informed that there were none, but if we looked through the Baltimores we might find some belonging to the plane[4]. So we got to work and found a few tools. By the time the day was finished we found that Accra was also the land of sweat and toil. One day Dakotas arrived. This was another aircraft we knew nothing about. Then we had our third change – Marauders" [5].

'At every station and staging post Royal Air Force "tradesmen" such as these were to be found, able to service and test all types of aircraft, of which many thousands passed through their hands before victory was won. Theirs was often a monotonous existence in places far removed from the bustle of Glasgow or Cardiff, the clamour of the Old Kent Road or the tranquillity of the English countryside from which so many of them came. Yet their task was something new in the history of war, something of importance and merit. . . .

'Very important persons, VIPs as they were called – to which, in the later stages of war, was added the refinement VVIP, were carried by Transport Command, many of them by No 24 Sqn flying Yorks and commanded by Wg Cdr H B Collins. In York LV633 he took the King to North Africa on 11 June 1943, and on 22 July 1944 to Naples. The Prime Minister, the Secretary of State for Foreign Affairs and other high personages were also conveyed in this and other aircraft[6] which travelled as far as Teheran, Adana and Moscow.

'Though the rate of loss due to weather or accident was very low, on occasion a York or a Liberator failed to arrive. . . .'

In summing-up the achievements of Transport Command over less than two-and-a-half years, the official history records that its transport aircraft – taking no account of reinforcement flights – 'flew more than a million hours between 1 April 1943 and the end of the war'.

---

4 The Air Ministry (AHB) Monograph on Maintenance (AP3397) says of Takoradi (and the same would apply to Accra) that 'difficulties over the lack of AGS (aircraft ground support) items and tools were, however, not so great with the American types as, in contrast to the British practice, each aircraft was packed with a bag of the essential parts and an efficient tool kit arrived in each craft'.

5 The Martin B-26 Marauder, which with its high wing loading was regarded as a very 'hot' type to handle. Its first RAF recipients were No 14 Sqn in the Middle East in 1942.

6 Liberators were the other VIP transport; and in 1940, for cross-Channel flights to France and internal UK visits, the elegant DH Flamingo.

Chapter VII

Reinforcement and Repatriation: The Trooping Programme (1945–46)

'For that, as it seems, they come home,
to Mens Businesse, and Bosomes'

Francis Bacon, dedicatory letter to his Essayes

'Immediately after VJ Day,' wrote the official historian[1], 'an Air Trooping Programme was initiated. So great was the importance of bringing back officers and men of all the Services for return to civil life, that special efforts were made, and as high a proportion as half the aircraft of Bomber and Coastal Commands were temporarily transferred to Transport Command for this task'. On 16 September 1945 the Chief of the Air Staff (Sir Charles Portal) had written to the Commander-in-Chief Transport Command, the Hon Sir Ralph Cochrane, to say that 'the air trooping programme will make a real contribution to the economic revival of the country'.

THE phrase 'the importance of bringing back officers and men . . . for return to civilian life' makes it sound as though air trooping was a one-way business. In fact it was two-way. Before the end of 1944 the Chiefs of Staff had approved a policy of large-scale air trooping after the defeat of Germany. This was to support Operation Dracula (originally Vanguard), a seaborne and airborne attack on Rangoon proposed by Admiral Lord Louis Mountbatten, Commander-in-Chief, South-East Asia. Subsequently the Air Ministry and the War Office assumed a planning date of 30 June 1945 for the defeat of Germany, and intended that UK–India air trooping should begin in July with an initial lift of 3,500 troops, rising to 17,500 by October. The main object of this trooping was to accelerate the redeployment for the war against Japan, whether or not Dracula were postponed or was carried out in modified form.

Perhaps the early planning figures were over-optimistic. At the eastern end of the line in New Delhi, HQ No 229 Group recorded on 12 October 1945 that 'October saw the launching of Large Scale Trooping and the target for the month was estimated at between 7,000 and 8,000 men in each direction (into and out of India). The outward figure exceeded this

---

1 Hilary St G Saunders, quoted in the previous chapter.

estimate though the full flow of trooping aircraft did not begin until 7th October.'

At the end of October Air Marshal Sir Ralph Cochrane sent the following congratulatory message: 'Please pass to all ranks engaged in the Large Scale Trooping programme my personal congratulations on the success achieved during the first month of operations. Target figures in both directions were exceeded and when much remains to be done to complete organisation of the route.'

The No 229 Group Equipment Branch ORB for October 1945 recorded later that month: 'The scheme for terminating all Trooping aircraft ex-UK at Mauripur [Karachi] and providing a Dakota feeder service beyond was augmented, and for this purpose Nos 10 and 76 Sqns were located at Poona and No 77 Sqn at Mauripur'. These were ex-Bomber Command Halifax squadrons which had been transferred to Transport Command in May 1945. The ORB added : 'Air Ministry advised that Halifax aircraft were to be used in a trooping role and indicated the requirements upon which the equipment packs would be based'.

Among the arrivals at Mauripur during that month was Dakota KN416 of No 525 Sqn, which came in on the 7th. It was captained by the writer of this history. He and his crew had picked it up at Habbaniyah under the 'shuttle' system whereby aircraft were taken on while the incoming crew rested at a staging post. It was flown with a load of freight to Bahrain, and of vegetables from there to Jask; from Mauripur it went on to Poona, returning on the same day. As there were no troops aboard for Karachi, it was presumably an aircraft which had got out of phase, perhaps because of unserviceability.

Its UK-bound trooping flight was interesting because the aircraft was routed via Masirah Island, Aden and Wadi Halfa, involving 11hr 10min night flying and 1hr 30min day. From Wadi Halfa the crew took another aircraft, KN487, to Lydda, El Adem and Elmas (Sardinia); then a third one, KN498, on the final leg to base (Membury).

This example of a trooping flight is cited because it gives some idea of the tremendous logistic problems which had to be solved by Transport Command in mounting this gigantic trooping operation: the provision of airfields (the Southern Arabian route was an alternative to the Shaibah–Habbaniyah one) and the setting-up of staging posts on them, with personnel who provided refuelling, servicing, Signals, meal facilities and accommodation.

Those aircrew who flew along those routes at that time with their loads of troops, whether outward bound to India or returning to the UK, took it for granted that all these amenities would be there. As soon as one's aircraft landed it would be refuelled, any unserviceability would be checked and rectified (unless a major defect was reported which involved sending for spares by a so-called 'Aircraft On Ground' (AOG) urgent message), the aircraft's position and its load would be Signalled to the next destination, the crew and passengers would be fed and – presuming there was a slip crew ready to take the aircraft on after two hours on the ground – the crew who brought it in would go off to their transit accommodation. This procedure applied to all Transport Command aircraft en route – Liberators, Yorks, Halifaxes[2], Stirlings and Dakotas – in the Large Scale Trooping Operation.

To give an idea of the number of movements involved, during November 1945, 361 aircraft arrived at Mauripur from the West and 375 left there for the UK. Early in that month, Nos 10, 76 and 77 Sqns began to operate on the internal movement of troops. Then during December, when No 229 Group despatched 15 empty aircraft from Mauripur to clear a backlog of troops which had accumulated in the Middle East, a total of 219 trooping aircraft reached India and 211 left there for the return.

In a post-war lecture on Transport Command[3] Sir Ralph Cochrane made particular reference to two types of aircraft on the trooping run, the Dakota and the York, and compared their capabilities. The Dakota's shorter range and slower speed made nine refuelling and rest points necessary on the round trip, as against five for the York. The longest stage on the Dakota route was 880 n.m. in a scheduled flying time of seven hours. For a York it was 1,300 n.m. in a flying time of seven-and-a-half hours – an increase of almost 50 per cent for only an extra half-hour's flying.

During January 1946 two related events occurred, in the UK and in India: the Government decided to reduce large-scale air trooping; and airmen of No 229 Group went on strike – a reaction by those on the ground who felt that their role of assisting the repatriation of other Army and RAF personnel meant that their own repatriation was being delayed so that they could continue to support this airlift. They feared that by the time they themselves got back all the civilian jobs would have been taken up by those they had helped to send on ahead.

Notification that trooping was being reduced reached No 47 Group, which controlled the long-range squadrons, in early January and on the 12th the stations concerned were notified. As the ORB put it: 'Signal AO 541 to Membury and Broadwell notified Cabinet decision (a) to reduce air trooping rate UK–India and return from 10,000 to 5,000 per month; (b) to reduce Dakota trooper all-up weight to 28,000lb[4] w.e.f. 12 January' – adding, however: 'Action to effect (b) later deferred to 1 February'. The ORB noted that for January 1946, large-scale trooping continued: a total of 2,809 troops were flown back to the UK and 2,766 flown out.

In India, however, there were rumbles of unrest, which the AOC No 229 Group, Air Cdre G T Jarman DSO DFC, encountered when he arrived at Mauripur on 20 January after inspecting the Jodhpur staging post. Shortly after his arrival there was a stoppage of work by corporals

---

2 No 229 Group noted in October 1945 that 'the arrival of Halifax aircraft has created a difficult servicing problem owing to lack of experience and particularly [of] Halifax ground equipment'. On 4 December, Stirlings were withdrawn from the trooping programme, and on the 8th the Equipment ORB stated that all Skymasters were to be returned to the USA.

3 Delivered at the Royal Aeronautical Society on 30 January 1947.

4 From 31,000lb.

and airmen. The ORB gave a blow-by-blow account of subsequent events;

'This was the first of several so-called "Strikes" which spread to units throughout India. The grievances varied with the unit, but in general they centred around repatriation and demobilisation. The AOC remained at Mauripur until the 25th January and the following is a resumé of his activities during that time.

'When at 108 Wing, the AOC was informed that several notices had been displayed in airmen's cookhouses at Mauripur, urging men to strike for a redress of grievances and in sympathy with strikers at the neighbouring station of Drigh Road. The AOC proceeded to Mauripur, where he visited the airmen's dining-hall and inspected tiffin [i.e. lunch]. There were numerous complaints dealing, not with the food, but with Release and Repatriation problems. The AOC discussed these grievances at length and arrived to meet representatives in the Station Cinema the following day. On the afternoon of the 21st Air Chief Marshal Sir Arthur Barratt KCB CMG MC, Inspector General, arrived at Mauripur from UK.

'The IG and the AOC arrived at Mauripur to discover that no airmen had reported for duty. At 1100hr the Inspector General addressed the men in the Station Cinema but without satisfactory result. The AOC addressed a further meeting at 1600hr that day and offered to send a signal to the C-in-C Transport Command, stating the demands of the men, requesting that they be brought to the notice of the highest Parliamentary authority. The men refused to resume work.

'The Indian Other Ranks joined the strikers and the AOC informed AMC BAFSEA [Air Marshal Commanding, Base Air Forces, South-East Asia] of the urgency and seriousness of the situation. Air Marshal Carr arrived at Mauripur in the afternoon to address the Indian Other Ranks in their dining-hall, as a result of which they gave assurance that they would resume work. The AOC later took details of the various individual and personal complaints.

'On the evening of the 23rd Air Marshal Carr addressed a large meeting of British Other Ranks and he assured them that their demands had reached the highest quarters. It seemed likely that the men would agree to return to work, had not someone announced that other 229 Group units and stations under 216 Group were on strike. The AOC signalled 216 Group and the main stations in 229 Group asking if there was unrest and on the morning of the 24th received negative replies. Another meeting of the men was held on the 24th and they agreed to return to work on the 25th. The AOC urged the men to return to duty by midday on the 24th but without success.

'The airmen resumed work on the 25th, but during the period of unrest both Trooping and Traffic Route and Internal Airline Squadrons were kept going by officers and Senior NCOs.'

During January, February and March 1946 the trooping operation gradually diminished. The industrial unrest at Mauripur came to an end on 25 January when the airmen resumed work, and from 22 February No 525 Sqn was withdrawn from the role[5]. In an ORB entry for 28 March, under the heading 'Large Scale Trooping', No 47 Group effectively wrote *finis* to the UK–India–UK trooping commitment:

'With cessation of LTH (246 Sqn – which operated Yorks from Holmsley South; the last letter of this code referred to the squadron, the LT to Large-Scale Trooping) and LTD (187 Sqn – Dakotas) – last departures from UK being 31 March and 17 March respectively – there are no trooping schedules operating, but w.e.f. 1st April any troops requiring passage will travel as passengers on the UKT and UM Services. . . .

'A total of 40 (26 LTH and 14 LTD) out of a possible 46 trooping services were despatched during the month, carrying 856 troops. 1,324 troops reached UK by the LTH, LTD and LTB (271 and 575 Sqns – Dakotas) Services (the last despatch in regard to the latter service being 28 February)'.

There are no figures for passengers and freight into or out of Membury during March 1946, nor were there any passengers leaving Merryfield. The Dakotas' trooping runs had ended.

In a public tribute to the air transport role of his Command during the war years, Sir Ralph Cochrane said that in the 21-month period from the beginning of 1945 to the end of September 1946 the RAF had flown more passenger miles than had British civil aviation in all its 21 years' existence. This was a remarkable achievement considering the very limited role of air transport in the RAF during the pre-war years.

In his lecture to the Royal Aeronautical Society Sir Ralph said that during the period some half-a-million troops and 200,000 tons of equipment had been carried and, in addition to the posthumous VC awarded to Flt Lt David Lord, more than a hundred decorations had been won by Transport Command aircrew. He cited also the contributions made by Air Commodores A Fletcher and H G Brackley (respectively the Command's first Administrative and Air Staff Officers) and by Air Commodore Whitney Straight. He also paid tribute to the sound foundations laid by his predecessor Sir Frederick Bowhill.

He quoted the impressive statistic that during 1945 no fewer than 3,000 pilots – three times the total of pre-war 'B' licence holders – had

---

5 In practice, trooping runs must have tailed off gradually, according to where aircraft were positioned on the route. The author's last run in a No 525 Sqn aircraft, from Lydda, ended at Membury on 8 March.

been absorbed into the RAF transport organisation, some of them transferred from other Commands but the majority coming from the training units with a total flying experience (dual plus solo) of only some 300hr[6].

He referred to the hazards of flying into high ground, or of collisions, when during the war traffic densities were a hundred or more times greater than those allowed by civil regulations, or of flying into cumulo-nimbus cloud. He said that only six aircraft had been lost in these dangerous cloud conditions during the 21-month period, and none due to collisions.

---

6 Pilots specially trained for ferry operations and posted to Takoradi in 1941 to fly on the West African Reinforcement Route (among them the author) had less than 200hr experience. After SFTS (Service Flying Training School) they had been posted to the Service Ferry Squadron at RAF Kemble, where they did a conversion course on to single- and twin-engined aircraft, including the Blenheim, Hurricane, Tomahawk and Maryland.

Chapter VIII

Post-war Reorganisation and Future Policy (1946–47)

'I am for "Peace, retrenchment and reform" '

John Bright, 28 April 1859

IN September 1945, Transport Command was a huge organisation: it had ten Groups, 24 Wings, seven airports, 103 stations worldwide and 55 squadrons. The Groups and their locations were Nos 4 at Heslington Hall, near York (taken over from Bomber Command); No 38 at Marks Hall, Colchester (transferred from Fighter Command in June 1945); No 44 at Gloucester; No 45 at Dorval, Montreal; No 46 at Bushey Hall, Watford; No 47 at Hendon; No 87 in BAOR; No 216 at Heliopolis, Cairo; No 229 in Delhi; and No 300 at Melbourne/Camden[1].

The impressive roll of squadrons numbered Nos 10, 24, 46, 51, 52, 53, 59, 76, 77, 78, 86, 102, 147, 158, 162, 167, 187, 190, 196, 206, 216, 220, 231, 232, 233, 238, 242, 243, 246, 267, 271, 295, 296, 297, 298, 299, 301, 304, 311, 353, 422, 423, 426, 435, 436, 437, 511, 512, 525, 570, 575, 620, 644, ADLS Sqn and Met Comm Sqn; plus 19 Flights and 18 Glider Pilot Regt Units – all in No 38 Group.

Some of these squadrons had been in the transport role pre-war or since the early days of hostilities, like Nos 24, 216 and 271; some were ex-Bomber or Coastal Command squadrons; some, like Nos 238 and 242, had former Fighter Command squadron numbers. The high numbers of the majority of the squadrons indicated that they were formed during the war years.

In addition to its stations, Transport Command had 163 staging posts and many other units located at 336 places throughout the world.

Its contribution to the air war of 1939–45 had been of four kinds: transport of passengers and freight, ferrying reinforcement aircraft to battle areas, airborne forces operations with the Army, and trooping to the Far East theatre. Inevitably some of these roles disappeared or were diminished with the end of hostilities, like the supply of Lease-Lend aircraft which had to be flown across the Atlantic or along the trans-Africa route. But there was still a need for air movement of Service passengers or

---

1 Formed in April 1945 from No 300 Wing, whose original purpose was to provide air services for the C-in-C British Pacific Fleet, its ambitions to evolve an efficient air service in the South-West Pacific were shattered by the Japanese surrender. It had two squadrons, Nos 238 and 243, and No 1315 Flight, all equipped with Dakotas. In his autobiography, *Heavenly Days Recollections of a Contented Airman* (Crécy Books, 1994), Gp Capt James Pelly-Fry DSO describes how he was posted in 1945 to command RAF Camden, which was 40 miles from Sydney. See maps overleaf for No 300 Group operations.

of whole squadrons, and for aircraft to be sent out to the Middle East or India (until the latter's Partition). Furthermore the Army still needed RAF support for parachute training exercises.

In a word, the Command had made itself so useful that it could not be ignored, but its responsibilities had to be re-defined and its activities would shrink dramatically in size from their wartime worldwide dimensions.

There was no question of Transport Command being disbanded. An Air Staff paper of 28 May 1945 said: 'Experience has shown that Air Transport has a lasting place in the RAF which cannot be filled by other forms of transport or by the Merchant Air Fleet'. At that time, although hostilities had ended in Europe, the Dakota squadrons of No 46 Group were involved in repatriating DPs (displaced persons) to their homelands – mainly Russians who had been employed as slave labourers in the Ruhr industries. They were flown to Luneburg, south-east of Hamburg, for onward transport to the Soviet Union. Also the great trooping programme which the No 47 Group squadrons undertook did not fully get under way until after the Japanese surrender in August 1945.

Early in 1946 the Air Council considered the organisation of Transport Command. At its meeting on 1 February VCAS (Air Chief Marshal Sir Douglas Evill) said that it had been designed to meet war conditions; it was somewhat unorthodox and had given rise to a division of responsibilities which had often proved difficult of interpretation in practice. Now that air trooping was coming to an end, it was recommended that Transport Command be brought into line with normal RAF practice and that responsibilities be re-allocated.

The Air Member for Supply and Organisation (Sir Leslie Holling-hurst)[2] confirmed that Commanders overseas had been emphatic that the present system of divided control led to difficulties. The new CAS (Lord Tedder) said it was most important to ensure the necessary safeguards in the case of the trunk routes, as at Staging Posts. AMSO assured the Council that such safeguards were provided; he also pointed out that, eventually, control of such routes would revert to the countries concerned.

The outcome of these discussions was a policy of decentralisation. On 3 February 1946 the Air Council decided that Nos 216, 232 and 229 Groups were to become Groups in Mediterranean/Middle East, South-East Asia and what was to become AHQ India respectively, instead of being in Transport Command. Thus one of the Groups from which the Command was originally formed, No 216, reverted to its former local status.

When the Council again discussed the organisation of Transport Command at its next meeting, on 7 February, AMSO said that a Directive giving effect to its decisions on this subject would be issued and would come into operation on 1 March, instituting a drastic slimming-down of the Command and transferring the responsibilities of its overseas Groups to the Middle and Far East Commands in which they operated.

---

2 As AOC No 38 Group he had been in the first Albemarle of No 295 Sqn from Harwell to fly over Normandy with its pathfinder paratroops of the 22nd Independent Company on the night of 5/6 June 1944.

No 300 GROUP DAKOTAS' ROUTE
DORVAL - SYDNEY & SOUTH WEST
PACIFIC ROUTES

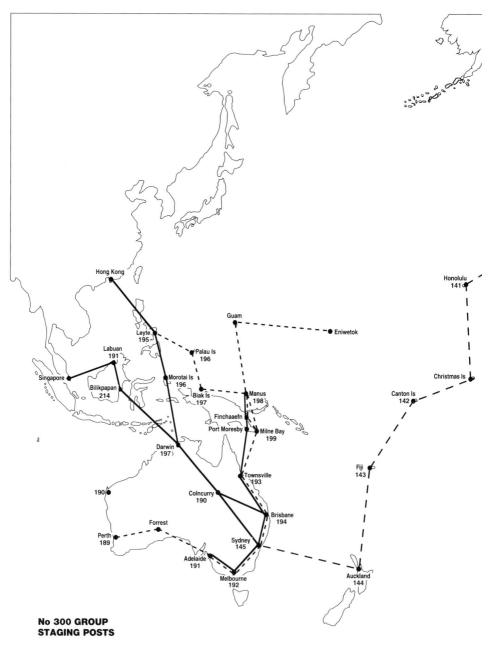

**No 300 GROUP
STAGING POSTS**

No		
145	MASCOT SYDNEY	
189	GUILDFORD PERTH	
190	LEARMOUTH W AUSTRALIA	
	Later COLNCURRY QUEENSLAND	
191	PARAFIELD ADELAIDE	
	Later LABUAN BORNEO	
192	ESSENDON MELBOURNE	
193	GARBUTT TOWNSVILLE	
194	ARCHERFIELD BRISBANE	
195	LEYTE PHILIPPINES	
	Later TOCLOBAN LEYTE	
196	PELELUI PALAU IS	
	Later MOROTAI NEI	
197	BOROKE BIAK IS	
	Later DARWIN N TERRITORY	
198	MANUS ADMIRALTY IS	
199	MILNE BAY NEW GUINEA	
	Later PORT MORESBY NG	
214	BILIKPAPAN BORNEO	

DORVAL - SYDNEY — — — —

DORVAL	- NASHVILLE	825nm
NASHVILLE	- DALLAS	521nm
DALLAS	- TUCSON	730nm
TUCSON	- RIVERSIDE	347nm
RIVERSIDE	- SACRAMENTO	347nm
SACRAMENTO	- HONOLULU	1997nm
HONOLULU	- CHRISTMAS IS	1042nm
CHRISTMAS IS	- CANTON IS	781nm
CANTON IS	- FIJI	995nm
FIJI	- AUCKLAND	995nm
AUCKLAND	- SYDNEY	1042nm

No 300 GROUP
ROUTES DEC 1945 ⸺⸺⸺⸺

SYDNEY	-	SINGAPORE	3907nm
SYDNEY	-	HONG KONG	4081nm
SYDNEY	-	MANUS	1997nm
SYDNEY	-	ADELAIDE	664nm

No 300 GROUP
ROUTES JUL 1945 - - - - - -

SYDNEY	-	MANUS	1997nm
SYDNEY	-	LEYTE	3560nm
MANUS	-	ENIWETOK	1736nm
SYDNEY	-	PERTH	1910nm

The change in size of Transport Command as a result of this policy was dramatic. According to its Order of Battle (ORBAT) at 19 February 1946 it had an establishment of 47½ squadrons and flights, 40½ of these being operational. But the compilers of the ORBAT warned that a re-organisation would take place on 1st March 1946. This would transfer the control of Transport formations and services in overseas theatres (including the British Air Forces of Occupation in Germany) from Transport Command to Overseas Theatre Commanders, retaining in Transport Command the home-based formations and units, and the control and operation of all trunk services. In future, therefore, the Transport Command Order of Battle would not show transport squadrons based in the overseas Commands.

When the next Order of Battle was issued on 15 March, it showed a total of 24½ established squadrons, of which 19½ were operational. Instead of a total UE (unit establishment) of 1,174 aircraft worldwide, for Transport Command it now became 541. The Command had relied heavily on US-built aircraft, principally Liberators and Dakotas. In this mid-March 1946 Order of Battle the total strength for these two types was respectively 125 and 232. With the ending of Lease-Lend they would have to be replaced by British aircraft.

However, the Dakotas would continue in service for many more years; eight squadrons of them were used in the Berlin Airlift of 1948–49. These famous Douglas Aircraft transports, which had made such an outstanding contribution to the Allied cause during the War, were going to be very hard to replace – and perhaps never would be.

At the 'receiving end' of the de-centralisation policy, the Organisation Branch of HQ No 229 Group noted in its ORB for March 1946, under the heading 'Transfer of Control': 'With effect from 15th March the control of this Headquarters passed from HQ Transport Command to HQ Base Air Forces, SEA. As from 0001hr on 16th March, 229 Group ceased to be a Transport Command Group and came under the direct administration of Air Headquarters (India)'.

The Transport Command changes did not escape the attention of commentators in the aviation Press. In its issue of 4 April 1946, *Flight* commented thus on the Air Ministry's demolition of the Command's wartime-created overseas structure:

'Transport Command, RAF, is being reorganised in such a way that the Command's Headquarters itself remains only responsible for home-based Transport Command forces and for the control and operation of all trunk air services.

'In the past the Command has had its own Group Headquarters in Canada, the Middle East and India, with Wings under these Groups, and these formations have controlled all transport units and routes operationally and, to a large extent, administratively. In fact, there has been a division of administrative responsibility between Transport Command and the Overseas Theatre Commanders.

'In future, Overseas Theatre Commanders will be responsible for the command and administration of all transport forces and units allocated to their theatre whether for support, airborne supply, or for internal services; also for the command and administration of all trunk route staging posts. In addition, Theatre Commanders will take over responsibility for the provision of all facilities necessary for Transport Command on the trunk route, and the ferrying and flying control of all aircraft in transit through the theatre.

'In his turn the Air Officer Commanding-in-Chief, Transport Command, will be responsible for the operational control and organisation of RAF trunk route scheduled services and ferry operations. The training of all transport crews, and the command and administration of transport and airborne assault experimental establishments, will also be his responsibility.

'Transport resources will be allocated to all theatres by Air Ministry, who will issue instructions to all Commands for the establishment of trunk route staging posts and necessary facilities. Air Ministry will also define RAF policy in connection with the use of transport aircraft, relying on the advice of Transport Command and Overseas Commands as necessary.'

Not only were there worldwide organisational changes. In the UK the long-range Group, No 47, was amalgamated with No 48 Group from the beginning of May and the latter – on the 15th May – disbanded. The new No 47 Group had its Headquarters at Milton Ernest Hall near Bedford and controlled three York and three Liberator squadrons. The Headquarters was established from 21st June 1946.

Avro Yorks had made a slow entrance into Transport Command because wartime production had been concentrated on the Lancaster bombers from which they were derived. The first ones to come into RAF service were specially equipped VIP versions, like LV633 which in March 1943 was delivered to No 24 Sqn at Northolt, fitted up internally as a flying conference room. Named *Ascalon*[3], it took Prime Minister Winston Churchill and his Chiefs of Staff to Algiers via Gibraltar on 25 May 1943 for the Casablanca Conference of Allied leaders. Other VIP versions were MW102 for Lord Louis Mountbatten when C-in-C South-East Asia Command, MW107 for Field Marshal Smuts and MW140 for HRH the Duke of Gloucester when he was Governor-General of Australia.

The first 'standard' York to enter Transport Command, MW104, a first-class passenger-cum-freighter version, was taken on charge by No 511 Sqn at Lyneham on 10 February 1944. This was the squadron which, during 1945, became the first to be fully equipped with Yorks – the first of eight such squadrons in Transport Command. The others were Nos 24, 40,

---

3 A coastal town in Palestine, birthplace of Herod the Great and later a stronghold of the Crusaders.

51, 59, 99, 206 and 242. No 246 which was also equipped with Yorks merged with 511 Squadron under the latter's numberplate on 16 October 1946. All eight took part in the Berlin Airlift.

As in the 15th Century Wars of the Roses, Yorks succeeded Lancasters. On the Avro production line the same wings, engines and undercarriages were embodied in both types. Features which distinguished the York were a high-wing configuration and three fins. Common to both the bomber and the transport was the throaty growl of four Rolls-Royce Merlins. Yorks were first proved on high-intensity operations by Transport Command in the 1945–46 trooping runs to and from India.

The three York squadrons which came under the re-formed No 47 Group were Nos 511 at Lyneham, 242 at Oakington and 246 at Holmsley South. They all operated scheduled services.

The three Liberator squadrons which operated trooping services were Nos 53 at Upwood, 59 at Waterbeach and 220, also at Waterbeach. Their days were numbered. On 25 May 1946 No 220 Sqn was to be reduced to a 'number only' basis, on 10 June No 53 ceased operations, and on the 15th both it and No 59 Sqn were also reduced to a 'number only' status.

Not only were there aircraft reductions in the post-war Transport Command; it also lost experienced personnel through demobilisation, with aircrew and groundcrew anxious to get back to civilian life. There were thus great problems in keeping up squadron and unit strengths. In the May/June 1946 ORB of No 47 Group it was recorded that the manpower position within the Command had reached such straits by the end of May as to force reduction in the working week of maintenance personnel from seven to five days, and severe curtailment of the 'slip crew' principle on scheduled services.

Shortages in specialised trades had been noted earlier in the No 47 Group Medical Branch ORB which recorded in March 1946 that Lyneham, the largest station in the Group, with an actual strength of over 2,500 had just lost its only medical NCO on posting.

In August 1946 the Air Council decided to modify its decentralisation policy in the light of experience and issued a new Directive, which was to come into effect on the 15th[4]. This said in its preamble:

'It has now been decided that control of overseas transport units and services may be de-centralised, with the prior approval of Air Ministry, to the Group or Air Headquarters administering the area in which the units concerned are situated. This Directive provides for the consequent changes in organisation and will supersede the previous Directive . . . with effect from 15 August 1946'.

Under the new Directive, certain air transport functions were reserved to the Air Ministry, including defining RAF policy for the use of transport aircraft and the allocation of transport resources between Transport Command and overseas Commands.

During 1946 the Air Staff gave much thought to the future of Transport

4 See folder Transport and Routes – PRO Air 20/7062.

Command itself, now without its overseas Groups. A paper on the RAF Transport Force, dated 5 December 1946 and re-issued on 30 January 1947, formed the basis of discussion at a meeting between VCAS (Sir William Dickson) and the C-in-C Transport Command (Sir Ralph Cochrane) at the Air Ministry on 13 March 1947. As a result of this meeting, what were called 'Notes on the Provisional Policy for the RAF Transport Force' were issued on 5 July 1947. These defined the tasks, within the limitations of their equipment, which all squadrons of Transport Command might be required to carry out in war as: (a) Transport Support Operations and (b) Route Transport Operations – which, in addition to the delivery of reinforcement aircraft, had been the Command's main roles during the war.

'Limitations of their equipment' was a key phrase here, for in its wartime operations Transport Command had relied heavily on American aircraft, especially the Dakotas, which had been used both in the air support role and also on the trunk routes and for trooping. With the ending of Lease-Lend a British type had to be introduced to take the place of the Dakotas. As the Statement Relating to Defence had put it in February 1947[5]: 'The Air Ministry programme provides for . . . a start to be made on the replacement of American transport aircraft and the introduction of a modern type for the carriage of Airborne Forces'.

When the Air Council discussed the RAF production programme for 1948/49 at its meeting on 8 September 1947[6] AMSO (Sir Leslie Hollinghurst) explained that it was important to proceed with Valetta production as this type would replace Dakotas. He pointed out that the Dakotas 'were still costing us dollars. We had an agreement with the USA under which we should progressively return to them the Dakotas then in use, and the longer we retained them the more dollars it cost'. The Secretary of State (P J Noel-Baker) suggested that it might even be advisable to ask for Valetta production to be accelerated.

Whereas previously Transport Command's role had been determined for it by the exigencies of war, in peacetime its roles would be decided by the long-term requirements of Defence policy. Inter-continental transport routes to the Far East and Westwards had to be sustained, the other Commands had to be supported in their operational deployments, and the Army – whose own aircraft were limited to 4,000lb a.u.w.[7] – had to be provided with airlift capability. This meant that transport aircraft designs had to be tailored to meet joint specifications.

But while this long-range planning was going on in 1947–48, at a time of great financial stringency, a major crisis blew up which was to test the nerve and the transport capabilities of both the RAF and the USAF. This was the need to supply Berlin by air after the USSR had closed the land access routes, a move which threatened the survivability of the Western sectors of the city. To have acquiesced in this *force majeure* would have been a major defeat for the Allies in the Cold War.

---

5 Cmnd 7042.   6 12/47

7 In *Soldiers of the Air The Development of Army Flying* (Ian Allan, 1967) Brigadier Peter Mead writes of 4,000lb being 'the statutory upper limit to the weight of Army aircraft'.

Chapter IX

Airlift into Berlin
(June 1948–May 1949)

'. . . their country's pride,
When once destroy'd, can never be supplied'

Oliver Goldsmith, The Deserted Village

THE British Government's decision was that Berlin – no longer the German capital but symbolically so – should be supplied by air to beat the Russian blockade. How was this to be achieved? It was estimated by the Joint Staffs in London that 4,000–5,000 tons of food, supplies and fuel a day were needed to keep the city going. The Chief of the Air Staff, Lord Tedder, told his fellow Chiefs of Staff on 28 June 1948[1] that the RAF would be able to arrange for a lift of 75 tons a day into Berlin by air immediately and that this could be raised to 400 tons a day within 48 hours. After 3 July when the Gatow airport runway had been repaired this figure could be raised to 750 tons a day, but at the cost of stopping all Service transport except to Berlin and Warsaw. The airlift was code-named 'Operation Plainfare'.

At the meeting of Ministers appointed to deal with the Berlin situation on 29 May[2] the Foreign Secretary (Ernest Bevin) said that it was estimated that to maintain the population of the three Western sectors of Berlin on their existing scale of rations a daily lift of the order of 2,000 tons would be required[3]. This could only be achieved if the USAF would co-operate in the airlift. The British Government had willed the end – the sustenance of Berlin by air – and the means had to be found.

But it could not be found only in Transport Command, even though this was the front-line Command in this crisis. The Command had eight Dakota and eight York squadrons in the UK; these were the aircraft which would deliver up to 750 tons a day into Berlin, less than half the amount required.

Fortunately the co-operation of the Americans was assured. In Washington, the resolve of President Truman needed no strengthening. He was adamant that the Western Allies should maintain their presence in Berlin. By the time of their meetings on 28–29 June the British Government knew that they could count on US support. Truman's instruction to James Forrestal (Secretary of Defense), Kenneth Royall (Secretary of the Army) and Robert Lovett (Under-Secretary of State), at

---

1 87th (48) CoS Mtg.

2 Gen 241/2nd Mtg.

3 An average daily total of 5,000 tons was supplied before land communications were interrupted (Cabinet, 46th Mtg, 1 Jul 48).

a meeting on 25 June, left no room for doubt; all resources were to be channelled into forming a robust airlift organisation[4].

But the Berlin airlift could not have found Transport Command in a much weaker state when it came to large-scale lifting capacity. To quote P R Wood of the Air Historical Branch, who made a special study of the operation: 'Defence expenditure had been budget-capped only nine months before; Transport Command in consequence was facing a period of severe contraction' – not the best circumstances in which to mount from scratch a major airlift, the like of which had never been seen before – an operation to 'hold the line while the diplomats explored Soviet intentions'. Whatever might happen, action was needed urgently, as with only a month or so's supply of essentials in West Berlin the Allied position there would have begun to crumble within two or three weeks were no supplies to be brought in. So, plans for an emergency airlift, a joint Anglo–American operation, were put in train within two days of the blockade being imposed.

On 21 July Lord Tedder told the Chiefs of Staff[5] that the USAF was investigating the possibility of putting an additional 50 or 100 C-54s on the airlift. These aircraft, with their ten-ton lifting capacity, were crucial to keeping up the Allied airlift of supplies; by early 1949 there were 226 of them in Western Germany. The fact that they were tricycle-undercarriage aircraft also made for easier loading and unloading.

As to aircraft overhaul and groundcrew support, a meeting called by the Secretary of State for Air (Rt Hon Arthur Henderson) on 27 July was told that arrangements had been made for the overhaul of 60 Dakotas a month by industry and that similar arrangements were being made for 40 Yorks; also that airmen in certain under-manned trades were being held back from Release during the airlift. But there was still a worrying net outflow of skilled men.

In August 1948 an Air Ministry official noted that the RAF was carrying into Berlin an average of 1,100 tons a day using Yorks and Dakotas from Transport Command, and flying-boats from Coastal Command[6]. The American contribution was averaging over 1,500 tons a day, and they intended to deploy a further fleet of C-54s. Estimates of the size of this fleet ranged between 72 and 125 aircraft.

In a signal to Commanders-in-Chief on 13 August, the Air Ministry said that all flying crews who were due for Release were to be retained until further notice. Initially Transport Command groundcrews had been boosted by the loan of 300 additional technicians transferred from other Commands. These however were now to be returned to their own units and the requirement would be covered – for the Yorks and Dakotas – by the civil maintenance arrangement.

On the 17th the Secretary of State informed the Foreign Secretary that it

---

4 For a full exposition of the airlift operation see: Robert Jackson, *The Berlin Airlift*; Patrick Stephens, 1988.
5 103rd (48) mtg.
6 Berlin Airlift (Operation Plainfare) file – Air 19/168 Pt 1.

would be necessary to withdraw a number of Yorks and Dakotas from the airlift in order that the training programme of Transport Command, which had been completely interrupted, might be resumed. The plan was to withdraw 32 aircraft, which would reduce the daily tonnage carried by the RAF by up to 400 tons. But the gross tonnage of supplies into Berlin would not be reduced. Twenty-seven American C-54s were due to arrive at Fassburg on the 20th, 21st and 22nd August, which would augment the airlift from the British Zone by at least 600 tons a day – making a net increase of about 200 tons. The Foreign Secretary in a letter of 23 August nevertheless asked the Air Minister to reconsider the withdrawal of the aircraft. He said he could not go on urging the Americans to increase their contribution if the British side started withdrawing aircraft at that stage.

When the Air Council discussed the airlift on 2 September[7] the following daily tonnages were reported:

USAF (from the American Zone)	1,587 tons (estimated)
USAF (from Fassburg)	682 tons (estimated)
RAF	1,145 tons
Civil	101 tons
Total	3,515 tons

At this meeting, when VCAS (Sir James Robb) referred to the USAF build-up at Fassburg he said that they were now operating an average of 20 C-54s from there daily and were shortly moving in two more squadrons of nine aircraft each. This had already meant arranging for the removal of 25 Dakotas of No 46 Group to Lübeck, and if the American build-up continued, more Dakotas would have to be withdrawn to there.

The question of withdrawing Yorks and Dakotas for training rumbled on at a meeting on 8 September[8], the Air Minister explaining that when the airlift had started, the RAF had put into the operation all the Yorks and Dakotas normally employed on aircrew training. It was now urgent that the training should be re-started. He said that they would wish to start the withdrawal on 12 or 13 September, and Lord Henderson of the Foreign Office undertook to discuss the matter with the Foreign Secretary urgently.

Eventually it was agreed at a meeting between the Air Ministry and the Foreign Office on 10 September that the first eight additional civil aircraft would be available by the 15th and that eight RAF Dakotas could be withdrawn by that date. A further ten civil aircraft would be available by the 22nd, and a further six Dakotas would then be withdrawn. The remaining four Yorks would be withdrawn as soon as possible after the 22nd.

Lord Henderson wrote to the Air Minister[9] on 30 September to say that since 10th September the civil charter fleet had been increased by four

---

7 Conclusions, 11(48).

8 File Berlin Airlift (Operation Plainfare) – Air 19/168 Pt 1.

9 The Air Minister at the time was the Rt Hon Arthur Henderson, who happened to be Lord Henderson's brother.

BERLIN AIRLIFT - OPERATING ROUTES

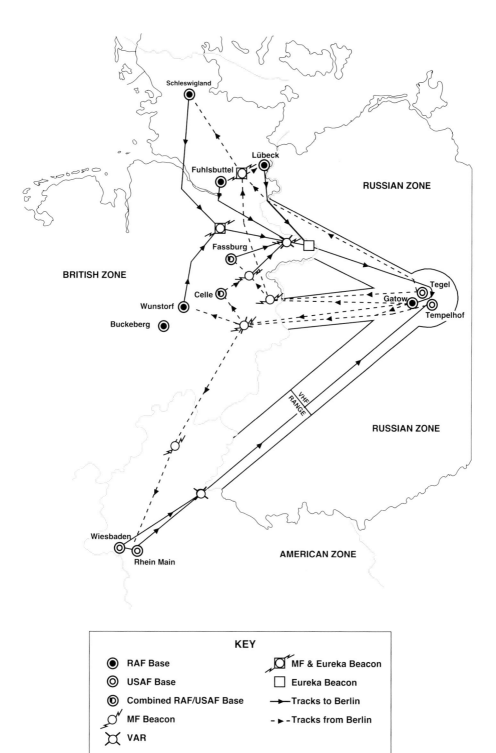

Airlift into Berlin (June 1948–May 1949)   77

Dakotas, three Halifaxes, two Wayfarers, one Hythe flying-boat, one Tudor and one Viking. But there had been a decline in the British lift, from an average of 308 sorties per day between 7 and 13 August, to 241 sorties per day between 17 and 23 September. He wanted to know what factors accounted for this and again stressed how important it was, at a time when the UK were pressing the Americans to increase their lift, that its effort should be maintained. Among many factors found to be responsible for the decline the poor serviceability of the York was the main one, and a revised organisation had been set up to improve the maintenance facilities.

Thus in mounting the airlift there were a number of difficulties to contend with. There was political pressure – from the Government through the Foreign Office, there were manpower and logistic problems, and there was the need for Transport Command to keep up its training and therefore wanting some of its aircraft back on its own stations. There were also payload limitations on some RAF types – the Dakotas carried half as much as the USAF C-54s. All these difficulties and pressures were in addition to the aircraft, aircrew, air traffic, airfield and weather problems of maintaining a sustained airlift to feed and fuel Berlin during the winter of 1948–49. Nevertheless, the months from October until early 1949 were marked by a very substantial expansion in the resources devoted to the airlift, in terms particularly of aircraft and bases.

The expansion of aircraft resources was chiefly caused by the additional USAF C-54s and by the introduction of the Hastings into the RAF fleet.

This four-engined aircraft, which carried 9½ tons, was introduced into No 47 Sqn of Transport Command in September 1948 and the Berlin Airlift was its first major employment. The Hastings moved into Schleswigland on 1 November and did their first operation from there on the 11th. This was one of three new despatching bases in the British Zone for British aircraft; the others were Lübeck for RAF Dakotas and Fuhlsbuttel for British civil machines. Schleswigland (opened in November 1948) was also used by civil carriers, as was Wunstorf, the base for the Yorks.

In outline the plan for the Airlift was that a northern corridor ran into Gatow and a southern corridor into Tempelhof. There was a 'time block' system, with every 24hr period being divided into four-hour cycles, and landing slots were allocated to each despatching base according to the number of aircraft it had available. From the point of view of flying operations the weather in the 1948–49 winter was typically dull, but at the same time it was unseasonably mild between early December and the end of February, which fortuitously reduced the demand for coal for heating.

Other factors helped the RAF–USAF organisers and controllers – the opening of Tegel airfield in early December, built from scratch in the French Zone and providing a third Berlin terminal; the discovery during January and February of hitherto unlisted stocks of coal; an improved standard of aircraft maintenance resulting from the milder weather; and the unscheduled arrival of 30 more C-54s.

But ironically the allocation of increased resources to the British Zone had worked to the detriment of the RAF. As more and more American C-54s and British civil aircraft (there were about 105 of these) moved in, the RAF share of the 350 or so sorties achieved along the northern corridor fell from that of the free-wheeling days of July to 69% in August and to as low as 37% in December.

The air traffic control problem was a complicated one. Civil carriers in the northern corridor were using 11 different aircraft types, in addition to the four Service ones, and there were six despatching bases. It was to regulate this mixture of traffic along the northern corridor that the time-block system was introduced. Even so, this had disadvantages for Transport Command aircraft. The four-hour cycle was ideal for the C-54, which by carrying standard loads and operating from bases near to the northern corridor could complete each round trip and be ready for the next comfortably in four hours. But the RAF aircraft, often hampered by carrying awkward loads, back-loading passengers and freight from Berlin to the British Zone, and being based at a distance from the northern corridor, generally took more than four hours to complete a round trip.

There were also other problems for the RAF in the airlift. The York, which carried eight to nine tons, had been designed as a long-range airliner and was not best suited to short trips carrying heavy loads (although its height off the ground was suitable for loading from a three-ton truck). The Hastings, because of its tailwheel configuration, suffered from cross-wind limitations. (This problem was eased on its civil successor, the Hermes, by the introduction of a tricycle undercarriage). The Dakota, although reliable, could carry only 3½ tons.

Finally there was still the aircrew shortage, caused not only by the aforementioned releases from service, but also because the Command was not manned to deal with the high utilisation rates demanded by the Airlift. The ratio of aircrew to aircraft on the USAF squadrons was double that of the RAF. This problem would have become critical if the crisis had lasted into a second year.

Fortunately it did not. The blockade ended as suddenly as it had begun, on 12 May 1949. By that time, over 1.6 million tons had been delivered to Berlin, and a further 713,000 tons were added to that figure before the airlift officially ended on 1 September 1949, when the Combined Airlift Task Force was disbanded.

The RAF (in effect, Transport Command) had had 20 squadrons and two OCUs involved in Operation Plainfare: Nos 10, 18, 27, 30, 46, 53, 62 and 77 (Dakotas); Nos 24, 40, 51, 59, 99, 206, 242 and 511 (Yorks); Nos 47 and 297 (Hastings – the first two squadrons to operate this new type); Nos 201 and 230 (Sunderland flying-boats, which caused a morale-boosting sensation when they appeared over Berlin, landing on the Havel See: ten were used); and Nos 240 and 241 OCUs (Dakotas and Yorks respectively).

What was the sum of experience for Transport Command as a result of the airlift? To quote from an article by P R Wood in the *Royal Air Force Quarterly* in the autumn of 1958[10]:

---

10 Quoted by Robert Jackson at the end of his book *The Berlin Airlift* (Patrick Stephens, 1988).

'It had made the most of a situation not of its own choosing. It had demonstrated at the beginning of the airlift how rapidly it could respond to an emergency; the Dakota and York force had been operating from Wunstorf within 24 hours of the order being given, and the tonnage which it delivered in July and August while the C-54s were deploying was vital in sustaining the Allied position. The first Hastings squadron too had been deployed to Germany well ahead of schedule. More significant, the emphasis which the previous Commander-in-Chief of Transport Command, Sir Ralph Cochrane, had put on training and accident prevention had been more than justified by the high standard of flying under the exacting conditions of the Airlift, and by the fact that there were only five serious accidents to RAF aircraft (three of them Dakotas – one of which, KP223, came down in the Russian Zone near Lübeck on 17 November 1948 when carrying out a BABS approach, one York and one Hastings). Sadly though, 17 RAF personnel were killed.

'In the end it was transport aircraft which won a notable victory and the RAF transport force which helped to sustain Britain's position in the alliance – 23% of the total tonnage delivered being perhaps no mean contribution in the conditions of the time[11].

'The irony of the situation, however, comes in the postscript. Success in the Airlift could not save Transport Command from further cuts, it being perhaps inevitable in the circumstances of 1949 that what money there was to spend would be devoted to other Commands. A resurgence of the transport force would have to await events beyond the confines of Europe.'

What then was the situation of, and prospect for, Transport Command as it entered the 1950s?

---

11 Additional information about the Berlin Airlift was presented at a Symposium on the subject arranged by the Royal Air Force Historical Society in June 1989 and recorded in the Society's *Proceedings*, Issue No 6.

Chapter X

The Lean Years

'O, wither'd is the garland of the war'

Shakespeare, Antony and Cleopatra, *IV xv*

A WORLDWIDE contribution to the Second World War had been followed by the concentrated Operation Plainfare effort on behalf of the Western Allies in the Cold War; but the garlands earned by Transport Command were soon to wither from under-nourishment, with priority being given to the build-up of a nuclear deterrent force.

When Air Marshal Sir Aubrey Ellwood took over as Commander-in-Chief at the end of March 1950[1] in the new Headquarters at Upavon[2] he can scarcely have viewed the future with confidence, for these were bleak times for his new Command. The Statement on Defence for 1950[3], referring to Air Force manpower strength, said bluntly that 'with the gradual build-up of Bomber Command there will be a reduction in the air transport force at home'. Early that year severe cuts in Transport Command's establishment were decided upon[4]. At an Air Council Standing Committee meeting on 20 January[5] it was decided that No 46 Group should be abolished forthwith and No 38 Group not later than the end of 1950, thus cutting out the intermediate layer of command at Group level altogether, and leaving Transport Command HQ to assume direct responsibility for transport squadrons in the UK. Conveying these decisions to a conference on future policy for airborne forces held on the 21st, the Assistant Chief of the Air Staff for Policy (Air Vice-Marshal D MacFadyen) also said that the medium-range squadrons in the UK were to be reduced to a total of two as soon as possible and the Transport Command Development Unit was to be disbanded.

Set against the prestige and size gained by Transport Command during the war, and coming on top of the recent demonstration of its immense capabilities during the Berlin airlift, this was the nadir of its status and fortunes.

Before the end of January 1950, instructions had been issued to the

---

1 He had been AOC-in-C Bomber Command since 1947.

2 The move from Bushy Park was made in April 1950.

3 Cmnd 7895.

4 See file 'Reorganisation of Transport Command 1950' (A35412/49), from which these details are taken.

5 1(50).

Command to disband four medium-range squadrons, and for one of the remaining two medium-range squadrons to take over the roles of the Transport Support Training Unit. The squadrons to be disbanded during February were Nos 10, 18, 46 and 206; No 27 Sqn personnel were to be posted and the squadron number-plate transferred to the Training Unit which was to be reorganised and provisionally located at Abingdon. No 24 Sqn was to be reduced to five or six long-range and three or four medium-range aircraft.

The Command now seemed to have heard the worst about its present and its future; the 1951 Government statements were slightly less pessimistic. On 29 January Prime Minister Clement Attlee announced a huge increase in defence expenditure – up to £4,700 million, which included the costs of an increase in Canberra production[6] and the first orders for V-bombers. A Memorandum by the Secretary of State for Air to accompany the 1951–52 Air Estimates said that the rundown of Transport Command had been halted.

Successive Statements on Defence reflected the variety of ways in which the Command was called on 'to support British policy' in unsettled times. (They also showed, incidentally, that the Hastings were the workhorses of the Command in the lean years of the early 1950s). 'Hastings aircraft of Transport Command have run a casualty evacuation service conveying wounded soldiers of the UN forces from Korea. . . . In October 1952 Transport Command accomplished, at short notice and without any mishap, the task of carrying large formations of British troops to the Middle East'.

The Korea evacuation flights, which became known as the 'Japan shuttle', were referred to in the Air Ministry Quarterly Liaison Report for the last quarter of 1950[7]:

'During the quarter under review, Hastings of Transport Command have undertaken a number of special flights to Japan in support of British forces operating in Korea. With the build-up of British forces in the area it is intended shortly to introduce a regular service to Japan. On return flights, these aircraft have been and will continue to be used for casualty evacuation to the UK. Casualties have included Turkish Army personnel who have been flown as far as Habbaniyah and taken on to Turkey in Turkish aircraft'.

The next Report[8] noted a new, routine development:

'A once-weekly Singapore–Japan service was inaugurated in February 1951 with Hastings. On return flights these aircraft are used for casualty

---

6 The then Chief of the Air Staff, MRAF Sir John Slessor, wrote in 1952: 'We ordered as many [Canberras] as we could get to build up a front-line force . . . in the UK . . . for the support of SHAPE' (see *The RAF Strategic Nuclear Deterrent Forces*, by Humphrey Wynn; HMSO, 1994).

7 Air Ministry Quarterly Liaison Report – Dept of the CAS – Report No 17 – Oct–Dec 1950.

8 Report No 18 – Jan–Mch 1951.

evacuation. In addition to a number of British personnel, Turkish, Greek, Dutch, Belgian, Indian and French casualties have been flown out on this service'.

The squadron which performed this regular service was No 47, based at Topcliffe, and its Operations Record Book for February 1951 recorded:

'Flt Lt Weller and crew positioned for the Japan shuttle on the 9th. This "shuttle" being a new service, consisting of an aircraft based at Changi, with a squadron crew detached there for four weeks, during which time four lifts are made to Japan – passengers and casualties being flown in and out, a new crew relieving after four weeks'.

These flights were made between Changi, Singapore, and Iwakuni, Japan, and the service continued for more than two years.

The world situation was becoming more and more unsettled. The 1953 Statement on Defence spoke of the continued tension in international relations, hostilities in Korea, Cold War conditions in Europe, anti-bandit operations in Malaya and unrest in Kenya. There was also, in 1953, natural disaster – the East coast floods and those across the North Sea, and Transport Command played a major part in relief operations. Valettas (which had entered service in 1948 as a Dakota replacement) were employed in this country and in Holland to drop dinghies and supplies. Aircraft of Transport and Coastal Commands also brought from abroad nearly three million sandbags.

What hopes did Transport Command have, however, of new aircraft and a defined role in Defence policy? In the early 1950s there was not much sign of either, and the Command was being cut to the bone – both organisationally and in numbers.

Using numbers as a yardstick, the forecast reduction in the size of Transport Command in relation to the other Commands becomes starkly apparent. In a planned RAF Order of Battle from mid-1950 to March 1954[9] Transport Command was to have in mid-1950 64 aircraft (long- and medium-range transports) as against 200 aircraft in Bomber Command and 442 in Fighter Command. By March 1951 it was to have only 32 aircraft, as against 200 for Bomber Command and 522 for Fighter Command. By March 1954 the gap was to be even greater: still only 32 in Transport Command, with 352 in Bomber Command and 944 in Fighter Command. This was at a time when, against an increasing Soviet threat, Britain's Defence budget had been increased to £3,600 million and then to £4,700 million over a three-year period. Clearly, offensive aircraft were getting all the priority during the Cold War period; Transport Command had acquired what came to be referred to as its 'Cinderella status'.

This grand total of 32 aircraft would have translated into just three long-range squadrons and one medium-range squadron, with eight aircraft in each. As one historian has commented of this period: 'as a result

---

9 S of S for Air file: Size and Shape 1950.

of the priority given to bombers the RAF capacity for air transport was woefully neglected for a number of years until Suez exposed its inadequacy' [10].

Fortunately the dire prediction of Transport Command being down to 32 aircraft by March 1952 was not fulfilled, but it had few enough squadrons to meet the demands made upon it and its capability was limited by the types with which it was equipped. As at 31 January 1950 it had four squadrons of Hastings C.1s – two at Topcliffe (Nos 47 and 53) and two at Lyneham (Nos 99 and 511), all in the long-range role; a Hastings/York Special squadron at Lyneham (No 24 (Commonwealth)); a Dakota/Valetta squadron at Abingdon (No 30) in the medium-range role; and a Communications squadron at Hendon with a miscellaneous collection of types – Ansons, Devons, Proctors and a Spitfire LF.16. The Command had an authorised total of 166 aircraft, with 186 actually on hand; but of these, only the Hastings could really be described as front-line aircraft. The Command's contraction had been severe, and it was not until the mid-1950s with the arrival of new types that its fortunes began to be revived and its status restored. Inevitably, the fewer the aircraft the busier the squadrons were kept, because the transport tasks did not diminish. Assurances of 'better times ahead' could do nothing to ease the day-to-day pressures when there was such a mismatch between demands made from the 'sharp end' and the means available to meet them.

What was it like for the Hastings squadrons in the lean years of the early fifties? No 47 Sqn at Topcliffe was one of the five Hastings squadrons to which the Command had been reduced, and it is clear that its resources were over-stretched – largely because of detachments in the Middle and Far East which took away aircraft and crews for weeks at a time. Reporting from the home base, for 12 days during July 1950 the Operations Record Book noted: 'No flying. No aircraft available', and a similar situation prevailed for nine days during August.

In addition to the Korean commitment there was an even larger task, occasioned by the need to position crews and aircraft at Fayid, Egypt, because of the international crisis which had blown up following the Persian intention to nationalise the Abadan oil refineries. Then in October–November a yet bigger Middle East commitment occurred: moving Army personnel from the UK to Castel Benito, Tripoli, and from there – and also from Nicosia, Cyprus – to Fayid. The Operations Record Book commented in November that this operation had lasted for 22 days, when 5,342 troops and 362,350lb of freight were uplifted without incident.

The Operations Record Book also noted the comment of an unnamed senior officer, that this was 'one of the most successful shambles ever carried out by the Royal Air Force'. Part of this comment may have been occasioned by the performance of the Army loading teams. To quote again from the Operations Record Book:

10 *Nuclear Politics – The British Experience with an Independent Strategic Force 1939–1970*, by Andrew J Pierre (OUP, 1972).

'It soon became apparent that the success of this lift depended upon the skill and enthusiasm of the crews, who had on occasions to regretfully override the decisions of the Army loading teams, who had a deplorable tendency to load all available freight against the rear Elsan doors. . . . Weight and balance problems, it is feared, remained a dark and unnecessary mystery to them, as did adherence to the request for accurate manifests; a load of 64 troops in marching order plus one kit bag appeared as 64 troops plus two kit bags, plus blanket rolls, Piat guns, Sten guns, mortars and trenching tools.'

The Air Council was not concerned with such immediate problems but with what was going to be the equipment of Transport Command in four or five years' time. At their meeting on 19 July 1951[11] they concluded that no time should be lost in notifying the Ministry of Supply of a firm requirement for the GAL[12] Freighter (which became the Beverley); that they accepted in principle a recommendation that the long-range squadrons of Transport Command be re-equipped in 1956 with high-speed transport aircraft, derived from an existing civil or military type, and designed for the rapid movement of personnel and equipment over long distances (types which eventuated as the Comet and the Britannia); and that the Council should authorise a supplementary bid for C-119s (Fairchild Packets) (which in fact never came to Transport Command).

The Secretary of State was clearly worried about the reduction in size of Transport Command and was concerned about the plan to have only three long-range transport squadrons during the 1953–55 period. He would have expected the Chiefs of Staff to say that a larger force was needed – say, five squadrons. He said that it might become necessary to state publicly that the needs of the bomber and fighter forces (i.e. Canberras, V-bombers, Hunters and Javelins) could only be met by this reduction in Transport Command. Even then the question might still be raised whether the reduction had not gone too far.

Another requirement touched on by S of S was for the provision of a tail-loading aircraft in the tactical transport role, which he said was becoming increasingly more urgent. This requirement would have been met by the C-119s had they been procured for RAF service. In the event it was not to be met until the Beverleys arrived.

In the early 1950s, as became apparent, the demands on the four Hastings squadrons were too great. To revert to the example of No 47 Sqn, most of the aircraft and crews were away on long detachments like the one at Fayid (which was open-ended because of the unpredictable international situation), or were in Singapore doing the shuttle service to Japan. Consequently, there were all too few crews and aircraft left at base – or even none at all – to fulfil one-off commitments. In November 1951 the

---

11 13(51) Conclusions.
12 General Aircraft Ltd had built the tank-carrying Hamilcar, largest Allied glider of the Second World War, which had participated in Overlord operations; GAL merged with Blackburn Aircraft in 1948 to become Blackburn and General Aircraft.

squadron still had eight Captains operating between Castel Benito, Nicosia and Fayid; in December it was still doing 'Fayid Specials', the Japan shuttle and catching up with the essential continuation training which had perforce been neglected earlier in the year because of the unavailability of aircraft at Topcliffe.

The year 1952 saw the end of production of the Vickers Valetta, the sturdy twin-engined, medium-range transport which had been developed from the Viking civil airliner to an Air Ministry Specification (C.9/46) and entered Transport Command service in 1948 (with No 240 OCU) in succession to the Dakota. Its C.1 version fulfilled many roles – troop and freight carrier, glider tower, supply-dropper and ambulance aircraft. It served in four UK-based squadrons – Nos 30, 78, 204 and 622 (No 622 being the only R Aux AF transport squadron).

As the militarised version of the Viking it had a strengthened fuselage floor and large loading doors on its port side (with a smaller door inserted as a paratroop exit), and lashing points in the fuselage floor and sides for securing cargo. In its troop transport role the Valetta could carry 34 fully equipped soldiers. In its airborne forces role it could take 20 paratroops, and as an air ambulance it could accommodate 20 stretcher cases with two medical orderlies. As compared with its civil predecessor, the Valetta had stronger, longer-stroke undercarriage legs to cope with rough, unprepared landing surfaces[13]. In Transport Command it was mainly used for routine airlift and training duties in co-operation with Airborne Forces and Army units. In the Middle East it took part with the Hastings in the reinforcement of and repatriation from the Suez Canal Zone in 1951. In the Far East it played its most dramatic role, participating in Operation Firedog – the Malayan Emergency, dropping supplies to troops in the jungle and supporting the psychological warfare operations when nearly 500 million leaflets were dropped into the communist-terrorist areas. It was also initially used there for 'loud-hailing' flights but was later supplanted by the Dakota when it was found that too much feed-back from the Valettas' engines was getting into the voice broadcasts[14].

In its final manifestation in the UK the Valetta became a VIP transport. The 31 January 1952 Order of Battle noted that two of the York aircraft of No 24 (Commonwealth) Sqn and the Valetta C.2 of No 30 Sqn (the only remaining Valetta squadron in the UK) were equipped to VIP standard to provide airlift for the Prime Minister, Cabinet Ministers, Chiefs of Staff and others. These Valettas had accommodation for nine to 15 passengers and an extra 116 gallons fuel tankage to extend their range. Valettas continued in service until the 1960s when they were supplemented by Andovers.

There was shining evidence that crews of the post-war Transport

---

13 Details from *Vickers Aircraft from 1908*, by C F Andrews (Putnam & Co, 1969). The Valetta was the first RAF transport aircraft for which rearward-facing seats were specified (OR/209/1, February 1946).

14 For fuller information on the RAF's role in the Malayan Emergency, see *Operation Firedog* by Raymond Postgate; HMSO 1992.

Command could display the same courage as had their wartime predecessors on operations against the enemy. Following a tragic accident to a Hastings in December 1950, the Commander-in-Chief wrote a letter of appreciation to the Station Commander at Lyneham. He recalled in graphic detail what had happened on the night of 20 December when TG574 was flying westwards from El Adem, en route from Singapore to the UK, with a crew of six and 27 RAF passengers. The letter first quoted from the Board of Enquiry:

'One blade of a propeller fractured and a large portion of this flew through the side of the fuselage, fatally injuring a member of the crew, Flt Lt S L Bennett, who was resting in a cot. It also severed the elevator and rudder controls and their trimming tabs, and the aileron trimming tabs. At the same time, the engine driving the unbalanced propeller fell out of the aircraft.

'It is clear from the evidence that in spite of all this, the crew and passengers kept perfectly calm and somehow the Captain of the aircraft, Flt Lt G Tunnadine, managed – although having no elevator or rudder control – to keep the aircraft on an even keel and trim it by moving passengers as necessary along the fuselage.

'Calmly, and with great skill and courage, Flt Lt Tunnadine and his crew – which then included Sqn Ldr James, who had taken the co-pilot's place – flew the aircraft in the dark to the nearest airfield, Benina, and not only flew it there, but somehow managed to make a successful approach to the airfield. They were, however, unable to effect a safe landing and hit the ground about 700 yards short of the runway. The aircraft turned over and in doing so killed a further four members of its crew, who were in the front of the aircraft.

'Owing entirely to the skill and courage of the crew, and the calmness and discipline of all aboard, the rest escaped with their lives'.

The Commander-in-Chief then mentioned the crew members who had been killed or injured. Flt Lt Tunnadine, first pilot and captain; Flt Lt S L Bennett, second pilot; Flt Sgt I A Johns, navigator; Sgt G J Bain, signaller – all of No 53 Sqn, all killed; Sqn Ldr W G James, check pilot and acting as co-pilot at the time of the crash – of No 99 Sqn, who was also killed; the two injured aircrew members – Sgts R E Walker, engineer, and W J A Slaughter, air quartermaster, both of No 53 Sqn. The letter ended in the following terms:

'I should also mention one of the passengers, Sqn Ldr T C L Brown of Abingdon, an RAF Medical Officer who went forward to the crew compartment and did what he could for the seriously injured co-pilot, Flt Lt S L Bennett, staying with him in the forward part of the aircraft until after the crash. As a result of this devotion to duty, Sqn Ldr Brown sustained serious injury'.

'This is a story of valour in which we in Transport Command can all take pride, and in particular No 53 Sqn, which, with the one exception, provided this gallant crew.

'I think the squadron might possibly like to have this letter and to keep it in memory of those who lost their lives, and as a record of outstanding airmanship'.

The appropriate historical comment is that of John Milton, in his sonnet addressed to The Lord General Cromwell in May 1652:

> Peace hath her victories
> No less renown'd than War.[15]

---

15 A similar encomium should be applied to the crew of Hastings WD 492 of No 47 Sqn which on 16 September 1952 landed inadvertently on the Greenland ice cap when doing a low-level (Soft) drop of supplies to the British North Greenland Expedition. The captain, Flt Lt M A Clancy, experienced a "white out" (ice haze blocking out the horizon) just after completing his second run and the port wing struck the snow: the aircraft then turned through 180°, there were two impacts and it slid tail-first for several hundred yards before coming to rest. There was no panic among the RAF, Army and one USAF officer crew aboard as they abandoned it; and although three of them were injured they survived sub-zero temperatures (down to −38°F) for nine days and through good discipline, high morale and common sense, assisted by air-dropped supplies and ground support from the BNGE – before being lifted off to safety by a Grumman Albatross (which picked up the three casualties) and a USAF C-47.

1 Liberator AL578 'Marco Polo' of RAF Ferry Command and No 45 Group when employed on the Return Ferry Service

2 Red-haired and with 'very direct blue eyes under bushy eyebrows': Air Chief Marshal Sir Frederick Bowhill, first AOC-in-C Transport Command

3, 4, 5 and 6 Hudson (above) and Dakota (right and below) casualty evacuation during
Operation Husky. The Dakota at right (above) is from No 267 Sqn. The Kittyhawks
in the background of the photograph at right (below) are of No 3 (RAAF) Sqn, Desert Air Force

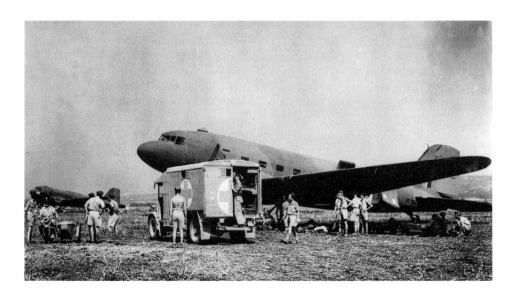

8   The AOC No 216 Group, Air Cdre Whitney Straight, makes a new friend on a visit
to a staging post on the West African Reinforcement Route. Pets were common at these isolated
SP airfields: the author recalls a cheetah at El Geneina and a lion at El Fasher

7 *Left*, The AOC-in-C,
Air Chief Marshal
Sir Frederick Bowhill,
inspecting aircrew of No 216 Sqn
on 11 February 1944 at Cairo
West airfield. Behind him
is the CO, Wg Cdr E M Morris

9 AOC and AOC-in-C: Air
Cdre Straight and Air Chief
Marshal Sir Sholto Douglas,
who was AOC-in-C Middle
East Command from December
1942

10 Flt Lt David Lord VC
DFC: a portrait of him as he
would have looked had he
survived the war

11 Coals to Berlin: a Hastings being unloaded during the 1948–49 Airlift

12 Yorks, Dakota and a civil Tudor in the Airlift

13 An Airlift concentration of Yorks: the nearest one, KY-N, is from No 242 Sqn at Abingdon (or Lyneham, to which it moved in mid-June 1949 before Operation Plainfare ended)

14 Hastings in Plainfare, their first operational commitment after being introduced into service

15 Stalwarts of Transport Command: a Vickers Valetta flanked by a Handley Page Hastings

16 Stars of the Command: Britannias Aldebaran and Rigel

17 Long rangers: a Britannia followed by a Comet 4 and its smaller predecessor the Comet 2, with RAF Lyneham as background

18 The business end of a Blackburn Beverley during a 1966 exercise at Larkhill on Salisbury Plain

19 Unloading a Westland Whirlwind helicopter from XB268, a Beverley flown by both Nos 47 and 53 Sqns

20 How many troops will go into one Britannia? – a demonstration using both ends of Capella

21 Talking Comets: the Rt Hon George Ward, Secretary of State for Air,
and Sqn Ldr G C McCarthy, one of the captains of No 216 Sqn who flew S of S to Buenos Aires
on his South American visit in 1958

22 Comet 2 XK670 unloading Service passengers at Gan

23 Air Vice-Marshal P G Wykeham, first AOC No 38 Group after its re-formation, greeting the Rt Hon Julian Amery, Secretary of State for Air from October 1960, on his arrival at RAF Odiham

24 Scottish Aviation Twin Pioneer of No 230 Sqn in a casualty evacuation exercise

25 Westland Whirlwind Mk 2 in Exercise Saucy Sue with No 16 Para Brigade Group

26 Seeing for himself: S of S for Air the Rt Hon Julian Amery answering questions after a flight in a two-seat Hunter of No 1 Sqn, which with No 54 Sqn operated FGA.9s in No 38 Group from 1960 to 1969

27 One of the Argosy's roles was paratroop dropping: here members of the 1962 Free Fall team depart from XN853 of No 114 Sqn

28 Rolling in the barrels: Britannia Aldebaran at Lusaka during the Zambian oil airlift from Kenya by Nos 99 and 511 Sqns

29 Tank transporter: unloading practice from the Shorts 'big lifter', a Belfast of No 53 Sqn, based at Brize Norton

30 Fast, high-capacity, long-range transport: a VC10 of No 10 Sqn

Chapter XI

Enter the Beverleys and Comets

The old order changeth, yielding place to new

Tennyson, Morte d'Arthur

FROM November 1950 the long-serving Dakotas, which had played their last starring role in the Berlin Airlift, had been succeeded in the medium-range transport role by Valettas, though "soldiering on" to 1952. But what about re-equipment for the long-range and the Army support roles?

The Statement on Defence for 1950[1] had some chilling words for Transport Command. It warned that with the gradual build-up of Bomber Command (as the nuclear deterrent force) there would be a reduction in the air transport force at home but that we should retain enough transport aircraft to meet essential needs, and '. . . to enable us to make an important contribution to another airlift operation should that become necessary'. In order words, Transport Command was to have a relatively lower priority in the nation's Defence calculations.

The only new transport aircraft in the production pipeline was the Beverley, a four-engined, high-wing, fixed-undercarriage freight and troop carrier resulting from a post-war Air Ministry Specification, C.3/46, which called for an aircraft with a still-air range of 500 miles and with a payload of 25,000lb.

It happened that General Aircraft Ltd of Feltham were in a position to meet this Specification and built the GAL 60 Universal Freighter. But before it reached the stage of its first flight from the nearby Hanworth Aerodrome, General Aircraft had merged with Blackburn Aircraft, so on 1 January 1948 the prototype was disassembled and transported to Brough for its maiden flight. As the Beverley C Mk 1 (named after the Minster city to the north of Hull) it entered RAF service with No 47 Sqn at Abingdon on 12 March 1956. Two more Beverley squadrons were formed in 1957, No 53 in February and No 30 in April, both of them – like No 47 – formerly equipped with Hastings.

The Beverley had a tremendous load-carrying capacity, lifting an equivalent of 22 tons, but it was slow. Typical ranges were 1,300 miles at 186 mph at 8,000ft with a 29,000lb load, or 160 miles at 170 mph at 8,000ft with a 50,000lb load. It could accommodate bulky loads and had STOL characteristics. When flown to the SBAC Show at Farnborough in September 1951 by Blackburn chief test pilot 'Tim' Wood it conveyed the

---

1 Cmnd 7895.

company's Land Rover and 22ft caravan from Brough and stole the show by the shortness of its landing run and the ease with which its vast bulk left the ground. When the Beverley was introduced into No 47 Sqn, it was the largest aircraft to enter RAF service at that time and the first specially designed for dropping heavy Army equipment. (In a demonstration in 1953 an Army gun and its support vehicle, mounted on a wooden platform, were successfully dropped at Amesbury, Wiltshire under a cluster of six 42ft parachutes)[2].

The origins of the de Havilland Comet, which came into the RAF in June 1956 only three-and-a-half months after the Beverley, were quite different. It entered Transport Command service after an unusual and tragic sequence of civilian accidents as a BOAC airliner; these all occurred to Comet 1s.

On 2 May 1953 G-ALYV took off from Calcutta for Delhi but while climbing to cruising altitude was inexplicably destroyed with the loss of 43 lives. This accident was repeated twice more in almost exact detail[3]. On 12 January 1954 G-ALYP took off from Rome and plunged into the sea near Elba from a height of 26,000ft with the loss of 35 lives. Then on 8 April G-ALYY, also after take-off from Rome, crashed off Stromboli with the loss of 21 lives. The Comet fleet was then grounded and a public inquiry and accident investigation were convened. It had been possible to salvage the wreck of G-ALYP from the sea. This was subjected to microscopic examination and reassembled at RAE Farnborough. As a result the cause of the accidents was accurately pinpointed. Structural failure of the pressure cabin had occurred, brought about by fatigue. It was the end of the Comet 1, but the lessons so disastrously taught were embodied in later marks[4].

The Comet 2, with heavier gauge skin for the fuselage and rounded (as opposed to square) windows, made its maiden flight on 27 August 1953. Trials showed that although its range was adequate for the South Atlantic route it was still not suitable as a civil airliner for the North Atlantic crossing. With four exceptions the Comet 2s were therefore delivered to No 216 Sqn, RAF Transport Command, which used them on scheduled trooping runs between Lyneham and Australia[5].

The Comet 2 had not originally entered the Air Council's calculations when they first discussed the need for a long-range aircraft to replace the Hastings. The Air Staff had issued an Operational Requirement (OR 315) for a pure jet passenger/freighter, the Vickers V1000, which was being developed on the basis of experience gained with the Valiant V-bomber.

A paper submitted to the Council at the beginning of the year[6] set out

---

2 I am indebted to A J Jackson's book *Blackburn Aircraft since 1909* (Putnam & Co, 1968) for these anecdotes.

3 *British Civil Aircraft 1919–59 Vol One*, by A J Jackson; Putnam, 1959.

4 A J Jackson, op cit.

5 Ibid – i.e. in 1959.

6 'The Re-equipment of the Long Range Transport Force' – Note by Deputy Chief of the Air Staff (DCAS) (AC (54) 7, 28 Jan 54).

the requirements for the long-range transport force against the background of defence strategy. The principal need concerned air mobility in Cold War conditions, the ability to move an Army division out to the Far East within a month. The Planning Staffs proposed a force of 24 V1000s and 32 Beverleys, whose numbers could possibly be reduced if civil aircraft could be engaged in the trooping role. Then under a radical review to meet a financial limit imposed by the Minister of Defence, this force was arbitrarily reduced to 12 V1000s and 24 Beverleys. A delay in the forecast availability of the V1000 then caused the Air Staff to consider the possibility of using the Britannia or Comet 3[7] instead. It had become clear though that the latter would not meet the Operational Requirement, mainly because its passenger load (78 maximum) would be only two-thirds of that needed; furthermore, despite suggested modifications, it would not be able to carry the items of freight specified in the Air Staff OR.

The Air Council paper had set out a comparison between the V1000 and the Britannia 250 and recommended that the V1000 should be the choice for the long-range force. But because the first V1000 could not be available before late in 1958 it was recommended that the gap be filled by replacing a squadron of Hastings with Comet 2s.

Throughout the rest of 1954 the Air Council's discussions about the long-range transport requirement continued, but without leading to a conclusion. At one stage four options were under consideration: Britannias; Comet 2s followed by the V1000; refurbished Hastings followed by the V1000; and Britannias with a 'speculative order' for perhaps four V1000s. The strategic scenario, which would influence the requirement, was itself a variable – as between hot or cold war conditions. Developments on the civil airliner side were also a factor in the equation. The Council nevertheless agreed that the V1000 was a firm contender and that an initial order should be placed for six[8]. Minutes of the Council's meetings continued to show uneasiness about how much reliance should be placed on the Comet, even as a stop-gap, but in December it was provisionally agreed that an order should be placed for six of them.

The V1000 continued to be the designated choice for Transport Command's long-range aircraft until mid-1955. By then it became clear that the forecast performance for the type was falling behind the Operational Requirement. Weight growth without a matching increase in engine thrust was going to cause the aircraft to be underpowered. This meant that the use of 2000yd runways would impose payload limitations which would prevent the aircraft providing the required range/payload. Cruising speed and LCN[9] were also out of line and it would not have been possible to operate the aircraft at its normal all-up weight from many of the airfields that the transport force was required to use. Furthermore the earliest in-service date had slipped to 1960.

---

7 Stretched version of the Comet 2, first flown on 19 July 54.

8 AC 8(54), 1 Apr 54.

9 'LCN' stands for 'Load Classification Number' and is a measure of the load which an aircraft imposes on runways and other surfaces when it is on the ground.

PRINCIPAL WORLD ROUTES
OF TRANSPORT COMMAND - 1954

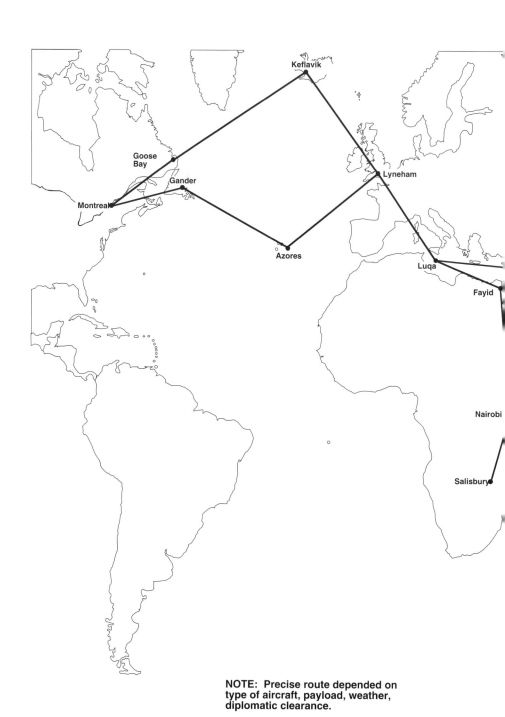

NOTE: Precise route depended on
type of aircraft, payload, weather,
diplomatic clearance.

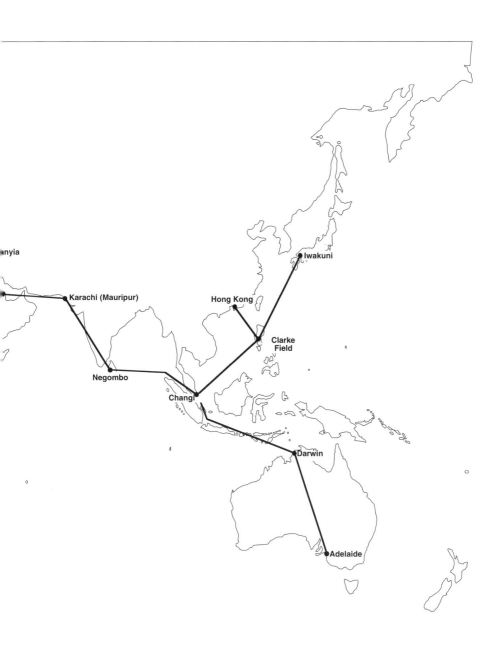

At the same time the nature of the requirement was itself shifting. Because of changes in strategic thinking there was less need for the new aircraft to be so closely associated with the operations of the V-force. The emphasis was moving more toward Cold War tasks, with the consequential requirement to provide quick reaction and long-range mobility for the army's Strategic Reserve. Payload and range were important, as was an early in-service date.

Accordingly at a meeting on 27 July 1955 the Air Council called for the cancellation of the V1000 order and recommended an order for Britannia 250s instead[10]. Transport Command's long-range force would thus consist primarily of Britannias, supported by a small number of Comet 2s.

Meanwhile the evolution of the strategic concepts prompted the Air Council to reconsider the future role of Transport Command. In a paper tabled for the Council on 27 June[11] it was proposed, first that the Command's primary role should be to provide support in the Cold War by giving mobility to the Strategic Reserve including the move of RAF formations overseas. Second, its use for scheduled operations in peacetime should be regarded as a bonus. Third, the transport force available for a hot war should consist of that developed to meet the Cold War commitment, with the addition of the civil fleets.

The new policy was endorsed by the Council, but not without a lengthy discussion on the place of route flying in the Command's order of activities. Route flying provided invaluable training of a kind which was essential to the efficiency of a military transport force; but the Command had never been established to undertake long-range scheduled services and freight transport. There was a danger that if the number of such tasks continued to rise then the Command would not be able in an emergency to fulfil its strategic mobility role. There was mention of the heavy commitment imposed by the task to fly people and equipment out to Woomera, Australia, in connection with nuclear weapon trials, a task which had fallen to Transport Command for reasons of security. It was now thought, however, that this task could be met by civil charter aircraft.

PUS hoped that the Council would accept this new Transport Command policy in principle, but he expected that it would need to be reaffirmed in the light of financial and other implications brought out in further papers promised by VCAS.

The next paper, the first of two, concentrated on short term aspects[12], while the second looked into the longer term. Transport Command had only Hastings squadrons and one Valetta squadron with which to undertake a large number of commitments. It was deemed unwise to reckon on any productive Comet flying in 1956 and the first Beverley squadron of 8UE would only be formed on 1 July. Thus, any substantial

---

10 AC 15/55 (Conclusions).

11 'Future Role and Policy of Transport Command. Note by VCAS' – AC (55) 33, 27 June 1955.

12 AC(55)59 – 2 December 1955. 'Implementation of Policy for Transport Operations – Short Term'.

improvement in the long-range element of the Command could not be expected for at least 18 months to two years. The purpose of the first paper, therefore, was to make recommendations on how best to bridge the gap between commitments and resources in 1956.

The main load for Transport Command in 1956 would fall on the Hastings fleet, for which the tasks were listed as: aircrew continuation training; air mobility exercises for the RAF; airlift for both the Atomic Weapons Research Establishment (AWRE) and for guided weapons development in Australia; aeromedical evacuation; additional special flights; training and liaison flights in support of other Commands; route training flights with freight; parachute training for army formations in the UK; and airlift for the Army's Strategic Reserve.

AWRE had already asked for eleven special flights to Australia and detachments of three or four Hastings in that country. There would be a requirement to continue the six return flights a month to Australia in support of guided weapons development. Three aeromedical flights to the Far East and four to the Middle East had already been scheduled. In addition, the requirement for the Army's Strategic Reserve would be to deploy air elements up to Brigade Group size. Finally, the Command could also be called upon to meet some of the many emergencies for which contingency plans had been made.

VCAS envisaged that from July 1956 the Beverleys would assist in providing logistic air support for the Army in Germany: one sortie a day each could be provided to 2 ATAF and Northern Army Group. This allocation might be supplemented by a major autumn logistic exercise using all 12 Beverleys, the main objective of which would be to make selected army formations independent of sea, rail and long-distance road transport for up to ten days.

With the exception of parachute training for army formations in the UK, the commitments for the Hastings force were considered to be inescapable. At the same time it was plainly evident that, even though some tasks might possibly be met by Civil Charter, the Hastings fleet was over-committed. The first step towards reconciling the difference between commitments and resources would be to negotiate a new agreement with the War Office on parachute training. Once the Beverley – which was designed with the requirements of parachutists in mind – became operational, it would clearly be uneconomical to use the longer-range strategic Hastings for tactical exercises. The intention, therefore, would be to offer uncommitted Beverley effort for this task.

At its meeting on 15 December[13] the Air Council took note of the likely tasks of the Hastings force in 1956 and, notwithstanding the limited resources available, agreed that additional effort should be devoted to air mobility exercises. The Council asked that CAS approach CIGS about a new agreement providing for the use of Beverleys instead of Hastings for Army parachute training, and called for a re-appreciation of the aircraft requirement in the light of the latest information on the best utilisation rate

13 23(55).

for the Hastings. The Council agreed that action should be taken to transfer to civil charter any suitable tasks that could not be undertaken by Transport Command, and took note that the recalculation of the charter requirement was a matter of urgency, in view of the approach of the Air Estimates and the likely commitments of the charter companies.

At this time the Command, whose future had thus been weighed up very thoroughly, still had only the small force of 37 Hastings and one squadron of 12 Valettas to support Bomber and Fighter Commands in the frequent overseas rapid-deployment exercises foreseen by the Secretary of State for Air in his Memorandum accompanying the 1955–56 Air Estimates. In this Memorandum S of S also referred to the V1000 long-range jet transport, for which the Comet 2 operations could be looked upon as providing a lead-in. Prior to the V1000 being cancelled in mid-1955 it was intended that, pending its delivery, the Comet 2 would give Transport Command crews the experience required to operate high-speed jet transport aircraft. These aircraft would be modified and strengthened to meet RAF requirements and would be put into regular use on the military transport service to Woomera, a role in which the Comet's speed would be of great advantage.

The Memorandum also looked forward to the introduction of the Beverley, which would improve the capability of Transport Command both in the heavy freighting role and for tactical airborne operations and supply dropping. Despite its limited strength, the Command continued to provide casualty evacuation and route transport services, the delivery of aircraft and equipment to overseas Commands, and collaboration with the Army in Airborne Forces training.

Even by mid-March 1956, however, doubts were being expressed by the Air Council as to whether the RAF should accept the Comet 2. Air Marshal Sir Thomas Pike, Deputy Chief of the Air Staff (DCAS), reminded his colleagues on 15 March[14] that the Minister of Transport and Civil Aviation (MTCA) had told the Commons on 16 February[15] that Comet 2s delivered to Transport Command would be required to obtain a full civil passenger-carrying Certificate of Airworthiness (C of A) before they could go into service. But the Air Registration Board were reluctant to issue such a Certificate because they claimed that the Comet 2 fell short in respect of certain factors.

DCAS's own view was that none of these was important in a military aircraft, or beyond the capacity of the operating pilot to cope with; he hoped that a long delay would be avoided by giving the aircraft a qualified C of A which would enable it to operate within such limitations as would be laid down in the flight manual. There was, however, a contrary view, that taking account of the unfortunate record of the Comet 1 it would be unwise to use the Comet 2 for trooping in the absence of a full passenger-carrying C of A.

The Permanent Under-Secretary (Sir Maurice Dean) pointed out that

---

14 5(56) mtg.
15 Hansard, Col 391.

it would first be necessary to know precisely in what respects the aircraft was deficient from the point of view of a full C of A, and that the Ministry of Supply was seeking this information from the Air Registration Board (ARB). In the light of these negotiations it would be premature for the Council to take any decision, and this line would apply equally to the two training aircraft which were due to be delivered in March. On this advice, the Council agreed to defer a decision.

A more hopeful note was struck when the Council met again on 29 March[16] when DCAS told members that the situation regarding the issue of a C of A was more promising: two of the three factors which had failed to satisfy the ARB had now been cleared; the third – relating to buffeting – would, he thought, take another two/three weeks to resolve. Matters moved a stage further in the following month: on 2 May DCAS told the Air Council[17] that it was hoped to get a full C of A from the ARB within the next month. Then at their meeting on the 17th[18] he reported that the ARB had recommended the Comet 2 for a C of A, which he expected fairly soon.

Meanwhile that famous old Middle East transport squadron, No 216, which since February 1951 had been operating Valettas from Fayid, was moved to Lyneham in November 1955 after 38 years' service overseas. Then in mid-1956, after jet conversion on Meteor 7s, two of its crews were detached to the de Havilland Aircraft Co at Hatfield for conversion on to Comets. The squadron's first operational flight with the type was to take the Secretary of State for Air (Rt Hon Nigel Birch) to Moscow on 23 June for the Russian Air Display at Vnukovo[19]. The aircraft was captained by the Squadron Commander, Wg Cdr B D Sellick, and the 1,490-mile flight took 4hr 2min.

This VIP journey was a prestigious inauguration for a type – the first RAF jet transport – which No 216 Squadron was to operate with conspicuous success, in its Mk 2 and then Mk 4 versions, for the next 19 years, from 1966 to 1975 being partnered by VC10s. The Air Council's caution over the introduction of the new type to Transport Command service had been understandable after the disasters which had befallen the Comet 1s. Once the 2s began to be flown worldwide with such speed and reliability they brought nothing but credit to the RAF.

The other new aircraft which joined Transport Command in 1956 – preceding the Comet by about three months – was the Blackburn Beverley medium-range/high-capacity transport: the first C 1 was flown from the manufacturer's airfield at Brough to RAF Abingdon on 12 March by

---

16 7(56) mtg.

17 10(56) mtg.

18 11(56) mtg.

19 On 23 April the Russian leaders N A Bulganin and N S Kruschev had visited RAF Marham. There was some embarrassment on a return visit to Moscow when the engines could not be started before a flight by Soviet Air Force officers. As Flt Lt P E Pullan AFC, one of the Comet captains, explained in an article in *Air Clues* ('First with the Comets', June 1957 issue): 'The trouble was found to be an internal fault in one of the aircraft's batteries. To offset any possible unfavourable impressions, a second trip to Moscow was made shortly afterwards'.

Squadron Leader A St J Price and his crew; it was the vanguard of replacement for No 47 Squadron of the Hastings they had operated since 1948.

The advent of the Comets and Beverleys meant the introduction of special conversion courses for Transport Command crews at both RAF stations and aircraft manufacturers. When the new No 216 Squadron was building up at RAF Lyneham in early 1956, crews not only carried out jet flying on the Meteor T.7 and courses with de Havilland, but some aircrew were sent to Bassingbourn to complete a Canberra course with 231 OCU or to Strubby for Meteor conversion. At the same time a Servicing Flight was built up which would be carrying out first-line servicing of the squadron aircraft, and Engineers were detached to de Havilland for the Comet Flight Engineers Course.

Jet flying familiarisation on the Meteor T.7 increased from 31hr in March 1956 to 85hr in May, by which time a second Meteor had been allotted. No wonder that, in its June ORB, the squadron could record: 'The handing-over to the squadron of the first Comet was very encouraging and a sign of real progress being made in the process of re-equipping'. No date is given for the actual hand-over, but it was on the 23rd – as already recorded – that the first operational flight was made, to Moscow, with the Secretary of State for Air on board.

The conversion process at Abingdon was not quite so drastic; it entailed going from the Hastings, with four Bristol Hercules engines, to the Beverley with four Bristol Centaurus engines. The No 47 Squadron ORB recorded the arrival of the first C.1 on 12 March for commencement of conversion, and this went on for the rest of that month, during the whole of April and for most of May. On 24 April a route-proving flight was made to Germany (Wildenrath and Wahn) by Flt Lt J McWicker; at the end of that month the CO, Sqn Ldr D P Boulnois, noted: 'The squadron was off to a good start on conversion. In view of the fact that the Beverley is a new aircraft both to the aircrew and the maintenance personnel, I feel justly proud of this month's achievement'.

By 6 June, when Flt Lt Sleeman collected a Beverley from Brough, No 47 Squadron reached its established strength of eight aircraft, and the following month saw proof of the capability of the new type. On the 11th, when Flt Lt P T Dudley was returning from Wildenrath on a scheduled flight he had to land at Koksijde in Belgium with engine trouble. The next day the CO collected the aircraft and, as noted in the ORB, 'returned to Abingdon on three engines – the squadron's first three-engine operation'. Clearly, confidence in the new type had been established.

By the middle of 1956 Transport Command was on higher ground, and had better future prospects than at any time since the end of the Berlin Airlift in 1949. In addition to its two new squadrons of Comets and Beverleys which gave it fast jet and heavy lift capabilities, it had four squadrons of Hastings, one of Valettas and one of Pioneer CC.1s – No 215, which had been reformed at Dishforth on 3 May. Commanded by Sqn Ldr J J Wood DFC, its role was 'to work in conjunction with the 24th Independent Infantry Brigade, located at Barnard Castle, Co Durham'. As will be seen in further references to Exercises in which it was involved, the Squadron practised air portability; its aircraft were dismantled and loaded into Beverleys to accompany the Brigade on Exercises overseas.

Transport Command itself, however, was to be involved in real-life operations overseas within four months in supporting the Anglo–French action of October–November 1956 against Egypt, Operation Musketeer.

Chapter XII

Supporting the Suez Operation

'We are not at war with Egypt. . . . We are in an armed conflict'

Sir Anthony Eden in the House of Commons, 1 November 1956

AIRCRAFT of all the main types in Transport Command took part in Operation Musketeer, the Anglo–French naval, air and land operation to recover control of the Suez Canal, before, during and after the period of actual hostilities (31 October to 6 November 1956). The Operation was a 'baptism of fire' for the newly acquired Comets (as high-speed passenger carriers) and Beverleys (as heavy lifters), backed up by the well-tried Hastings and Valettas.

The Beverleys made an early contribution, transporting 100 tons of bitumen from El Adem to Cyprus during August for the resurfacing of Tymbou airfield, which would supplement Nicosia and Akrotiri. (A further 700 tons was carried to the island by sea – 200 in tank landing craft and the rest by civil ships from Tobruk). The Air Historical Branch account of Operation Musketeer says that supplies were drawn from Amman and Habbaniyah where there were Maintenance Units (No 115 at Mafraq and No 116 at Habbaniyah), recording that 'tentage, refuellers, mobile generators, water bowsers and barrack equipment needed under field conditions were uplifted'. This was the first occasion on which the Beverley had operated under semi-tropical conditions, but the Operations Record Book of No 47 Sqn (Abingdon) recorded that performance and serviceability were impaired by the high temperatures and humidity. Among the varied and bizarre loads carried during Musketeer were a 47ft radar scanner, an 18,000lb signals vehicle, three 9,000lb trailers and 270 tons of oil – all airlifted from Cyprus to Port Said in 21 flights[1].

The AHB account records that the MEAF transport force [one Hastings and two Valetta squadrons] had been heavily committed before Musketeer began, with the pre-positioning of personnel and equipment. Supplemented by aircraft from Transport Command, the force provided the essential lift for the airborne assault on Gamil and was subsequently committed to scheduled re-supply services to the airhead until the evacuation was complete.

The new Comets of No 216 Sqn provided VIP transport. On 1 September a special flight to Cyprus in XK669 captained by the Squadron Commander, Wg Cdr B D Sellick DSO DFC, took out Air Marshal D H F

---

1 *Blackburn Aircraft since 1909*, by A J Jackson (Putnam & Co, 1968).

Barnett, the Air Task Force Commander, Air Cdre R A C Carter, Senior Air Staff Officer of Transport Command, Brigadier J Butler of the Parachute Regiment and Commander Mouie of the French Airborne Force. On 6th September the same Comet and captain took the C-in-C Transport Command, Air Vice-Marshal A McKee, to Malta.

A study of No 47 Squadron's Operations Record Book for this period shows that the flight times for the Beverley from Abingdon to Luqa (Malta), staging through Istres in France, were about 7hr 30min, and that those from Luqa to Nicosia varied between 4hr 30min and 7hr 30min. The whole of No 47 Sqn followed this well-worn track, for during October 1956 all available Beverleys were required for the airlift to Cyprus, and the regular service to Wildenrath, Germany, which had begun in July, had to be suspended.

During November the No 47 Sqn aircraft flew over 500hr and could have flown more but for an unproductive detachment to Nicosia when an aircraft was held at standby awaiting tasks which never materialised. Clearly when very bulky loads had to be transported the new RAF freighter came into its own; when these were not available its unique capacity could not be fully utilised.

In December 1956, the squadron ORB recorded that the Nicosia standby was continued by a relief aircraft and crew for the first three weeks of the month, and again this appeared an unnecessary drain on the squadron's resources as only one freight run was ordered and the aircraft only flew for 3hr 35min during the detachment. However, during that month No 47 Sqn made six special flights to Malta and Cyprus, those to Cyprus being specially authorised to carry up to 80 passengers on the return flight in connection with the return of personnel from Egypt. Those who flew home by Beverley were carried in the upper tail boom fuselage of the aircraft, an area of its airframe quite separate from the cavernous interior into which freight was loaded[2].

The other component of Transport Command support for Operation Musketeer was contributed by the Hastings and Valettas. At that time (September 1956) there were three long-range squadrons of Hastings, Nos 53, 99 and 511, all based at Lyneham, and there was one medium-range Valetta squadron, No 30, based at Dishforth. The Command's routine resources were therefore limited and fully stretched, as was quickly apparent when any large operation was mounted and had to be supported. The Headquarters ORB records that during October two Hastings carried Avon engines from Lyneham to Luqa and Nicosia for Bomber Command (for Valiants and Canberras) and that four Hastings were engaged in 'Goldflake' rotations from Marham to Luqa. 'Goldflake' was the code-name for the deployment of Valiant squadrons to Malta for Operation

---

2 Three members of a No 47 Sqn slip crew were killed and a fourth (the captain, Flt Lt V T R Hurring) injured in an accident to a Beverley of No 53 Sqn, XH117, on 5 March 1957. Formed at Abingdon in February 1957, No 53 was the second Beverley squadron and operated jointly to Khormaksar, Aden, with No 47 Sqn, supporting a detachment there. The primary cause of the accident was found to have been the incorrect fitting of the non-return valve in the No 1 port tank, resulting in fuel starvation of No 2 engine.

Musketeer. At the same time, by one of those ironic coincidences of history, the Hungarian uprising against Soviet occupation was put down brutally by the Red Army and led to a stream of refugees – some 100,000 – across the Austrian border, and to an emergency airlift of food and supplies to Vienna.

Transport Command's ORB records that this airlift was made by Valettas, Hastings and Beverleys flying out via Wildenrath. Three Valettas went from Dishforth and Benson and two from Abingdon; four Hastings went from Abingdon and five from Dishforth; and one Beverley from Abingdon: a total weight of 112 tons of supplies was carried out and some refugees were brought back to the UK.

The Command also had a large part to play in Operation Challenger – bringing back personnel who had taken part in the Suez operation. In his book *Wings in the Sun A History of the RAF in the Mediterranean 1945–1986*[3] Air Chief Marshal Sir David Lee writes that the withdrawal from Malta of troops who had taken part in the Suez operation caused a very large increase in the volume of transport aircraft through Luqa and reached its peak between 20 and 24 December 1956.

The number of personnel required to support Operation Musketeer – planning and administrative staff – can be gauged from the number of airlifts from the UK to Malta and Cyprus mounted by Transport Command in October 1956 – 58 sorties, all but three of them by Hastings (the three exceptions being those by Comets).

The bulk of the Operation Challenger flights were from Bomber Command airfields to Luqa and Nicosia: for example, eight Hastings picked-up Bomber Command personnel from Marham, Upwood and Waddington and flew them out to Luqa and Nicosia and eight Hastings did a similar airlift from Honington and Waddington to Nicosia. Army HQ staff were also airlifted to Akrotiri from Lyneham on three separate occasions – the first time by eight, and the second and third times by three, Hastings.

On one occasion three Comets carried out Coastal Command slip-crews from Lyneham to Luqa. Shackletons were used to supplement Transport Command lifting capability. As the Memorandum by the Secretary of State for Air accompanying the 1956–57 Air Estimates put it: 'further Army reinforcements have since been moved to Cyprus by Transport Command and Shackletons of Coastal Command. The Shackletons will be a most useful adjunct to Transport Command in an emergency and will be used when necessary to increase the strategic mobility of the RAF and the Army'. This proved to be the case in Operation Musketeer.

Looking back on that operation in the following year the Secretary of State for Air (George Ward) in his Memorandum accompanying the 1957–58 Air Estimates said: 'Both before and during the landing, transport aircraft of Transport Command and of the Middle East transport force played an important part in deploying air and ground

3 HMSO, 1989.

forces, including airborne forces. A battalion of parachute troops was dropped with great precision at Port Said'.

Partly because aircraft and crews from the UK supplemented the resident Middle East transport squadrons, and partly because of the vagueness of many Operations Record Book entries, the contributions of individual Transport Command squadrons to Operation Musketeer are difficult to determine.

Of the UK-based transport squadrons, No 511 (Hastings) was probably the most closely involved, as its ORB for November 1956 records: 'This month the Squadron took part in Operations in the Middle East. Three aircraft were on detachment to Nicosia and were engaged in dropping leaflets and paratroops at Port Said and in shuttle services between Nicosia and Gamil. In these operations one aircraft was slightly damaged by hostile fire. In connection with these operations, 28 flights were made to Cyprus and eight to Luqa'.

Two other squadrons involved were Nos 30 (Valettas) and 53 (Hastings). Twelve aircraft and crews of the former squadron left Dishforth for service in the Middle East. During November they were involved in Operation Jinx and the crews detached for that operation did not return to base until 22 December, having completed 167 Nicosia/Gamil flights.

No 53 Sqn did several airlifts of Bomber Command personnel to Luqa and Nicosia supporting the Valiant and Canberra squadrons. During November the squadron became actively involved in Musketeer operations: three crews formed part of the Hastings task force which was detached to Nicosia for the purpose of dropping parachutists over Port Said after the landings, on 5 November.

Transport Command still had a ferrying role at this time, and its No 147 Sqn at Benson was involved in flying out Hunter 5s and Venoms. The former got as far as Malta but then had to return, as El Adem – a necessary refuelling stop – was closed to them. The Venoms had to be flown direct from Luqa to Akrotiri, and the speed with which No 8 Sqn there accepted them and flew them on operations was remarkable. The two aircraft delivered on 3 November by Flt Sgt H C Farmer and Plt Off R E Maxwell were airborne on an operational mission four hours after landing, then inspected, refuelled and re-armed. The abortive Hunter delivery had taken place on the 1st: the two aircraft returned to Benson on the 6th.

Soon 1956, with its curious climax of the Suez operation – not a war but an 'armed conflict' – came to an end; 1957 was to bring more specific and peaceful successes for Transport Command, particularly with its jet transports.

Chapter XIII

Confirmation of the Comets

'While self-dependent power can time defy'

Samuel Johnson (added to Goldsmith's Deserted Village)

WITHOUT question 1957 was the Year of the Comet in Transport Command. Doubts about its reliability were dispelled and the way was smoothed for its regular operation to the Far East by the development of Gan in the Maldive Islands as a staging post. The Air Council had been adamant that this stepping-stone in the Indian Ocean should be established. If the Treasury raised opposition to its development, said the Secretary of State (Mr Nigel Birch) at the first meeting in January 1957[1] the matter should be referred to the Defence Committee.

The Council was told that a reconnaissance party of works and signals experts was going to the Maldives to determine the requirements for erecting an aerial farm for communications, and another working party was being sent from Cyprus. The Air Council had clearly made up its mind about the development of Gan.

Next, a Comet proving flight to the Far East was on the cards. If that were successfully accomplished the new jet transport would be given additional long-range roles.

In a Note on the use of the Comet 2 for aero-medical evacuation put to the Council on 24 January[2] VCAS (Air Chief Marshal Sir Ronald Ivelaw-Chapman) said that subject to a proving flight and to Transport Command achieving a total of 3,000hr flying by its Comet fleet without serious incident, a scheduled aero-medical service evacuation from the Far East should be instituted. He also proposed that Service personnel of either sex – but not their families – should travel by Comet when required to move under trooping or routine deployment arrangements.

In response the Council authorised a Comet proving flight to the Far East, agreed – subject to its success – that a detailed examination should be undertaken to determine the minor structural alterations necessary to allow for the fitting of 7–9 stretchers in the Comet freight compartment (on the assumption that they would be readily removable), and approved the carriage of aero-medical patients and serving personnel in Comet 2s – subject to the completion of 3,000hr flying without serious incident.

When the Air Council made its decision about the future use of Comet

---

1 Conclusions, 1(57).

2 AC(57)1.

2s, No 216 Sqn had already made many flights to the Far East; during January 1957, for example, there were three routine training sorties to Changi (Singapore), and return. But it was not until June, with the squadron having been involved in many VIP flights up to that time including taking the Queen and the Duke of Edinburgh from Norfolk to Scotland and back to London Airport on the 4th (the first Royal flight using RAF Comets), that preparations could be made for a regular Far East and Australia service. The squadron ORB recorded that June saw the start of the first intensive slip trials to Singapore and Australia. This was the first time since the Comet entered service in the Royal Air Force that it had been used in its role of providing a high-speed passenger service to the Far East and Australia.

In an interview with *Flight*, published in its 28 June 1957 issue, the C-in-C Transport Command, Air Marshal Sir Andrew McKee[3], said that the Comet 2s – all ten of which had been delivered – were performing extraordinarily well and had really put the Command on the map.

One of the long-distance proving flights by one of the ten Comet 2s, XK695, was made by the No 216 Sqn CO, Wg Cdr B D Sellick, to Australia and New Zealand between 9 and 26 March. The graceful new RAF jet transport was given an enthusiastic reception. At RNZAF station Ohakea the aircraft was open to the public, who took full advantage of the chance to inspect it at close quarters. On the return flight the Aden-Nicosia leg – 2,400nm, covered in 6hr 25min – was the longest ever flown by a Comet 1 or 2.

The British Press had also been given a chance to size-up Transport Command's new acquisition, when on 8 March a party of air correspondents was flown to Malta for lunch in Comet XK699 captained by Sqn Ldr W I Harris. In a subsequent leading article in its 29 March issue, *Flight* emphasised the significance of the Comets in the light of that year's Air Estimates. It commented that

'Whatever gloom may be cast by the Air Estimates, it can hardly cloud the outlook for RAF Transport Command. A report on page 403 bears witness that DH Comet 2s have placed the Command squarely ahead of any similar formation; and the lead will be held until, some months hence, the KC-135s [developed from the Boeing 707] become operational in the USAF. Even then the 480mph Comets will remain unchallenged in respect of field performance, as their current operations testify. That the ten Comet 2s already acquired will eventually be joined by later, large machines of the same family is an entirely reasonable expectation. [The first Comet C.4s went to No 216 Sqn from February 1962 onwards.]

'Bulkier, heavier loads will be lifted over longer ranges, at a speed only

---

3 A New Zealander, Air Marshal Sir Andrew McKee CB DSO DFC – known as 'Square' McKee – took up his appointment on 15 Oct 55. He had previously been Senior Air Staff Officer, Bomber Command.

80mph less, by a fleet of 13 Britannia 253s, to be delivered from the autumn onwards [the first was formally handed-over to No 99 Sqn in June 1959]; and further Britannias may yet be procured.

'As a short/medium-range loadlifter and heavy dropper the Blackburn Beverley makes its own massive contribution to the mounting strength of the Command. . . .'

The Air Council's cautious hopes for, and faith in, the Comet 2 had been justified. At its meeting on 18 July 1957[4], when members discussed the carriage of Service families in the Comet 2, VCAS (Sir Ronald Ivelaw-Chapman), whose Note[5] prompted the discussion, said that the limitations of the aircraft when it had first been introduced to Transport Command had gradually been removed as experience with it had been built up. The object of his paper was to remove the last remaining restrictions, by permitting the carriage of Service families whenever this was necessary or desirable.

He said that the Comet 2 had acquitted itself with such success as to make it universally useable – although there had been incidents in the last few months connected with the inter-tropical front. These extreme conditions had caused engine flame-outs attributed to compressor stall, but rapid progress was being made in the fitting of cloud and collision-warning radar, which would enable aircraft captains to avoid centres of disturbance within the front and so avert incidents of this nature.

In September 1957 No 216 started regular services to Christmas Island where the Operation Grapple nuclear tests were taking place, culminating in the dropping of a hydrogen bomb from a Valiant of No 49 Sqn over Malden Island on 15 May 1958. In its entry for September 1957 No 216's ORB recorded:

'For the first time the Squadron started a regular westbound service to Christmas Island. The new staging posts include Keflavik, Goose Bay, Offutt AFB, Travis AFB and Hickam Field in Honolulu. The first person to make this flight was the C-in-C Transport Command, Air Marshal Sir A McKee. . . . The captain of the aircraft, which left Lyneham on 5 September, was Sqn Ldr D J Harper'.

One difficulty with Comet flights to North America was that of the supply of appropriate fuel. Since the USAF did not use JP.1 (Avtur) in any bulk the fuel had to be positioned at Goose Bay before the arrival of the Comets.

An interesting example of the Comet's speed advantage over its piston-engined contemporaries occurred in February 1958, when a joint Army-Air Reinforcement Exercise took place involving Transport Command and No 24 Brigade Group. The squadron flew four return sorties to Idris (Tripoli) in support of this exercise, Operation Quickstep, on

4 17(57).
5 AC(57)50.

February 17th, 18th, 19th and 20th. The first aircraft to leave Lyneham conveyed press correspondents to Idris. Due to the superior speed of the Comets over the Hastings and Beverley transports, journalists were able to watch both the embarkation of troops from Lyneham and their disembarkation at Idris. (The flight times of the three Comets involved were 3hr 30min, 3hr 25min and 3hr 25min).

In his interview with *Flight* the C-in-C said that there was a need to press home the advantages to Britain's military communications of long-range, high-speed transport; the Britannia 253, 13 of which were at that date being built for the RAF, would provide a very large amount of the trunk-route capacity for the movement of the mobile reserve. It was hoped at that time that the Britannias would come into service in 1958 but the first of them did not arrive until 1959, No 99 Sqn beginning its Britannia conversion on 19 March and No 511 Sqn not getting the first of its aircraft until the squadron reformed on 15 December.

Meanwhile in mid-1957 the Hastings was still the backbone of Transport Command, which at that time had 38 of them in three squadrons – Nos 24, 99 and 511.

The C-in-C also referred to the Beverley, which he said had given an entirely new significance to the term 'air portability' – its huge freight compartment literally opening the doors to a vast new range of Service equipment and military stores which hitherto could not have been carried by air, although other aspects of its performance still proved disappointing. More will be said about this remarkable aircraft later in this history.

At its meeting on 24 October[6] the Air Council, considering a Progress Report on New Weapons, agreed that a recommendation should be put to the Chiefs of Staff that Orion engines should be fitted to the Britannias for the second squadron. But this did not in fact occur; the Proteus icing troubles were eventually overcome though the Orion option was kept open until early in 1958. At the Air Council meeting on 20 December 1957[7] the Secretary of State for Air (Mr George Ward) said he had attended a meeting of the Lord Mills Committee[8] on the icing troubles of the Proteus. There was now general confidence that these could be overcome with a multi-duct engine, and the Financial Secretary to the Treasury had approved expenditure on R&D.

Further delays in the Britannia's entry into service occurred during 1958. A gloomy note was struck by VCAS, Air Marshal E C Hudleston, at the Air Council's meeting on 15 May[9] when he said that the aircraft had slipped some four/five months in its acceptance trials at A&AEE Boscombe Down. He asked whether Controller, Aircraft (CA) (Air Chief Marshal Sir Claude Pelly), could accelerate the work and whether it would help if some of the trials were done in squadrons.

---

6 22(57) Item IV.

7 28(57) Item I.

8 Lord Mills, an industrialist and politician, was Minister of Power 1957–59 in the Macmillan Government.

9 11(58) Item II (20).

CA countered by saying that it was not intended to subject the Britannia to full-scale trials; the main object was to prove the differences between the civil and military types. He did not think that squadron help would accelerate Release to the Service; in fact, lack of proper equipment in the squadrons would slow down the trials.

A further cause for delay was brought to the Air Council's notice on 31 July when DCAS (Air Marshal G W Tuttle) said that 'when in 1955 we had ordered the Britannia we had specified only half a freighter floor. A year later we had changed the design to call for a freighter floor all over. This was a modification of some magnitude.' Admiral Slattery, the Chairman of Shorts[10], admitted that there was a production delay, for which Shorts must accept a measure of responsibility. He had said that the order would be completed by the end of 1959, whereas the Air Council's estimate was a year later. The Council then discussed how to put pressure on the firm. The Secretary of State said he would be willing to see the Chairman of Bristols, with Ministry of Supply agreement. The Council invited CA to see what action he could take at an official level in the light of the discussion.

In the event, Britannias made an initial appearance in March–April 1959, when No 99 Sqn received two 252s (XN398 and XN404) for conversion/route training.

A Poorly-equipped Command

In 1957–58 therefore, Transport Command was equipped with Comets, Beverleys and Hastings, one squadron of Valettas and one of Pioneers. Despite its C-in C's brave words, the glittering achievements of the Comets and the promise of the Britannias, it was still poorly equipped compared with the all-jet Bomber and Fighter Commands – the former with Canberras, Valiants, Vulcans and Victors and the latter (which was soon to get Mach 2 Lightnings) with Hunters and Javelins.

The Comet had come into Transport Command from civil aviation. It had been a replacement for the cancelled V1000, and the RAF had proved the Mk 2 version to be a safe and reliable aircraft after the Mk 1 disasters in BOAC service. The Beverleys, despite their huge capacity and ability to take-off and land on limited-length runways and unprepared strips, had restricted performance in speed and range. The Hastings, reliable old warriors, had entered service during the Berlin Airlift and had the outmoded tail-wheel configuration; the Valetta had never proved to be quite the Dakota replacement it was intended to be. The Command needed more up-to-date equipment, and was not to start getting it for a further 18 months with the arrival of the Britannias and the promise of Argosies, Belfasts and Andovers.

Lockheed C-130s (Hercules) had been discussed by the Air Council during 1958 when at the 31 July meeting[11] S of S for Air (Mr George

10 Rear Admiral Sir Matthew Slattery, Chairman and Managing Director of Shorts, who were building the Britannias.
11 18(58).

Ward) said that there was no aircraft which could be made quickly available, and within the price level, which matched up to the C-130A. 'We should buy enough AW660s[12] to supplement and eventually replace the Beverley and Hastings and order some C-130s'. But the Hercules was not to come into squadron service until 1967, just after Transport Command had disappeared and been replaced by Air Support Command.

The C-130 was an aircraft which offered a combination of virtues – speed, range, carrying capacity, low-loading capability and general adaptability to different circumstances and environments. The resources of the RAF, the Army and British aerospace industry had never quite been able to bring such a capable and versatile type into being, perhaps because too many compromises had had to be made, militarily, politically and industrially.

By 1957 Transport Command was a self-contained formation, without Groups (unlike Bomber, Fighter and Coastal Commands). In addition to VIP flights, supporting the deployments of other Commands, scheduled services and ferrying, it had the responsibility of getting Army forces and equipment quickly to wherever they might be required; mobility was the key.

These transport support operations involved regular training and exercises with Army formations for the specialised activity of delivering troops, equipment and supplies to the battle area. As in 1943–45, the Command was also responsible for paratroop training and supply dropping.

As in the wartime years too, it was still responsible for ferrying aircraft, both within the UK (which had been the role of the Air Transport Auxiliary during the war) and overseas. Four squadrons fulfilled these roles. There was No 187 at Aston Down and No 173 at Hawarden (stations in Maintenance Command, from whose Maintenance Units aircraft were picked up for delivery); these two were responsible for internal deliveries. And there were Nos 147 and 167 Squadrons at Benson which were responsible for overseas deliveries. The ferrying role was to come under Air Council scrutiny in 1958–59.

At the Council's meeting on 5 May 1958[13] the Air Member for Supply and Organisation (Air Chief Marshal Sir Walter Dawson) tabled a Note with the title 'Economy in the Ferry Organisation'[14]. Sir Walter recalled that at their meeting on 4 July 1957 the Council had agreed that both the two home and two overseas ferry squadrons should be amalgamated and deployed at Benson as Nos 147 and 167 Sqns, which were eventually merged (in September 1958) as the Ferry Squadron. His Note examined the pros and cons of allowing squadron pilots to undertake the ferrying of aircraft within the UK, and considered whether maintenance and servicing for the Ferry Organisation should be put to civilian contract. The Council had asked for an analysis of the accident statistics which had led to

12 The Armstrong Whitworth AW660 was to be a military version of the AW650 civil freighter aircraft then under development. See Chaps XIV–XVI.
13 10(58) Item III.
14 AC(58)23.

a change to a centralised ferry system, and of the proportion of the overall work of the organisation which was taken up in ferrying aircraft between user units and MUs in the UK.

It transpired that major accidents in ferrying in the UK were reduced from 15.6 per 10,000hr to 2.5 per 10,000hr after the establishment of the Ferry Organisation, an improvement of 84% compared with an improvement of only 22% in the RAF as a whole during the same periods. Sir Walter feared that this trend might well be reversed if ferrying in the UK were carried out by squadron pilots; accordingly, no change in the organisation was recommended. Nor was servicing by civil contract recommended, since for a variety of reasons the Ferry Organisation was considered to be a particularly unsuitable unit for maintenance by civil contract. The rate of flow of ferry aircraft was uneven, much of the flying was done outside normal working hours, and there would be difficulties over the supply and housing of skilled labour in the Benson area.

Sir Maurice Dean, Permanent Under-Secretary, pointed out that while the statistics in the paper showed that the aim of reducing the high accident rate in aircraft delivery had been achieved, they did not show that the reduction was directly attributable to the formation of the Ferry Organisation. Only about one-fifth of delivery flying before 1952 was done by Commands; thus the reduction of the accident rate from 19.5 per 10,000hr in 1949 to 1.5 per 10,000hr in 1956 was mainly an improvement in skill in ferrying, not a change from one method to another. The Chief of the Air Staff (MRAF Sir Dermot Boyle) drew attention to the fact that aircraft being ferried were, however, not always fully equipped as regards radio and other aids, whereas operational squadron pilots were accustomed to flying aircraft with their equipment complete and in full working order. Ferrying was therefore in a different class from operational flying, one for which ferry pilots were specially trained.

The Controller of Engineering and Equipment – Air Marshal Sir Raymund Hart – agreed. In delivering aircraft from the manufacturer to the MU the ferry pilot gained experience of flying with the minimum equipment, usually just the basic VHF radio. Even when the aircraft had been prepared at the MU with its equipment complete there was no air-testing of its efficiency in terms of operational standards. In practice the ferry pilot was accustomed to delivering aircraft whose equipment might not be working to full efficiency, while a squadron pilot might well be confused in a situation where his flying aids were only partially effective, and this could lead to an increase in accidents.

US of S commented that Bomber Command collected V-bombers from the manufacturers and delivered them to squadrons. It was possible that Fighter Command might ask in due course that the Lightning should be ferried by squadron pilots. Should such a request be rejected?

PUS said that on balance he would not disagree with the view that ferrying from MUs to squadrons in the UK should continue to be carried out by the Ferry Organisation. He thought though that if Commands strongly urged on training grounds that V-bomber practice should be extended to aircraft in their own Commands such requests should be considered on their merits.

US of S nevertheless felt moved to point out to his colleagues that if they did not succeed in finding economies in the non-operational areas they might find economies being forced onto the planned front line. The case for continuing the present ferry organisation had not been conclusively proved. The current arrangements might be continued for the time being, but the position ought to be reviewed in a year's time or earlier if there were a good reason for doing so. Such a reason might come about if, for example, Fighter Command asked to collect its Lightnings direct from the manufacturer for delivery to squadrons.

As regards servicing for the Ferry Organisation, PUS said that the arguments against putting this out to civil contract were not decisive. The uneven rate of flow of ferry aircraft, weather conditions and the fact that much of the flying was done outside normal working hours were not peculiar to this particular commitment, while the question whether or not a contractor could obtain sufficient labour or accommodation was a matter for him to decide.

CAS still felt that the Ferry Organisation was not a suitable unit for maintenance by civil contract, but he accepted that there were other examples where the work was more routine and less technical, where civilianisation would be more appropriate.

US of S summed-up by saying that the majority view of the Council appeared to be that on balance the Ferry Organisation was not a suitable choice for maintenance by civil contract. It must be recognised however that the difficulties in bridging the Service manpower gap would increase with every decision to oppose civilianisation, a factor which 'might force us to change our view in this particular case'.

Ferrying of aircraft was indeed discussed a year later by the Air Council, on 30 July 1959[15], on the basis of another Note by AMSO on Economy in the Ferry Organisation[16]. He said that it was already the practice for crews from operational squadrons to ferry four-engined aircraft and helicopters, and recommended that ferrying between Maintenance Units and squadrons in the UK and Germany should be progressively transferred to the squadrons themselves over a period of 15 months. The process should be a gradual one and a close watch should be kept on the accident rate.

A large part of the ferry organisation's task was nevertheless concerned with overseas ferrying. Squadron pilots could not undertake this because of the long absences involved, nor could squadron pilots be spared for ferrying between MUs and contractors. The possibility of undertaking these tasks by civil contract should be examined and if satisfactory arrangements could be made the Ferry Wing should be disbanded.

After its discussion the Council agreed that, starting with Fighter Command, there should be a progressive decentralisation over the following 15 months of ferrying to user units in the UK and Germany. The possibility of contracting out the ferrying for Maintenance and overseas

---

15 18(59).
16 AC(59)69.

Commands was to be examined, and if this seemed favourable then the Ferry Wing should be disbanded.

In its ORB for January 1959, RAF Benson had described the activities of the ferry organisation centred there:

'The role of the Station is the ferrying of all aircraft in the RAF, at home and overseas, except four-engined types (Hastings, Beverley and V-bombers) and helicopters. These exclusions are due mainly to the fact that the numbers of aircraft to be ferried do not justify the training of ferry pilots specially for the purpose'.

Its description of operations indicated that little had changed in procedures since wartime days:

'The principle of operations is quite simple: internal ferries are made direct from dispatching unit to receiving units, the pilot being delivered and collected by Benson taxi aircraft. Overseas ferries are made from Benson; this involves bringing the aircraft here from the MU or contractors' airfield, preparing it to the required standard, and then delivering it. The Benson taxis do not collect pilots from overseas Commands except from Germany. The others either return by civil airline or ferry another aircraft back to Benson. This is called a "return ferry" and results in some unexpected and dilapidated presents for Technical Wing to puzzle over'.

There was one difference, however, in peacetime years:

'Not only RAF aircraft are ferried; quite a number of British types bought by foreign Governments are delivered to the purchasers by Benson pilots. A notable case is that of the re-equipment of the Indian Air Force with Hunters, which are at present being ferried through Benson'.

However, all this was to change, following Air Council decisions about the Ferrying Organisation.

The history of RAF Benson later recorded that the Ferry Wing at Benson was disbanded in 1960 and squadrons then became responsible for the collection and ferrying of their own aircraft. This marked the end of a long-standing role for Transport Command – one which, with its predecessors ATFERO, the West African Reinforcement Route and Ferry Command, it had performed for the past 20 years.

Early in 1960 a new policy was announced for Benson – that it was to become Transport Command's base for the AW660, to become known as the Argosy.

Chapter XIV

Tactical and Strategic Freighters; a Light Transport/Helicopter Force

'. . . argosies of magic sails,
Pilots of the purple twilight . . .'

Tennyson, Locksley Hall

WITH its Comets well in service and Britannias at least on the horizon, the next need for Transport Command was a replacement (or replacements) for its 30 Beverleys and 32 Hastings, and the determining factor was the Army's requirements. Two types were wanted: a long-range strategic freighter to replace the Hastings, and a medium-range tactical freighter to supplement and eventually replace the Beverley. Final decisions about the long-range freighter and the numbers of each type required would be made by the Chiefs of Staff Committee and the Defence Committee.

The Deputy Chief of Air Staff (DCAS – Air Marshal Sir Geoffrey Tuttle) told the Air Council in July 1958[1] that no new aircraft was being designed to take the place of the Beverley. This requirement should be met by buying the military version of the Armstrong Whitworth AW650 which was being produced as a civil freighter, thus saving on R&D costs and concentrating R&D expenditure on the development of the long-range freighter.

The military version of the AW650 (the AW660) could not carry certain items of Army equipment but the Air Staff's view was that the requirement should be tailored, so far as possible, to fit a freighter type likely to be available, thereby avoiding the heavy R&D costs which would arise from developing a new aircraft with little prospect of civil application. The Council might agree to retain a reduced Beverley force in service until about 1970, to take care of the small amount of the requirement which could not be carried in the AW660.

The Secretary of State (Mr George Ward) asked when, if ordered, the AW660 could enter service. CA (Air Chief Marshal Sir Claude Pelly) estimated that delivery would take about three years and the cost of militarising the AW650 would be relatively modest. By comparison the Blackburn B.107A (the developed Beverley) would cost £4.9M on R&D and the production price would be £1.3m each.

CA added that the Short and Harland Britannic (later re-named

---

1 Air Council. 18(58) Conclusions.

Belfast) would cost £3.9M on R&D and that the production price would be £1.34M each on the basis of an order of 20. The Britannic had been suggested by Sir Matthew Slattery (Shorts' chairman) as a private venture on the assumption that the RAF would order some of the production aircraft.

The CAS (MRAF Sir Dermot Boyle) wished to know whether the acquisition of more Beverleys had been ruled out? His question generated some comments on the type's performance. Its main deficiency was that it was underpowered. The only possible substitute engine was the Dart or Tyne, but if the Beverley were re-engined this would probably involve other modifications and the end result would, in effect, be the B.107A, which would entail heavy R&D costs.

Thus the alternatives for the medium freighter requirement appeared to be to buy more Beverleys or to go for the AW660. The latter course would require that a part of the Beverley force be kept in service after 1964 expressly to meet certain Army requirements. CA saw an inconsistency in this. He thought that the combination of AW660s and Beverleys would not be particularly suitable. It would mean retaining the Beverley to take relatively small loads and introducing another aircraft, the AW660, which would not meet the Army's requirements.

DCAS felt however that a combination of AW660s and Beverleys appeared to be the best way of solving the problem in the shortest time and more economically than any other method. Such an arrangement would last until 1970 and enable R&D funds to be concentrated on the long-term development of a strategic long-range freighter. The choice was between the proposal in the paper, which would nearly but not entirely meet the War Office requirement until about 1970, and a Beverley replacement, which would probably not reach the Service before 1968.

CA then referred to the Blackburn B.107A and Short Britannic, which would both have a superior performance in range and load-carrying capacity, as would the Lockheed C-130A (the type the RAF eventually received), which should be available in a year. Comparative delivery dates for entry into squadron service for the other types were three years for the AW660, 20 months to two years for more Beverleys, and nine years for a new design replacement for the Beverley. The long-term requirement was by no means clear. If vertical take-off (VTO) or near-VTO were to be specified[2] this would mean that the aircraft would arouse no civil interest. A long-range freighter in terms of the B.107A or Britannic could be available in five years.

S of S said it was unlikely that we could afford to buy two aircraft, a medium- and a long-range freighter; if we were to buy one new type, then that should be the AW660 since there was no other aircraft under development which could be produced in the time-scale and which would be any better at meeting all the Army's requirements. This would allow R&D money to be concentrated on a new-design advanced type, possibly

---

2 The AW681 project, cancelled by the Labour Government in 1965, had V/STOL capability.

with a VTO capability. The only design deficiency of the AW660 to be mentioned was that the main spar occupied the middle of the fuselage. On the positive side it used the proven Shackleton wings, and the Dart power unit already fitted to the Vickers Viscount.

The general view of the Council was that there was a need for a Beverley replacement in the tactical role and that the only aircraft which could fill this role within a reasonable time was the AW660. Since this could not carry all the loads needed by the Army 'we would have to continue to use the Beverley'.

At the same time there was a need for a long-range freighter which could be employed in both the tactical and strategic roles. There was no aircraft which could be made quickly available within the price level which matched the Lockheed C-130A, so there might be merit in buying a few American aircraft to get them quickly and avoid R&D costs. Subject to verification by CA of the performance claims and further consultation with the War Office, enough AW660s should be bought to supplement and eventually replace the Beverleys and Hastings in the tactical role, and some Lockheed C-130s ordered. The preparation of an Operational Requirement for the Beverley/Hastings successor could then be deferred to the longer term.

The War Office should be asked whether it might be possible to modify some of their target items of equipment which seemed outside the capacity of the AW660 and the Beverley. The numbers of both types would also need discussion with the War Office.

In principle, therefore, Transport Command was set to receive AW660s in 1961, if an order were placed later in 1958. In fact, as will be seen, the RAF received its first Argosies (as the AW660s were named) at the very end (November–December) of 1961.

The Britannic long-range freighter, re-named the Belfast, entered service in 1966.

Transport Command's situation in 1958 was summed-up in the Defence Statements published in February of that year. The overall *Report on Defence Britain's Contribution to Peace and Security*[3] said: 'At present [the] Command is equipped with Hastings and Comet aircraft for long-distance lifts and with Beverleys for transportation within the theatre of operations. These will be supplemented by Britannias, of which 20 have been ordered. This will greatly expand the Command's long-range troop-carrying capacity'. By this time the Comets had already completed 10,000hr flying with the RAF and were being used on the aero-medical service from the Far East as well as providing a regular service to and from Christmas Island.

As to the Beverleys, they were in service at home and overseas; Army airborne forces had all been converted to the type and an exercise programme had been carried out with both Regular and Territorial Army airborne forces. As the Britannias were introduced the Hastings would supplement the Beverley for the movement of heavy freight and for

---

3 Cmnd 363.

intra-theatre tasks. They gave a better lift than the Valetta, which was being withdrawn.

Valettas had been in service since 1948, as long as the Hastings, and they continued to serve in the Far East with No 52 Sqn until 1966. The type was finally retired in June 1969 when the last Valetta, VX573, left RAF Wildenrath in Germany on its way to the RAF Museum at Hendon.

At the beginning of 1959 the Air Council considered the choice of a strategic freighter for the RAF – Vickers VC10, Short Britannic or Handley Page HP111. When these alternatives were discussed at the 14 January meeting[4] S of S cleared the ground by saying that, contrary to what was suggested in the paper before them[5], the decision to abandon the V1000 and OR323[6] had been taken on military grounds. He said secondly that while it was right that the Council's recommendation on the choice of a strategic freighter should be based on the military requirement, it would be wise to recognise that the final decision would have to take other considerations into account. The choice had previously appeared to lie between the VC10 and the Britannic, but on the facts now available the HP111 must be seriously considered[7]. In DCAS's view the HP111 would be the most suitable aircraft; if it were not selected the VC10 looked preferable to the Britannic despite greater difficulties in loading and the shape of its cargo compartment.

Even so, the ability of the aircraft to meet the military requirement was the major consideration. With a few exceptions the HP111 and the Britannic could carry all the items of equipment specified by the War Office. A large number of items could not be carried in the VC10, and there was concern about its cargo-handling limitations and the length of runway it would require. The choice seemed to lie between the HP111 and the Britannic; the former seemed preferable provided its cargo compartment was adequate. If a recommendation in favour of the HP111 was not accepted, there were doubts as to whether the VC10 was an alternative. The Secretary of State said there was an advantage in presenting Ministers with a straight choice between two aircraft only. These should be the HP111 and the Britannic, with the former being preferred on operational grounds. The Council agreed that a recommendation should be put to the Defence Board along these lines.

A couple of days after this Air Council meeting, the 16 January 1959 issue of *Flight* carried an item headed 'Augmenting Transport Command' in which it said:

---

4 2(59) Special.

5 AC(59)6.

6 OR323, for a medium-sized transport to replace the Valetta, but with rear loading and capable of longer range and greater payloads, had been issued in 1953 with 1958 as a target date for first production.

7 The HP111 was to be based on the Victor V-bomber, a circular-section transport employing many components common to the Victor B.2, able to carry a 53,000lb payload for 3,330nm in still air with a cruising speed of 472kt at 41,000ft. It is described, with a three-view drawing, in C H Barnes' *Handley Page Aircraft since 1907* (Putnam & Co, 1976).

'It was announced last week that the Minister of Defence had authorised an expansion in the carrying capacity of RAF Transport Command, in fulfilment of the Government's policy of increasing the mobility of the Armed Forces, and that accordingly it was proposed to adopt a military version of the Armstrong Whitworth Type 650 freighter (i.e. the AW660). The number of AW660s to be ordered for the RAF has not been disclosed'.

Re-equipping Cinderella

This news item was complemented by a leading article in the same issue under the heading 'Equipping Cinderella':

'It looks as though RAF Transport Command is in for a happy New Year. The first Bristol Britannia 253 (for No 99 Sqn) has taken the air at Belfast, the Minister of Defence has authorised an increase in the Command's carrying capacity and the adoption of AW660s, and the first Argosy has successfully flown at Bitteswell. Thus when Air Marshal Sir Denis Barnett takes over from Sir Andrew McKee in May as C-in-C he will have under his direction a transport arm potentially more muscular and flexible than any the RAF has previously possessed.

'This is not to say that all is as well as can be, and that Transport Command is no longer a Cinderella. The Britannias will reinforce the Comets on fast long-range operations, and the AW660s will supplement the Beverley. What is still needed is a faster and longer-range heavy freighter. We hope that the phrase "an expansion of carrying capacity" signifies a further Government intention in that direction'.

As has been evident from the Air Council's discussions, the 'faster and longer-range heavy freighter' was to be either the HP111, or the Britannic, which – as the Belfast – eventually emerged as the successful contender. *Flight* was right to use the soubriquet 'Cinderella'. For years Transport Command had been expected to do the routine drudgery, faithfully fetching and carrying, but without the promise of new hardware. Now it was getting some.

In his Memorandum accompanying the 1959–60 Air Estimates, the Secretary of State had described the Command's involvements and its proposed augmentation:

'In 1958–59, Transport Command, supported by transport aircraft of overseas Commands, was heavily engaged upon inter-Service operations overseas; upon support for nuclear weapons trials in the Pacific; upon urgent freight and passenger carrying; and upon casualty evacuation and the normal programme of training exercises with other Commands and the Army. The build-up of the air transport force continues.

'The first of 20 Britannia 253s on order is undergoing clearance trials at

Boscombe Down and is due to be delivered to the RAF shortly. The Comets continue to give excellent service. As a further step to increase our freight and passenger-carrying capacity, particularly in the tactical role for Army support, an order is being placed for the AW660. Since this is a military version of the civil Argosy . . . it will minimise the need for a special development programme. Looking further ahead, there will be a need for a strategic freighter. . . . An order is being placed for the Britannic 3 for this purpose'.

Subsequently, at its meeting on 4 June 1959[8], the Air Council agreed that the Britannic 3A should be ordered, rather than the Britannic 3. The reason for this was that heavier fuselage components were required for the Britannic 3 (ten of which were on order) and this would reduce the payload to 25,000lb over 3,600 miles. The original choice of the Britannic 3 as a strategic freighter had been made on the basis of advice that it would be able to carry 29,000lb over 3,640nm. This was against an Air Staff Requirement for a payload of 30,000lb over 3,600 miles, with a possibility of development to carry the same load over 4,000 miles.

Shorts had proposed a revised version, the Britannic 3A, with a new wing centre section increasing the wing area from 2,077 sq ft to 2,454 sq ft, higher maximum all-up weight and greater fuel capacity. This was expected to be able to carry a 30,000lb payload over a staging distance of 4,100nm with 20% fuel reserves. DCAS proposed that an order should be submitted for the Britannic 3A since the Britannic 3 no longer met the specification on which the Ministerial decision had been based.

Technically the 3A was a better conception than the Britannic 3 and the Ministry of Supply believed that it had better prospects in the civil market. It also had greater development potential in that engines more powerful than the Rolls-Royce Tyne 12 Mk 101 turboprops could be accommodated if they were later required. The estimated Release-to-Service date was January 1965, which was some nine months later than had been estimated for the Britannic 3. For an order of ten the total increase in Government cost, as compared with the Britannic 3, would be of the order of £1.5M. A smaller order would not mean a proportionate reduction in costs. As the large items of Army equipment for which the freighter was particularly required would not be available until 1965, the later delivery date should be acceptable to the War Office.

In its conclusions the Air Council recorded that it saw little prospect of reopening the case for a pure jet aircraft, and agreed that the Britannic 3A should be ordered, rather than the Britannic 3. When the production contract was signed, late in 1960, the type name Belfast C.1 was chosen and this was the aircraft which went into service with No 53 Sqn at Brize Norton in January 1966. During operational trials at Boscombe Down the fifth Belfast (XR366) had been flown at up to $2\frac{1}{4}$g with a military payload of 77,400lb. It had also flown to New Zealand and back carrying a 12,500lb

---

8 AC(59)43.

SR.N5 hovercraft over maximum-range stage lengths, on one of which its take-off weight was 230,610lb[9].

The first of the Britannia 253 long-range transports was handed-over to No 99 Sqn at Lyneham on 9 June 1959, and from December 1959 No 511 Sqn would soon be similarly equipped. With the Comets of No 216 Sqn now being supplemented by Britannias, Transport Command was beginning to have a much more impressive and up-to-date look; and this was happily symbolised by naming all the aircraft of its long-range force after stars and constellations[10].

Unhappily, this year of achievement for the Command was marred by a fatal accident to one of its aircraft, Hastings TG522 of No 36 Sqn, at Wadi Seidna, Khartoum, where it had landed when en route from Christmas Island to the UK on 29 May, after taking off for El Adem[11].

Light-transport/Helicopter Force

Another development in Transport Command at this time (1959–60) was the creation of a light transport and helicopter force in support of the Army. At an Air Council meeting on 8 June 1959[12] VCAS reported that the War Office wished to press for a much larger force than the Council had suggested[13]. The requirement submitted by the War Office was based on the need for sufficient utility helicopters to permit a lift of two companies, with supporting elements, to be undertaken in the UK and in all major overseas theatres, and for substantial increases in the number of light cargo aircraft, both VTOL and STOL.

The War Office had estimated that this would involve the provision of about 132 utility helicopters, ten heavy helicopters and 12 three-ton light cargo STOL aircraft – an assessment which did not, however, allow for unserviceability, training and other factors. The Air Staff estimated that to meet the War Office requirement about 250 aircraft would be required. VCAS felt that the War Office proposals did not take sufficient account of

---

9 These details are taken from *Shorts Aircraft since 1900*, by C H Barnes (revised version by Derek James; Putnam, 1989).

10 E.g., *Taurus* (XK669), *Corvus* (XK670), *Aquila* (XK671), etc.

11 No 2 engine failed and was feathered. The captain, after jettisoning fuel, obtained clearance to land on Runway 180, but as the Hastings was incorrectly positioned for that runway he was given permission to land on Runway 360. On the final turn on to this heading the port wing centre section stalled. The Captain mistook this for vibration of No 1 engine and feathered this one too so there was now no power on the port side. The by-then low level and low speed of the aircraft forced the Captain to make a crash landing one mile south of the 36 Runway threshold. The Hastings caught fire on impact. All the crew members except for the AQM were killed and four of the 26 passengers were seriously injured. The No 2 engine had failed owing to cylinder seizure, and the accident investigators concluded that the primary cause of the accident was the Captain's error in flying his circuit on asymmetric power at too low an altitude and airspeed, the low airspeed causing a pre-stall judder, a contributory cause being his mistaking this for No 1 engine vibration and feathering that engine, thus aggravating the stall.

12 13(59).

13 AC(59)51.

the possibility of reinforcing one theatre from another, for example by airlifting Whirlwinds and single-engined Pioneers by Beverley. They also under-estimated the extent to which the Beverley and AW660 themselves could supply forward areas by the use of short strips or by parachute dropping, so reducing the number of light cargo aircraft required. Some allowance ought also to be made for helicopters of the Commando Carrier, due to be stationed east of Suez from early 1961. It should be possible to meet the Army's requirements by an increase, against the planned figures, of four Bristol 192s, four Twin Pioneers and 45 turbine-engined Whirl-winds. The cost of this force over the next five years might be about £12M – compared with perhaps £90M for the force which would be required if the War Office proposals were to be met in full.

The Secretary of State (Rt Hon George Ward) nevertheless felt it was important that the Council should be seen to be taking a positive attitude towards the War Office proposals. He further believed it would be wrong to suggest that helicopters from the Commando Carrier should be regarded as contributing to the Army's requirement but agreed that the other proposals in VCAS's paper should be used in the Chiefs of Staff discussion on the Army's requirements. These discussions were the genesis of a mixed light-support (Pioneer and Twin Pioneer) and helicopter (Whirlwind and Sycamore) force which came into being in Transport Command early in 1960.

A step in this direction, the formation of a helicopter squadron, resulted from a decision by the Air Council in September 1959 to convert JEHU (the Joint Experimental Helicopter Unit) into a short-range transport squadron[14]. The JEHU's aircraft strength was nine Whirlwinds and four Sycamores which had originally been bought by the Army. The unit's trials commitment would be completed by the end of 1959. VCAS proposed that thereafter the unit should be disbanded and its aircraft purchased by the Air Ministry, to enable a Royal Air Force squadron of six Whirlwinds and six Sycamores to be formed for short-range transport duties in the first quarter of 1960. This in fact became No 225 Sqn, formed at Andover at the beginning of that year.

---

14 Conclusions 19(59); AC(59)75.

Chapter XV

No 38 Group Revived

'Shall brithers be for a' that'

Robert Burns, A Man's A Man for A' That

THE Air Council had discussed the future role, size, command and location of what in 1960 became No 38 Group at its meeting on 5 November 1959. VCAS explained[1] that the build-up of the Britannia force would allow the Beverleys and Hastings to be used increasingly in the tactical role from 1960 onwards. There would be a considerable increase in the amount of inter-Service training. As an example, whilst there had been only three airborne and air transport exercises in 1956 there were 45 in 1959 and already 50 were planned for 1960. There must be a properly organised staff to control tactical and short-range transport operations and exercises. VCAS believed that a separate Group Headquarters was required under a Commander of Air Vice-Marshal rank. On historical grounds this might appropriately be called No 38 Group. It should work closely with the Army formations of the Strategic Reserve and a number of staff posts should be filled by Army officers. The new Group HQ should come into being at the beginning of 1960. Initially it might be located at Upavon but it should subsequently move to Netheravon, which was conveniently closer to the Army's Southern Command.

The Secretary of State was sceptical about such a separate formation. He accepted the need for additional staff to control the growing Tactical Transport Force but questioned whether it would not be better to increase the staff at Transport Command HQ rather than set up a new Group. He wondered about the relationship during operations overseas between a Group-level Headquarters for tactical transport and the Command-level Headquarters which covered RAF formations abroad.

VCAS explained that a separate Group HQ would permit closer cooperation with the Army. Experience had shown that to get the best utilisation of resources the Mobile Operations Centre, which at present existed at Transport Command HQ, had to deploy overseas in emergencies or for exercises, to control the tactical force. The Group HQ would provide a mobile controlling element in the same manner. PUS supported the proposal and felt it was important to take the initiative in making proper arrangements for the control of the tactical force. In its conclusion

---

1 AC(59)90

the Council agreed that the separate Group should be established under Transport Command on the lines proposed in VCAS's paper.

A notable choice was made when Air Vice-Marshal P G Wykeham was appointed the first AOC No 38 Group on its reformation on 1 January 1960, with HQ at RAF Odiham. He had had first-hand experience of Army/RAF cooperation during the Second World War in the Western Desert, during the initial engagements there in 1940 with the Italian Army and Air Force. Serving with No 274 Squadron, which until September 1940 had Gladiators but then became the first Hurricane squadron in the Middle East, he was the first of its pilots to engage the enemy. He was shot down, but successfully baled out and made his way back to 8th Army lines. He was awarded the DFC in November 1940, then a Bar to it in 1941 while commanding No 73 squadron – another Hurricane squadron – in the defence of Tobruk.

After the desert air war, during which he was credited with having destroyed 15 enemy aircraft, he next distinguished himself by leading No 23 Squadron Mosquitos on intruder operations from Malta over Sicily and Italy and was awarded the DSO in 1943. He then commanded No 140 Wing in No 2 Group, leading a precision attack by 24 Mosquitos on Gestapo HQ in Aarhus, Denmark, on 31 October 1944 and being awarded a Bar to his DSO.

After the war he became a test pilot at the A&AEE, Boscombe Down, where he flew all modern types of jet aircraft. He later went to Korea where he acted as adviser to the USAF, flying B-26 intruder sorties. On his return in 1951 he was awarded the AFC and the United States Air Medal, becoming the first Briton to be so decorated. He commanded two fighter stations, North Weald and Wattisham, in 1951 and '52 and in 1953 went to Allied Air Forces Central Europe as Chief of Operations. Subsequently he was Director of Operations (Air Transport and Overseas Theatres) in the Air Ministry from May 1958, before taking up the new post of AOC No 38 Group – one for which his operational and command experience well qualified him.

The motto of the revived Group was 'Par Nobile Fratrum' – 'A Noble Pair of Brothers', symbolising the close association with the Army Airborne Forces, and its badge was an eagle's leg grasping a sword. The Group initially had a thin time as far as equipment was concerned. It did not appear as a separate formation in the Operational Commands' Order of Battle until June 1960 and then with only three squadrons, two at Odiham (Nos 230 and 225, with Pioneers/Twin Pioneers and Whirlwinds/ Sycamores respectively), and one detached to Aldergrove (No 118 with Sycamores). The same situation continued throughout 1960 and into 1961 when No 118 Squadron disbanded on 14 April and re-formed. Not until 1962 was there a significant increase in strength when two Hunter FGA.9 squadrons, Nos 1 and 54, were transferred to it, giving the Group an offensive close-support role.

In November 1961 the Group's helicopter element was augmented, with the formation at Odiham of No 72 Squadron with the Belvedere. Another Belvedere squadron, No 66, had already formed at Odiham two months earlier, but was destined for the Far East Air Force as from June

1962. It left its first complement of aircraft behind at Odiham and these went to form another Belvedere squadron, No 26[2].

The Group was now a fully going concern. All these Odiham-based units, of Pioneers, Twin Pioneers, Whirlwinds (another squadron of which, No 230, was equipped wholly with Mk 10s, to supplement No 225 Squadron), Sycamores and Belvederes, were in addition to and worked with the tactical squadrons of Transport Command – Nos 114 with Argosies at Benson, Nos 24 and 36 with Hastings at Colerne and Nos 47 and 53 with Beverleys at Abingdon.

While all of this was taking place the requirements for the future of the strategic force had also come under consideration.

Strategic Force Requirement

Before the end of 1959 the Air Council discussed a replacement for the Comet 2[3]. Their discussion was based on a Note by DCAS (Air Marshal Sir Geoffrey Tuttle) on The Comet 2 Replacement[4], in which the VC10 was first discussed as a Royal Air Force transport aircraft. The DCAS submission examined whether there was a requirement for a jet transport aircraft after the Comet 2s had come to the end of their fatigue life in 1963 or 1964.

The main question was whether, judged against the likely reinforcement tasks, there really was a need for a jet transport, to supplement the Britannias and Belfasts. On this basis it appeared that a Comet replacement would be desirable rather than essential. DCAS believed that there could be no question of developing an aircraft specially for the RAF or of purchasing a foreign type. On considerations of payload and range, the only aircraft which appeared likely to meet RAF needs were the VC10 or Comet 5. (The type that eventually succeeded the Comet 2s was the Comet 4). The Council considered whether the life of the Comet 2s could be prolonged but learned that on current utilisation the fatigue life would be exhausted by 1963/64. It would be possible by replacing the wings to extend the life by perhaps 5,000hr but this would be very expensive. The Secretary of State recalled that the adoption of the VC10 had previously been opposed on the ground that the planned transport force provided adequate capacity, that we could not afford the additional manpower required, and that although we were attracted to the concept of the pure jet transport the VC10 was unsuitable, particularly because of its runway requirements[5]. Although the Council did not come to a decision at this meeting it agreed though that the acquisition of a jet transport was

---

2 RAF helicopter developments have been fully documented in *RAF Helicopters The First Twenty Years*; HMSO, 1992, by Wg Cdr J R Dowling MBE DFC AFC, who played a leading role in introducing the Belvedere into service and was OC the Belvedere Trials Unit at Odiham.

3 22(59)

4 AC(59)83. This paper used the term 'Comet II' but 'Comet 2' is preferred in this history.

5 A rather strange statement, in view of the fact that operations from 'hot and high' runways formed part of the design philosophy of the VC10.

desirable if a suitable aircraft could be obtained on acceptable terms. A Working Party was to examine the requirement and its implications.

Only four days later, on 9 November[6], the Council made reference to three other Transport Command types of aircraft when it discussed 'Weapons Systems Not Yet Fully Released': the Britannia, Bristol 192 helicopter, and Valetta/Anson replacement. There was concern that the Britannia, which had entered service only eight months before, was showing a high level of unserviceability and its Proteus engine was subject to icing problems. Fortunately the manufacturer had already proposed two modifications which ought to resolve the problem. The concern attached to the Bristol 192 (Belvedere) was that its entry into service would be delayed until third-quarter 1960 and that this delay would aggravate the existing shortage of helicopters. It might be possible to bring forward the Release to Service by introducing the aircraft with initial limitations to its clearance. (Considerations of this kind seem to accompany almost every aircraft's Release to Service.) In the end, as mentioned earlier, the Belvedere started its operational life with No 66 Squadron, at Odiham in September 1961.

Thirdly there was the replacement for the Valetta and Anson in the communications role, for which recommendations were to be tabled within a month[7] (The Valetta replacement was eventually the Hawker Siddeley Andover, which entered service in July 1966, the last full year of the existence of Transport Command.)

The Secretary of State summed up the ongoing state of affairs in his Memorandum accompanying the 1960–61 Air Estimates[8]. During 1960 the introduction of the Britannia would be completed when No 511 Sqn had got its full complement, and the strategic force would then be equipped entirely with Britannias and Comets, to be supplemented in due course by the Belfast.

For the medium-range tactical role an order had been placed for the military version of the Argosy (AW660), and production was proceeding satisfactorily. More Whirlwinds were being ordered to provide increased tactical transport support for the Army in the field, and a more advanced helicopter was also to be developed for this purpose. In January 1960 the new Group, No 38, had been formed, as related earlier.

Clearly this was a time of consolidation and achievement. During the decade 1950–1960 Transport Command had achieved a three-fold increase in air transport capacity. 'Cinderella' had come into her own.

---

6 23(59) meeting.

7 The Avro Anson had been in service with the RAF, in one role or another, starting with No 48 Squadron in Coastal Command, since June 1936.

8 Command 950.

Chapter XVI

A Strategic and Tactical Force

'Git thar fustest with the mostest'

Gen Nathan Bedford Forrest, Confederate General, US Civil War

DURING the 1960s Transport Command acquired its greatest strengths at both ends of the operational scale, strategic airlift and tactical support for the Army.

At the end of 1959 the Air Council had considered the implications of two squadrons of Britannias[1]. On the introduction of the first squadron the carriage of all high-priority RAF freight would be undertaken by Transport Command. On the introduction of the second squadron the resultant surplus routine capacity should be made available to all three Services.

Production of the first 20 AW660s was in hand, and Treasury approval was being sought to order a further 20. There was news also about the Britannic; discussions with the manufacturers were being pressed ahead with a view to agreeing a Standard of Preparation for the aircraft. Target date for the first flight remained February 1962.

At the Air Council's 4 April meeting[2] the question of a Comet replacement was discussed. The Council agreed that five Comet 2s should be reconditioned, three to replace Comet 2s in Signals Command and two to replace the VIP Hastings in Air Forces Arabian Peninsula and FEAF. But the more important and inspiring decision was that five Comet 4Cs and five VC10s should be ordered to replace Transport Command's Comet 2s.

During 1960, two aircraft names which were to become famous in Transport Command were decided on by the Air Council. At its 16 June meeting[3] the Council agreed that the Hawker Siddeley/Armstrong Whitworth AW660 should be named Argosy, a name once upon a time applied to a large merchant vessel – particularly one of Venetian origin, or (poetically) to a ship or a trading venture[4]. (In more down-to-earth terms, the RAF were later to dub the Argosy 'the whistling wheelbarrow' because

---

1 26/59.

2 5/60.

3 8(60).

4 'He hath an argosy bound to Tripolis, another to the Indies, . . . a third at Mexico, a fourth for England', says Shylock in *The Merchant of Venice* (I.iii).

of its distinctive twin-boom structure and the high-revving sound of its Rolls-Royce Dart turboprop engines.)[5]

The other naming was in fact a re-naming, because the Short SC5, the freighter version of the Britannia being built at Belfast, had for at least 18 months been referred to as the 'Britannic'. At its meeting on 15 September[6], however, the Council agreed that the Britannic should in due course be re-named Belfast.

This change of name can be explained by reference to the history of Shorts Aircraft[7], which recounts that in August 1957 the company put up to the Air Staff a strategic freighter named Britannia 553 (based on the Britannia), and that the Air Staff approved the design and undertook to place initial orders with the development costs being spread over 30 aircraft. (In the event only ten of the Short freighters were ordered and built.) This design was indexed as SC5, and in April 1958 was named 'Britannic'.

The Shorts history explained that with so much divergence from the original dimensions it was thought appropriate to drop the name Britannic; in April 1959 the definitive aeroplane offered to the Air Staff was described simply as the Short SC5/10. When in 1960 a production contract was signed for ten aircraft the type name 'Belfast C.1' was chosen.

Air Mobility

During the 1960s the emphasis in Defence planning was on air mobility, which meant Transport Command carrying the Army into its operational theatres, and supporting it and RAF squadrons in long-range deployments. The Indonesian Confrontation of 1963–66 provided a perfect example of this long-range logistic support. Many bomber squadrons – Victors, Vulcans and Canberras – sent detachments from the UK, Germany and Cyprus to reinforce the Far East Air Force, and all these deployments were supported by Comets and Britannias of Transport Command carrying technical and support personnel and spares. This back-up was assumed and built-in to the Operation Orders under which bombers and fighters were detached overseas. Transport Command was part of the warp and woof of RAF operations; its efficient support was taken for granted.

The three major air mobility exercises mounted in 1960 – Starlight, Holdfast and Natation – were all planned by No 38 Group. Since the Group had under its own control only a small force of short-range transports and helicopters it had to depend on the Command for the participation of medium-range transports (Hastings and Beverleys). The inclusion of resources over which it did not have direct control could cause friction between Group and Command, as will be seen in the case of

---

5 There had been an earlier Argosy, a three-engined Armstrong Whitworth biplane which went into service with Imperial Airways in 1926.

6 12(60).

7 *Shorts Aircraft since 1900*, by C H Barnes; Putnam, revised edition, 1969.

Exercise Holdfast. Planning for the first exercise involving the Group had begun in November 1959, before it had set up its Headquarters at Odiham. It was an exercise to test strategic and tactical mobility, which was of prime importance to the nation's overseas defence policy.

The formation of No 38 Group in January 1960 eased the problems of detailed planning for Starlight and the Group took over the tactical phase of the exercise, which saw the deployment of a Brigade Group of over 4,000 troops, 300 vehicles, 175 tons of equipment and 14 helicopters, to an area south of Tobruk (where the 8th Army had fought the Afrika Korps in the bitterest battles of the desert war). The whole business took from January until April, from the time when a small-scale exercise was mounted to test the airhead organisation (there was a strategic air terminal at El Adem and a tactical airhead at Tmimi, 50 miles to the north west), to the return of the Pioneers and the Whirlwind helicopters to the UK, with the latter being flown back in Beverleys. In addition to the Whirlwinds and the Single and Twin Pioneers there were Beverleys and Hastings, as well as ground-attack fighters – Hunters of No 54 Squadron and Sea Venoms from HMS *Albion*. Britannias were also employed, being used for the first time on a large scale in a strategic airlift, plus Comets for special duties. The air side of Starlight was commanded by the AOC No 38 Group, Air Vice-Marshal P G Wykeham, with Major General R G S Hobbs as Director of Army Operations.

The Beverleys used a new container, a skeleton of nylon webbing on a pallet containing a 1,000lb load. In later years Air Marshal Sir Peter Wykeham (as he became) retrospectively praised their contribution to the exercise. Writing a Foreword in 1983 to a book about the Beverley[8] he said:

'I remember their remarkable performance in Starlight, the last big three-Service overseas deployment exercise from UK into North Africa, and how the General Commanding 3 Division and I rode back to El Adem in an empty Beverley when the exercise was over and realised that we could have played badminton in the hold if we had brought rackets and a shuttlecock'.

After Starlight No 38 Group got to work on another big exercise, Holdfast, which was to take place in September 1960 and involved 16 Parachute Brigade landing on a DZ by the Kiel Canal, defended by German and Danish Divisions against Orange Forces. It was the largest airborne operation since 1944. It was also an exercise in which some clash of interests arose between the Group and its parent Command.

The 1960s No 38 Group had two main roles, the planning of exercises (a very complicated business since every logistic aspect, down to shoe repairs and sports kit, had to be foreseen), and training the airborne forces. It worked closely with 16 Parachute Brigade Group. In Exercise Holdfast

---

8 *Blackburn Beverley*, by Bill Overton; Midland Counties Publications, 1990. Sir Peter Wykeham also recalled the verdict of a USAF captain seconded to fly the Beverley: 'It's a fine machine, but it'll never replace the aeroplane'.

some difficulty was experienced with Transport Command owing to conflicting demands for the Hastings and Beverley medium-range transports. As an exhaustive Report of October 1960 on Holdfast[9] put it:

'Though it appears logical that Transport Command should plan a strategic move and 38 Group confine itself to the tactical work, the disadvantage is that Hastings and Beverleys carry out both strategic and tactical moves as part of one and the same exercise or operation. To save these units trying to serve two masters it is considered more logical that 38 Group should plan all aspects of the operations of the medium-range force, Transport Command confining itself to the Britannia and Comet force. When 38 Group becomes autonomous it is understood that this course will be adopted'.

Matters presumably were amicably resolved between Group and Command, because in 1961 No 38 Group controlled Exercise Fabulist (27 April to 7 May) which required a large participation by Britannias, Beverleys and Hastings. This was an Army/RAF exercise in Cyprus designed to practice the mounting of an airborne assault from an overseas base, with offensive support and air re-supply. It involved 16 Para Brigade, and the figures for air drops were impressive: 1,864 troops, 77,712lb of freight and 52 platforms. The flying out and conduct of the exercise involved four Britannias from Lyneham, ten Beverleys from Abingdon and nine Hastings from Colerne (attached to Nicosia, with six Hastings already based there). Eight Hunter FGA.9s of No 165 Wing at Stradishall were deployed to Akrotiri to give offensive support.

Beside the major exercises there were also operational contingencies. During July 1960 Comets, Britannias and Beverleys moved some 1,500 officers and men of the Ghanaian Army plus 60 tons of stores and 45 vehicles into the Congo, and Hastings aircraft operated between Ghana and the Congo in support of the Ghanaian contingent in the United Nations force. Transport Command also helped to carry food and other supplies to the Congo at the request of the United Nations. Civil war had broken out in the newly independent Republic following the secession of the copper-producing province of Katanga.

The aviation magazine *Flight* in its 5 August issue had referred to 'two big airlifts, to Kenya and to the Congo; in the former some 700 men of the 1st Battalion the Duke of Wellington's Regiment and supporting units were flown from Lyneham in seven Britannias of Nos 99 and 511 Squadrons; in the latter over 1,200 Ghanaian troops and 27 tons of freight and vehicles were flown to the Congo by two Comets, two Britannias and three Beverleys, made available to the Ghanaian Government'.

Large-scale parachute training for the Army continued. During 1960 there were some 36,000 jumps from aircraft and the Army's training programme for 1961–62 included more than a hundred air-mobility exercises using RAF transport aircraft.

---

9 In Air 25/1669.

All these commitments were in addition to the Command's task to maintain its regular programme of scheduled services, almost world-wide. What exactly was the equipment state of Transport Command at this time? Inside the back cover of the Defence White Paper for March 1961 there was a diagrammatic description of the transport force. This showed, in the Strategic Force, 23 Britannia C.1/2 and ten Comet C.2; in the Medium-Range Force, 48 Hastings C.1/2, 32 Beverley C.1 and 12 Valetta C.1/2, plus the Argosies still to come; in the Short-Range Force, 15 Single Pioneer and 27 Twin Pioneer, plus four Pembroke; and under Transport Support Helicopters, three Belvederes (most of them still to come), plus Whirlwind 2/4/10 and Sycamore 14s. The full complement of Britannias had been delivered, and the Comet fleet was to be upgraded by the placing of an order for the Comet 4C. This had a longer fuselage so could accommodate 94 passengers as against 44 in the C.2, and had greater power, with 10,500lb st Avon RA.29s instead of 7,350lb st Avon 117/118s, giving a maximum cruising speed of 542 mph compared with 480 mph.

As to the Belfast strategic freighters, the contract had been placed for ten. These heavy lifters would have a payload of over 35 tons and be the largest aircraft ever in RAF service, intended mainly for the rapid deployment in emergency of bulky and complex equipment such as armoured cars and guided weapons, with a normal maximum range of over 4,000 miles which could be extended by air-to-air refuelling.

Year of the Argosy

Also to come were the Argosies, due to reach the Service in 1961. RAF Benson in Oxfordshire had been prepared with new buildings to receive them, and in July 1961 its ORB noted: 'It was announced that the first Argosy squadron at Royal Air Force Benson would be No 114 Squadron and that it would be formed on 1 October 1961' (a date which in fact proved to be over-optimistic). In September the ORB reported: 'Major works projects are going ahead. New boiler houses, central heating systems, extensions to the Officers' and Airmens' Messes, and an Electronics Centre are going up'. The first Argosy aircraft arrived in October. There were many people waiting to get them moving as soon as the clearance came through.

Meanwhile, pilots, navigators and engineers were going through manufacturers' courses, whilst trained crews were at Boscombe Down and in Aden carrying out flying trials – in other words, the Argosy action was taking place in other environments as well. In November the station at last began flying the new type, being operated by the Operational Conversion Unit commanded by Squadron Leader G C McCarthy MVO AFC. The first aircraft (XN821) took off from Benson at 1408Z on 21 November to carry out a local familiarisation flight and acceptance test.

In December two more aircraft were handed-over and, after acceptance checks had been completed, started flying with the OCU. The first two route-proving flights were undertaken, to Gibraltar and Cyprus. By January 1962, with seven Argosies available, flying hours on the new type increased considerably, up to a total of 312hr. No 114 Squadron was formed on the 1st of that month – or reformed; it had operated until September 1961 with Hastings. But it did not begin Argosy operations until 26 February when XN847 departed for Malta on a training flight, captained by Wing Commander W I Harris AFC (who was to command the second squadron, No 105).

Before the Argosy went into squadron service it had started a round of Intensive Flying Trials, based at Benson. The first phase of the trials had been completed by March 1962 and the second phase was due to begin on 2 April. Its requirements were for two aircraft to fly as intensively as possible until 500 flying hours had been accumulated. The two aircraft were XN847 and XN849, in the freight role. March 1962 was the first full month of operations for No 114 Squadron, which by then had four crews and had flown a total of 140hr.

Thus two Argosy activities were going on in parallel at Benson in the spring of 1962 – training crews at the OCU and flying two machines to their limits. These Intensive Flying Trials were in marked contrast to the introduction of other new Transport Command types like the Comets and Britannias which had been derived from civil airliners. The Argosy had been in civil service as a freighter and was in fact the first Armstrong Whitworth machine to go into RAF service since the Albemarle (which had been designed as a bomber but was utilised as a glider tug; it entered service in 1943 and won its spurs in Operation Overlord).

1962 was undoubtedly 'the year of the Argosy'. From the beginning of April the parent station, Benson, became part of No 38 Group and therefore part of the UK mobility forces. A second Argosy squadron, No 105, was formed in February and in June departed for Khormaksar, Aden. In July three Argosies took part in a mobility exercise with one of the No 38 Group fighter/ground-attack Hunter squadrons, No 54, whose personnel and equipment it deployed from Waterbeach to Kemble and back four days later (Exercise Owl Song). In September there were two bigger events and, it could be said, the Argosy came of age. The first was a major NATO exercise in Greece; the second was the prestigious Lord Trophy Competition, named after Flight Lieutenant David Lord VC who, as recorded earlier, was awarded the VC for his supreme courage over Arnhem in 1944. The Trophy was competed for annually by all the medium-range squadrons in the Command. The Benson ORB noted the signal success of a new squadron with new aircraft:

'Two Argosies were detached to Luqa and Larissa (Greece) to take part in the Lord Trophy Competition and Exercise Falltrap. Flight Lieutenant D C Miller (captain), Flight Lieutenant J L B Boutin (co-pilot), Squadron Leader C C Bevan MBE DFC, Flying Officer D Crowson (air engineer) and Sergeant Ellis (AQM)[10], representing the Argosy Force and No 114 Squadron won the Lord Trophy at the first attempt against

---

10 Air Quartermasters had been awarded aircrew status from 16 May 1962 (AMO A117/1962).

all other aircraft types and squadrons in the Medium-Range Transport Force of No 38 Group. This was a splendid effort'.

Exercise Falltrap (26–28 September) was the live-play part of NATO Exercise Fallex 62 and had as its aim the destruction of 'Orange' forces which had penetrated into Northern Greece. In addition to the transport aircraft and airborne forces, four Hunter FR.10s of No 2 Squadron, RAF Germany, took part. Assessing the exercise from the air transport point of view, No 38 Group judged it to have been a complete success. The force employed was the largest to have been flown in a 38 Group exercise, and it was believed that the drop was the largest since Arnhem.

By January 1962 deliveries of DH Comet 4Cs to the RAF had begun with the arrival of the first at Lyneham, where they were to be operated by 216 Squadron, which at that time was commanded by Wg Cdr (later Air Vice-Marshal) Norman Hoad AFC[11]. Five 4Cs were scheduled to be in service by the summer, supplementing the ten Mk 2s which the squadron had been using since June 1956. The 17 May issue of *Flight* summarised Transport Command's roles at that time:

'World routes are flown by the Command, which also has responsibility for rapid deployment of the UK Strategic Reserve. Carriage of troops, freight and mail, and casualty evacuation, plus major participation in the Army's training programme is effected by Britannia, Comet, Beverley and Hastings aircraft, plus Whirlwind helicopters and short take-off Pioneers and Twin Pioneers.

'Argosies have recently been introduced in the tactical freighter role, and 38 Group, which controls short and medium-range transports and No 1 Parachute Training School, has Hunters for ground attack duties.

'Transport Command is responsible for the Queen's Flight[12], an examining unit, an operational conversion unit and the Metropolitan Communications squadron'.

One role which *Flight* did not mention was the support given by Transport Command to Bomber Command, now at the height of its deterrent power with a full complement of V-bombers. Bomber Command's operational dispersal procedures and overseas deployments depended implicitly on the support of Transport Command, which thus became a key component of the nation's nuclear deterrent force.

The annual Micky Finn exercises in Bomber Command to test QRA (Quick Reaction Alert) procedures were likely to involve the dispersal of groups of V-bombers with their logistic support to airfields throughout the

---

11 Who in addition to commanding No 216 Sqn was distinguished as an aviation artist.
12 This unique unit, although based at a Transport Command station (Benson), nevertheless operated directly under orders received from Buckingham Palace. See *The Queen's Flight Fifty Years of Royal Flying*, referred to in Chapter II.

UK. After one of these exercises in 1964 the Chief of the Air Staff reported to the Minister of Defence that all 17 of the Transport Command aircraft required to move the V-force squadrons' personnel and equipment had arrived at the main bomber bases exactly on schedule – a tribute to the Command's operational efficiency and high level of performance, in which its crews justifiably took great pride.

Chapter XVII

New Government, New Aircraft – The Mid-1960s

'No Government can be long secure without
a formidable Opposition'

Benjamin Disraeli, Coningsby, *II i*

IN its last years (1963–67) before its transformation into Air Support Command, Transport Command continued to make a busy and impressive contribution to UK defence policy. From 1 December 1963 it had a new Commander-in-Chief, the formidable Air Chief Marshal Sir Kenneth Cross, who had served for the previous seven years in Bomber Command, first in command of No 3 Group and then as Commander-in-Chief. He moved to a Command which over many years had had a close operational relationship with Bomber Command. He was to remain in command until the beginning of 1967, the year of change, when he was succeeded by Air Marshal Sir Tom Prickett.

During 1964–67 Transport Command received three new types of aircraft, the VC10, Belfast and Andover (all in 1966); it could offer high-speed, long-range transport and also carriage of, and tactical support for, ground troops and airborne forces. The Defence policy of those years, characterised by the change to a Labour Government in October 1964, was largely geared to the swift reinforcement of the Far East theatre. It was a policy that was to be accentuated by the new Government, for its decision to withdraw from bases east of Suez carried with it a corollary. In place of the commitment to support the Far East with forces based in the theatre, as in the past, there was now the requirement to support the region with forces based in the UK should the need arise. When the Air Council discussed the future size and shape of the RAF at its meeting on 7 November 1963[1] one of its conclusions was that the Transport Force proposed was the minimum to meet the commitment, approved by the Government, to reinforce the Far East in a given time.

For this, Transport Command had its Lyneham-based force of Comet 4s and 2s and the Britannias, and the No 38 Group squadrons: Nos 24 and 36 of Hastings at Colerne, No 47 of Beverleys at Abingdon, and Nos 114 and 267 of Argosies at Benson.

To look at the work-sheet for these squadrons in a typical month is to realise how heavy their commitments were; they were tasked to the hilt. In December 1965, for example, the Comet 4s had 500 flying hours available; their tasks consumed 499hr of these, chiefly on the Far East run (293hr).

---

1 Conclusions 18 (63).

The Comet 2s were tasked to do 333hr out of 360hr available. Theirs were the shorter schedules – to Gibraltar, Idris (Libya), Luqa (Malta), El Adem (Tobruk) and Aden, plus the transatlantic services.

The two Britannia squadrons were tasked with 2,389hr out of 2,400hr available. They were also involved in Far East flights to Changi and services to Aden and Akrotiri (Cyprus). In addition there were flights to Australia and New York, Polar flights and the support of a V-force detachment to Darwin, Northern Australia. They also had a heavy exercise commitment.

The two Hastings squadrons had 1,680hr available and were tasked with 1,410hr. They also had a heavy exercise commitment which soaked up 456hr of their total.

Neither the Hastings nor the Beverleys flew scheduled services; the largest part of the Beverleys' available flying time (480hr) was taken up with training tasks and with getting to and from Akrotiri (62hr).

The Argosy squadrons had 1,540hr available and were tasked to use 1,148hr. The largest single amount of this (360hr) was devoted to continuation training and conversion in the process of forming four squadrons, two of which went overseas. Quoting the Statement on Defence 1964[2]: 'The build-up of the Argosy force is virtually complete. Squadrons are based in the Middle and Far East (Nos 105 and 215 respectively) as well as in the United Kingdom (Nos 114 and 267)'.

This Statement went on to look forward to new equipment: 'A version of the HS748 (later the "Andover") will be used for communication flying this year. The freighter version will follow in 1965 and will augment the short-range transport force'. It also recorded the previous year's operations:

'Transport Command and the theatre transport forces have continued the support of Malaysian and British troops deployed in Borneo [during the period of Confrontation with Indonesia]. In June, troops and equipment were flown to Swaziland; in July to British Guiana; and in December and January to Cyprus. In addition these forces played a major part in the deployment and support of British forces sent to East Africa in January at the request of the Governments concerned'.

These varied commitments demonstrate the variety and ubiquity of Transport Command operations which had characterised its work since its formation in 1943. There were also its many exercises with the Army and Royal Navy – over a hundred a year. The 1964 Statement recalled:

'Last year Transport Command participated in 113 exercises for all three Services. In the autumn, for the tri-Service exercise Triplox West, Britannias, Argosies, Beverleys and Hastings of Transport Command and the Near East Air Force flew some 5,000 men, 280 tons of equipment, together with 280 vehicles and four Whirlwind helicopters

---

2 Cmnd 2270.

from England to Libya and back again. Troops were re-supplied by air during the exercise, in which ground-attack Hunters and Whirlwinds and Belvederes of No 38 Group also provided tactical support'.

The Statement mentioned other aspects of Transport Command operations at this time:

'Route training flights by medium-range aircraft to Germany and the Near and Middle East are being used increasingly for the carriage of priority freight. Regular aero medical evacuation services are maintained to all the main overseas theatres, and 258 flights were made in 1963'.

During November 1964, Britannias of Transport Command undertook a major airlift between Denmark and Cyprus at the request of the Secretary General of the United Nations, rotating 1,700 troops of the Danish contingent in the island with their equipment – an airlift provided free of charge. The new UK Government made it clear however that in view of other British contributions to the UN peacekeeping force this was a service that could not be repeated on the same terms[3].

After the Labour Government's assumption of office in October 1964 the new Administration carried out a searching Defence Review which was to have major consequences for all three Services. As far as the RAF was concerned, changes inaugurated in 1965–66 led to the end of Transport Command as it had been known since 1943, to its loss of a STOL transport project (the HS681) and to its acquisition of the C-130 Hercules to replace the Hastings and Beverley, and eventually the Argosy.

On 16 November 1964 the new Secretary of State for Defence, Denis Healey, took the Chair for the first time at a meeting of the Air Force Board (successor to the Air Council and renamed after the formation of a unified Ministry of Defence in 1964), and heard a Progress Report on New Weapons and Aircraft. Looking at the list of R&D projects, and extrapolating costs from 1956/6 to 1974/5, the cost of the TSR.2 was found to be £182m, that of the P.1154 supersonic V/STOL fighter to be £166m, and that of the HS681 STOL transport to be £70m.

Sadly the HS681 project did not survive the Labour Government's examination of the Defence costs, inherited from the previous Administration. The project was cancelled early in 1965 on grounds of being so costly as to impose an unacceptable burden on the Defence Budget (Statement on the Defence Estimates 1965)[4]. The Statement announced that to replace the Hastings, the Beverley and eventually the Argosy, it was proposed to order the C-130.

The Lockheed C-130 had first flown in prototype form on 23 August 1954 and had been in service with the USAF since December 1956. It was used by many other air forces in Australia, Brazil, Iran, Pakistan, South

---

3 Statement on the Defence Estimates 1965 (Cmnd 2592).
4 Cmnd 2592.

Africa and Turkey. The decision to order it for the RAF, which involved reopening the production line at Marietta, Georgia, was one of the best taken by the Labour Government in the 1964–65 Defence Review.

The C-130 was the sort of tactical/strategic transport the RAF had needed for years. It is significant that the Lockheed aircraft and the Beverley had entered service in the same year; but how different they were in performance. True, the Beverley had a very large hold and could take bulky loads, but its maximum speed was 238 mph and maximum range 1,300 miles. The C-130's maximum cruising speed was 368 mph and its range with maximum payload was 2,430 miles. With a 20,259lb payload it was 4,780 miles. Furthermore, its short-legged tricycle undercarriage provided very convenient low-loading access.

Initially, 48 C-130s were ordered, but on 31 January 1966 the Air Force Board decided to increase this by 18, bringing the total buy to 66[5].

The introduction of the Belfast and VC10 cast long shadows in advance because a new base had to be developed for them, Brize Norton in Oxfordshire, which had been one of the No 38 Group stations for Operation Overlord in 1944. During the 1950s–60s Brize Norton had been used by B-47s of the USAF 7th Air Division, Strategic Air Command, but in March 1965 it was vacated by them and reverted to Transport Command. Part of the new development was the installation of an Autoland blind landing system.

At its 5 March 1964 meeting the Air Council had agreed that the HS748 MF and VIP versions should be named Andover, and later that year the new recruit for the short-range transport force reached the stage of acceptance trials. As the aviation journal *Flight* put it[7]:

> 'The first production rear-loading STOL 748MFs will be delivered later this year to the A&AEE at Boscombe Down for official acceptance trials in the tactical transport's several roles – paratroop and supply dropping; troop, vehicle and freight transport; and casualty evacuation. Six straight adaptations of the civil 748 Series 2 airliner with 2,100 hp Dart RDa 7 engines are also being built for Transport Command for special passenger-carrying duties. Two of these aircraft will be assigned to the Queen's Flight and will enter service later this year'.

Meanwhile the Air Force Board heard some discouraging news about the Belfast[8]. Limitations imposed by the engine anti-icing system called for a reduction in maximum cruising height, which would cause great difficulty on some routes and in the worst conditions would mean that the stage from Cyprus to Bahrain could not be flown. Even in less severe conditions it was probable that the payload would be halved[9].

---

5 Conclusions 2(64).
6 Conclusions 4(64).
7 23 April 1964 issue.
8 AFB Conclusions 9(64) (Special), 13 July 1964.
9 PUS(RAF) (Mr B Millan) told the Air Force board on 31 January 1966 (Conclusions

Anxiety about the Belfast's performance continued during 1965. At the AFB meeting on 27 May[10] DCAS said that there was considerable cause for alarm over its increase in drag, resulting from the need to fix vortex generators to improve the stalling characteristics. This rise in drag would have a serious effect on performance.

Meanwhile, work on the base for the big new transports was going ahead. In its 19 August issue *Flight* reported:

'Contracts have been awarded for the work of converting the former USAF SAC base of Brize Norton as the parent base of RAF Transport Command's Belfasts and VC10s. Under one contract worth £1.74M a VC10/Belfast hangar is being built together with annexes, aprons, taxiways and external services. The second contract, worth £684,000, is for alterations and additions to existing buildings. Other contracts, yet to be let, will cover the construction of a transit hotel, electronics centre and a squadrons' headquarters complex'.

In mid-1965 there was an unhappy reminder of the vulnerability of the ageing and hardworking Hastings of Transport Command and of the need for them to be replaced, when a No 36 Squadron aircraft flying from Abingdon with a crew of six and 35 Army and RAF parachutists crashed on 6 July near Dorchester, Oxon, with the loss of all on board. Two days later the Ministry of Defence announced that all Hastings would be grounded as a precautionary measure. The finding of the Court of Inquiry into the accident was that it had occurred owing to the fracture, through fatigue, of the two upper attachment bolts of the starboard elevator outrigger.

In view of this tragic accident it is of interest that No 36 Squadron was the first to equip with C-130s, and actually received the first of their new aircraft on the day that Air Support Command was formed, 1 August 1967.

During 1965, the Air Force Board considered whether the RAF C-130s should be re-engined with Rolls-Royce Tynes, but concluded that the performance benefits would not justify the time and cost likely to be involved. There were nevertheless a number of other items being considered for fitment at a total estimated cost by the manufacturer of £70,000 per aircraft.

Rolls-Royce did not give up hope for the Tynes and at their meeting on 31 May[11] the AFB were told that the company had come forward with a further offer, which was under urgent examination.

The Hercules were still a matter for the future but meanwhile the HQ of Transport Command and No 216 Squadron must have been cheered by a glowing tribute to their Comets which appeared in *Flight* in August 1965:

2(66)) that the Air Force Department 'was discussing with the Ministry of Aviation the question of financial compensation from Shorts for the shortfall' – no pun intended – 'in performance'.

10 9(65).

11 10(65).

'RAF Transport Command, one of Britain's best airlines, is just entering its tenth year as a jet transport operator. The Command was the first military force after the RCAF (Comet 1As) to operate jet transports, when 216 Squadron introduced Comet 2s in June 1956. For three years now the bigger Comet 4C has been in service, having flown some 30 million miles, according to an RAF spokesman. If RAF Transport Command, which operates meticulously to airline standards, flies its Comet 4Cs at anything like the average block speed of BOAC, each of the five aircraft has therefore averaged about 1,000hr a year over the past three years.

'The RAF's Comets have in the course of their service been seen at most major airports in the world, and at many small ones. Their safety record has been perfect.

'In October the first of 14 Standard VC10s for the RAF is due to fly, and according to a British Aircraft Corporation spokesman, should start to supplement the Command's jet fleet some time in 1965'.

But not everything was going as well as this and at the other end of the speed and size scale there were difficulties with the Belvedere helicopter which was proving to be very unreliable. Although modifications were available to cure some of the Belvedere's problems there were doubts on the part of the Air Force Board as to whether the future operational life of the aircraft was likely to be long enough to make the cost of the modifications worthwhile. In the end the full modification programme went ahead, but at the same time thought was being given to finding a replacement aircraft, and a report on possible options was awaited from a team which visited the USA in September 1965[12].

Even so, the Belvedere had provided significant service and had enlarged the scope of helicopter capabilities. Recalling its contribution to Army/RAF operations, the Chief Flight Test Engineer of Westland Helicopters, David Gibbings, wrote[13]:

'The full potential of the helicopter in the Armed Services was not fully realised until the first gas turbine machines became available. For the Royal Air Force, this came with the big twin-rotor Belvedere which entered service with No 66 Squadron at Odiham in September 1961.

'The Belvedere opened a whole new era. It was capable of carrying a 6,000lb underslung load or 18 fully armed troops. Belvederes operated

---

12 This was the Air Staff team which went to Washington as a result of the Labour Government's review of the Defence programme after it assumed office in October 1964 and which resulted in an option on the TFX (F-111A) to replace the TSR.2 and also – as an outcome of subsequent visits – in a purchase of Boeing–Vertol Chinook twin-rotor helicopters.

13 In his contribution on Autogyros and Helicopters to *75 Eventful Years, A Tribute to the Royal Air Force 1918–1993*, edited by Tony Ross, DFC; Wingham Aviation Books, 1993.

with No 26 Squadron in Aden and East Africa, and also with No 66 Squadron throughout the campaign in Brunei 1962–66, offering a new standard of mobility to jungle warfare.

'A Belvedere of No 72 Squadron was used for a much-publicised task, to place the spire (in the form of a fleche, surmounted by sculpture)[14] on the top of the new Coventry Cathedral. Belvederes of No 26 Squadron operated from HMS *Centaur* on Commando operations into Tanganyika in 1963.

'In the eight years they remained operational the Belvederes transformed many of the preconceived ideas regarding the use of helicopters and placed the foundations for a new arm of the Service'.

---

14 For a full appraisal of the Belvedere, which had an unhappy Service career, there can be no better authority than Wg Cdr John Dowling MBE DFC AFC, who not only commanded the Belvedere Trials Unit at Odiham in 1960 and successively formed the three squadrons but also wrote a history – *RAF Helicopters The First Twenty Years*, published by HMSO in 1992 – in which he carefully appraised (pages 384–389) the merits and liabilities of the big Bristol twin-rotor helicopter.

It was Wg Cdr Dowling who captained the Belvedere which successfully performed the difficult and dangerous operation to which Mr Gibbings referred – placing the 'spire' and sculpture on Coventry Cathedral in April 1962.

Chapter XVIII

1966 – A Year of Re-equipment: Belfasts, VC10s and Andovers

'Big is beautiful'

Aircraft industry aphorism (origin unknown)

WHEN one recalls Transport Command's 'Cinderella years' of the 1950s during which, as far as equipment was concerned, it had to play second fiddle to the Cold War priorities of Bomber and Fighter Command, the mid-1960s were years of plenty. During 1966 three new types were introduced into squadron service and a fourth was ceremonially handed over to the RAF by Lockheed Aircraft Corporation.

No 53 Squadron was the beneficiary of the first Short Belfast – the first of ten – at Brize Norton on 20 January 1966. It was to be in service with No 53 Squadron for ten years, and could carry – as occasion required – a Chieftan tank, or three Saladin armoured cars, or ten Land Rovers and trailers, or three Whirlwind or two Wessex helicopters, or two Polaris missiles, or three Bloodhound missiles with launching equipment.

This 'heavy lifter' was to the RAF what the Douglas C-124 Globemaster and the Lockheed C-5A Galaxy were to the USAF. As a troop carrier it could transport 150 soldiers, and it had a range with a maximum 77,500lb payload of 1,000 miles, and a cruising speed of 315 mph at an altitude of 24,000ft.

The Belfast had been introduced into RAF service on 10 January when XR367 was delivered to Brize Norton by Denis Tayler DFC, chief test pilot of Short Brothers & Harland. No 53 Squadron, which with No 47 had been one of the three Beverley squadrons and with which it had merged in 1963, had been reformed at Brize Norton on 1 November 1965. Its CO, Wing Commander A D A Honley AFC, was the first RAF officer to be converted to the new type.

Wing Commander Honley and Flight Lieutenant Laurie went off to Short Bros on 21 March to assist in Belfast flight development trials and along with Wing Commander M R Ingle-Finch (who during his wartime career had been a Typhoon pilot with No 56 Squadron) delivered a second Belfast, XR368, to Brize Norton. With two aircraft flying, conversion for squadron personnel got under way during April. On 23 May the CO took the new type on its first trip abroad when he went on a five-day tour of the Mediterranean, visiting Malta, El Adem and Cyprus.

There was some jollification at Brize Norton on 15 May when No 53's 50th anniversary was celebrated, but progress toward operational status was slowed down when the squadron had to move to Fairford for the rest of the year while alterations were made to the runway at Brize Norton. So it was to Fairford that the third Belfast, XR369, was delivered on 7 July, almost immediately going off on a trip to Singapore. The new aircraft was settling into its role. In September No 53 Squadron began flights to Gibraltar, Luqa, Lajes and Akrotiri, and in November XR367, with a nine-man crew, went off to Changi, Singapore.

On 1 December 1966 No 53 Squadron became operational with the Belfast, and on the 2nd one of its aircraft, XR368, with two complete crews set off for the United States, testing the 'Westabout' route with stops at Offutt, Hickam, Wake and McClellan AFBs.

Britannia Oil Lift

While the Belfast was being introduced the Britannias of Nos 99 and 511 Squadrons at Lyneham performed a remarkable operation which for intensity of purpose and emergency succour rivalled the Berlin Airlift. Its object was to keep Zambia supplied with oil after its normal sources had been cut off following the Rhodesian UDI (Unilateral Declaration of Independence) in 1965. For almost a year these fine turboprop-engined transports, the last emanations of a long line of Bristol aircraft for the RAF, created and sustained what was in effect an aerial pipeline between Kenya and Zambia.

A blow-by-blow account (or should one say, 'drum by drum' in view of the means of conveyance of the oil) of this remarkable operation (which actually began from Tanzania in December 1965 but was moved to Kenya following political objections), was given in an article in *Air Clues* for January 1967 which referred initially to the end of the airlift:

'At 0815hr local on 31 October 1966 the last sortie of the RAF oil lift departed Lusaka for Nairobi. After many rumours the oil lift to Zambia was officially over. For about a year, Britannia aircraft and crews of Nos 99 and 511 Squadrons had flown an average of 5½ loads of 50 full oil drums every day into the Zambian airfields of N'dola and Lusaka. In addition, full logistic support was given to No 29 Squadron (Javelins) and associated radar units, RAF Regiment units and personnel serving with COMBRITZAM. The range and scope of this support alone was staggering. . . .

'The oil lift operation started on 20 December 1965, using Dar-es-Salaam as a base. In early January 1966 when the civil charter companies joined in the lift, the RAF Britannias moved to Nairobi/ Embakasi Airport where they remained for the rest of the operation. The Royal Air Force Britannias operated daily and were joined for a short period by civil charter aircraft and USAF and RCAF C-130s.

'The base at Embakasi Airport expanded from one small hut into a sizeable operations and technical site. Oil trucks rolled in day and night from Mombasa – a journey of 300 miles over dirt roads; one was charged by an elephant and suffered severe damage – the truck, not the elephant.

'The loading and unloading of the Britannias at all airfields was carried out by MAM (Mobile Air Movements) teams detached from Abingdon, Cyprus and Aden, supported by locally employed labour. Using a 12,000lb forklift, 12 × 45 gallon drums, weighing approximately 375lb each, could be swung into the aircraft each time. At N'dola and Lusaka only 6,000lb forklifts were available, but nevertheless, the teams became so expert that 50 full drums could be unloaded and 92 empty drums back-loaded in less than 25 minutes. It became, indeed, a slick operation[1].

'Superimposed on the oil lift, several other tasks were undertaken by the Britannias operating at Nairobi. They included the withdrawal of the majority of personnel and equipment from Zambia and the positioning of Majunga detachment personnel and freight at Nairobi for onward movement to Malagasy by medium-range transport aircraft.

'In just under one year about 3,500,000 gallons of fuel, or 75,000 drums, was lifted into Zambia. During 1,560 sorties, 10,300 flying hours were achieved on the oil lift alone. In addition to the fuel, just under 2,000,000lb of freight and 3,731 passengers were carried in the oil aircraft.

'To the accompaniment of bagpipes played by an Air Electronics Operator of No 99 Squadron (Flt Lt I H Lewis), passengers walked out to the last Britannia to leave Nairobi for the UK – but the rain lashed down to provide a very damp ending to the operation. The last Detachment Commander, Squadron Leader E Reeves, No 511 Squadron, was the last person aboard.

'Lord Shackleton, Minister of Defence (RAF), sent the following message to the Commander-in-Chief on 1 November 1966 to mark the end of the oil airlift:

> "Since last December three-and-a-half million gallons of fuel have been carried into Zambia by means of the RAF oil airlift which comes to an end today. I realise that this has been achieved in the face of considerable difficulties and has only been made possible by a great deal of hard work and sacrifice, including separation from families and dislocation of normal Service activities. I should be most grateful if you would pass on to all concerned my warm congratulations on a job of great importance thoroughly well done".

'The Commander-in-Chief added his own congratulations, and similar congratulatory messages were passed on from the Prime Minister and Mr Herbert Bowden, the Secretary for Commonwealth Affairs.

---

1 But no doubt very hard on the fuselage floors of the Britannias. By chance the Airport Commandant of N'dola at that time was a former (1944–45) CO of No 216 Sqn, Wg Cdr J H Williams AFC.

'This operation brought to the forefront once again the excellent co-operation that can be achieved between aircrew and groundcrew under difficult circumstances. Over 500 groundcrew from Lyneham were rotated on detachment at one time or another; all aircrew of the two Britannia squadrons did three or four tours (each of four weeks' duration); and the percentage of on-time departures of Britannias from Nairobi was 92% – a figure of which all aircrew and groundcrew can be justifiably proud'.

By contrast with the *Air Clues* article, the Operations Record Book entries by the Lyneham squadrons were terse and statistical. No 511 Squadron confined itself to recording the number of Nairobi-based trips from February to November 1966, rising from 63 initially to a peak of 96 in May and totalling 633 over the ten-month period.

No 99 Squadron recorded the number of hours flown – rising to a peak of 1,237hr in September and totalling over 10,000hr – and provided some comments about the priority given to the operation. The March entry noted that 'apart from a few trips to the Far East, Canada and Norway[2] the main task continued to be the Nairobi detachment of three weeks' duration for each crew involved'. Then, in August: 'The carriage of fuel from Nairobi to Zambia still provides the major task, with a sharp increase of effort at the end of the month when the squadron was engaged in the withdrawal of No 29 Javelin Squadron from N'dola to Lusaka'.

It had been a long, monotonous, unglamorous operation, but comparable in the context of the times to the carriage of fuel and ammunition to the 8th Army in the Western Desert by the Dakota and Hudson squadrons of No 216 Group in the year when Transport Command was formed. It was an example of the type of unexpected task the Command had been called upon to perform in the subsequent years of war and peace, and which it took in its stride.

Belfast Capability

Meanwhile in 1966, as the Britannias continued to prove their worth in the long-range role, the Belfasts continued to make their weighty presence felt. A note on the history of No 53 Squadron in the Air Historical Branch of the MoD made these comments on the Belfast's heavy lift capability:

'This remarkable aircraft carried a variety of large and heavy items: rockets for ELDO (European Launcher Development Organisation) to Woomera, Australia, a pair of Abbot self-propelled guns, a stonecrusher weighing over 52,000lb from Sharjah to Masirah, and complete helicopters, including the Puma'.

---

2 What might be called a throwaway line, but strikingly indicative of the international outlook Transport Command had had since its inception.

In an article in *Air Clues* for October 1975 when the Belfast had been in service for nearly nine years, Sqn Ldr G Robertson and Flt Lt J E Copsey said that 'the aircraft had had its share of teething troubles when introduced, and being a big aircraft, not unnaturally the troubles were of the same magnitude'. Major modifications had been required to reduce the drag caused by the rear-end configuration. It was not until 1971 that the squadron received its full complement of ten fully modified aircraft – at that time renamed the 'fastback', because all aircraft now had the modifications to reduce the rear-end drag. No 53 Squadron was possibly unique in that it operated the entire production line of one aircraft type and had even had all ten aircraft airborne in formation together.

The Belfast came in for some friendly derision during its operational career. The authors of the *Air Clues* article recorded that when air traffic control asked a pilot for his aircraft type the reply 'Belfast' would be met with a puzzled silence. Transatlantic ATC would add the supplementary question: 'Say, what kind of aircraft is that?' – getting the standard replies, 'It's a Texan C-130'. A Belfast crew at Chicago heard a controller give a PanAm aircraft the taxiing instruction: 'Follow that flying banana passing in front of you now'. The article went on:

> 'Unlike the other strategic transport squadrons, very little of No 53 Sqn flying is on scheduled services. Over 80% of the flying effort is devoted to support of exercises by the three Services, and special tasks on behalf of the Services and other Government agencies. In an average year the squadron moves 34 million lb (or 17,000 short tons) and some 20,000 passengers to all parts of the world.

> 'One day an aircraft would be on its way home from the Southern Hemisphere with the hulk of an old Walrus amphibian for the RAF Museum and, a few days later, the same aircraft may be over the Northern wastes of Canada with a load of gleaming new weaponry for cold weather trials'.

Enter the VC10s

No 53 Sqn Belfasts supported Concorde trials to Japan and the Far East, as well as Strike Command squadrons in their many deployments. Clearly, these ten aircraft added new dimensions to Transport Command's long-range weight-lifting capability. The Belfasts shared their Brize Norton base with the other big acquisition of 1966, the VC10s. No 10 Sqn, the designation given to the VC10 squadron, was one of the No 4 Group, Bomber Command, squadrons which had been taken over by Transport Command in 1945. It had been converted from Halifaxes to Dakotas and sent to India. It took part in the Berlin Airlift then in 1953 became a Canberra B.2 squadron, converting to Victors in 1958 and flying them until 1964, when it was disbanded on 1 March. It reformed at Brize Norton on 1 July 1966 under the command of Wg Cdr M G Beavis, who as a Vulcan captain with No 617 Squadron had made a non-stop UK–Australia flight (Scampton to Sydney) in June 1961, covering 11,500 miles in 20hr 3min 17sec – an average speed of 573 mph, so he was no stranger to fast flights in big jet aircraft over long distances.

As a measure of how far Transport Command had advanced in point-to-point times since the Second World War, the author recalls that in January 1946 it took him almost as long to reach Elmas in Sardinia in a Dakota from the UK as it did later for a VC10 to fly from the UK to the Persian Gulf. Comparable flight times were 6hr 25min for the Dakota flight, a distance of 870nm, and 7hr 15min for the VC10 flight – a distance of 3,470nm.

The first of 14 VC10s for Transport Command had been formally handed over by British Aircraft Corporation in a ceremony at Wisley airfield, Surrey, on 7 July 1966 when Sir Kenneth Cross received XR808 from the Chairman of BAC, Marshal of the RAF Lord Portal. This was actually the third military VC10; the first and second were engaged on acceptance trials at A&AEE, Boscombe Down.

Differences between the military and the Civil Standard VC10 as used by BOAC were that the former was designed for worldwide operation as a troop transport, freighter and casualty evacuation aircraft, so it had to have the equipment for these various roles, capable of easy installation and removal.

The RAF version had a standard VC10 fuselage with a strengthened floor, side-loading freight doors and more powerful engines – Rolls-Royce Conway RCo 43s of 22,500lb st. With rearward-facing seats[3], the RAF VC10s were designed to carry 150 troops and their equipment non-stop over some 4,000 miles. Because the aircraft were likely to carry Service families their interior was designed to airline standards, while allowing for lashing points for freight – in which role the Transport Command VC10s could carry 59,000lb. In the casualty evacuation role there was room for up to 78 stretcher cases, with six medical attendants, two AQMs (Air Quartermasters) and medical equipment.

Flying on routine schedules, the VC10s took 19½hr from the UK to Singapore, with refuelling stops at Bahrain and Gan, and 22hr to Hong Kong. The time to Singapore was 4½hr faster than that of the Comet 4s and 12hr faster than the Britannias – a significant improvement.

Andovers at Abingdon

The third new type of aircraft to come into Transport Command service during 1966 – the Hawker Siddeley Andover twin-turboprop tactical transport – began operations with No 46 Sqn at Abingdon towards the end of that year. This squadron, famous for many years in Fighter Command, had had a brief post-war period (1945–50) in Transport Command when it was equipped with Stirlings and then Dakotas. In 1939–40 it had been commanded by the then Sqn Ldr K B B Cross when it had Hurricanes and

---

3 Rearward-facing seats were introduced into Transport Command with the Specifications for the Hastings (C3/44) and the Valetta (C9/46).

was sent to Norway[4]. One of the last visits paid by Air Chief Marshal Sir Kenneth Cross before he relinquished his appointment as Transport Command's Commander-in-Chief on 27 January 1967 was to his old squadron at Abingdon on 13 December 1966. A Press Day was held there to introduce the Andover, and to show off its STOL capabilities and its unique 'kneeling undercarriage', giving it a low-loading posture.

No 46 Sqn was reformed for its new role at Abingdon on 1 September 1966; its establishment was for nine Andover C Mk 1s. On 28 November the first aircrews were posted to the squadron from the Andover Conversion Course, and the three aircraft they had flown on the course – XS603, XS604 and XS605 – were transferred to the squadron. The groundcrew had begun to assemble from the 7th onwards when a number of them were posted-in from the Engineering Wing at Abingdon.

When the Press Day came round nine Andovers were lined up – three of No 46 Sqn, three of No 52 Sqn (which was shortly to go overseas to Seletar, Singapore), and three of the Conversion Unit. In a flying demonstration the Andover unstuck in an estimated 300yd and landed in about the same distance. A report on the occasion in *Flight International* for 22 December said that the excellent short-field performance derived from the use of high power-loading – the Rolls-Royce Dart 12 engines producing 3,245 ehp each – together with an efficient, high-aspect-ratio wing and four-position Fowler flaps, the type of flaps used on the wartime Lockheed Hudson which actually increase the wing area.

The report described another unusual factor contributing to the Andover's STOL capability: 'For landing, the airscrews may be selected into reverse pitch while the aircraft is still flying, thus providing not only power braking but also an immediate dumping of lift over a large part of the wing'. It will be immediately obvious that there was a danger attendant on this technique, and a rider was added: 'Some caution is clearly necessary here, but the sturdy undercarriage, designed to cope with descents of up to 14.5ft/sec, should prevent any expensive noises resulting from a really hard landing'.

The other distinctive feature of the Andover was its 'kneeling undercarriage' which, once the aircraft was on the ground, could be operated to provide any degree of ground clearance between 40in and 86in at the ramp hinge. The pilot armed the appropriate hydraulic circuit from the flight deck while a crewman at the external panel, below and aft of the port loading door, controlled the actual undercarriage movement to give the exact height required. One engine, normally the starboard, was kept running in order to provide the hydraulic power needed for the operation.

During early 1967 No 46 Sqn started to perform those roles which were its *raison d'être* in Transport Command. In February it began aero-medical special flights to Germany – one proving-flight and two actual aero-

---

4 In 1940 all of No 46 Squadron's aircraft, and those of No 263 Sqn with which it had fought gallantly in Norway, were lost when the aircraft carrier HMS *Glorious* was sunk by the German battleships *Scharnhorst* and *Gneisenau* in the North Sea after the evacuation from Norway, only two of the pilots surviving. See *Straight and Level*, the autobiography of 'Bing' Cross (Grub Street, 1993).

medical evacuations – and in March took part in a helicopter support exercise on Salisbury Plain. Its task in this was the dropping of fuel and ammunition to ground forces: a total of 80,160lb was dropped, involving some 300 runs in various DZs.

By the spring of 1967 the squadron was very much part of the No 38 Group scene. In April it took part in two exercises, both involving sorties to El Adem in North Africa. The first included the airlift of Army/RAF personnel and Forward Air Controllers to Libya with their supporting freight. The second was rather different – the deployment of a Bloodhound SAM squadron to El Adem which took place at the very end of April. In subsequent months the number of exercises, the variety of loads and the range of destinations continued to increase. To cite a further example, in June the squadron was authorised to start training in the one-ton container dropping role. The Andover had quickly become a 'maid of all work' in Transport Command.

The introduction of the Andover, the Belfast and the VC10 had been relatively straightforward, even though basing the two latter types had required major building works. But there were special problems with an American type like the C-130, and the Chief of the Air Staff (Air Chief Marshal Sir Charles Elworthy) told the Air Force Board at their meeting on 16 May 1966 that there was a vast amount of work to be done in a very limited time to provide the necessary supporting facilities. A new flight simulator had to be designed and produced, training aids and manuals commissioned and instructors and servicing personnel trained. The normal provisioning cycle for spares and other equipment had to be accelerated and arrangements made to supply the US contractors with certain equipment of British manufacture. The selection of suitable airfields for the deployment of the aircraft had given rise to a number of problems, and now that decisions had been taken a considerable programme of works services had to be planned and executed.

These new tasks had to be carried out concurrently with the normal day-to-day management of the RAF and by the same staffs. The total staff of the Air Force Department was no greater then than when the unified Ministry of Defence had been formed, in spite of the fact that additional posts had had to be created to deal with the introduction of new types of aircraft.

Sentiments not unlike these have continued to echo down the years.

Chapter XIX

End of an Era: Transport Command Transliterated

'Ring out the old, ring in the new'

Tennyson, In Memoriam, CV

THE change from Transport Command to Air Support Command on 11 August 1967 was not only a change of name but of operational concept. The searching review of Defence policy which the Labour Government had initiated when they came into office in October 1964 had looked at the former Imperial commitments and, in the words of the Defence Estimates 1967[1], had aimed 'to foster developments which will enable local peoples to live at peace without the presence of external forces' – thereby allowing British forces to withdraw from the Middle and the Far East and from Aden.

The implications of this policy were that Britain should nevertheless maintain obligations to friends and allies across the world and should retain a capacity for contributing to the maintenance of peace. Thus, as the Supplementary Statement on Defence Policy 1967[2] put it: 'In the next decade, new aircraft will enable us to move forces across the world faster and in larger numbers than was possible even a few years ago'. While Britain would continue to stand ready to provide support, this could now be provided from long range. It was furthermore felt that 'as our friends and allies outside Europe build up their own forces, the most valuable contribution we can make is the sophisticated elements which they may find it difficult to provide for themselves. While the visible presence of even small forces – not necessarily dependent on large and expensive base facilities – may be a good deterrent, it will be more economical to rely mainly on sending forces from Britain in a crisis'.

How were they to get there? Of course, by means of Transport Command. But that time-honoured title was becoming too limited for the role the Command was to play and, combined with the decision to reorganise the RAF Command structure in the UK, the title Air Support Command was considered to represent more accurately this new role called for in Defence policy. 'Transport' was considered to be less comprehensive and appropriate than 'Air Support', but – somewhat confusingly – references to the roles of the new Command in Defence Statements were headed 'Air Mobility Forces'. In the Statement on the

---

1 Cmnd 3203.
2 Cmnd 3357.

Defence Estimates 1966[3] the roles and equipment of these forces were described:

'Air Mobility Forces are made up of the strategic transport force; the tactical transport force (both medium and short-range aircraft); the tanker force; communications aircraft; headquarters, bases in the UK and overseas; and Service and joint-user airfields used as staging posts'.

A significant difference between this and the role statement for Transport Command was the mention of the tanker force – hitherto the perquisite of Bomber Command, which had created this force in the late 1950s and subsequently deployed tankers in support of its own and Fighter Command aircraft.

In describing the Air Mobility roles the Statement went on:

'The role of the strategic and tactical transport forces is to move men and equipment of all three Services as quickly as possible when reinforcements are required in other theatres, and to support them in operations. Tactical transport aircraft, based in the United Kingdom, can also reinforce other theatres and support operations in those parts of the world where transport aircraft are not normally on station'. (This was a contribution of the "sophisticated elements" Britain's allies might find it difficult to provide for themselves, as mentioned previously).

Quoting a planned annual rate of flying for all types of 224,000hr, the Statement described the size of the force required in terms of aircraft and flying personnel, saying that the total of airborne hours covered the operation of some 400 aircraft of about 25 different types and marks, with an aircrew strength of approximately 2,700 officers and senior NCOs. It added that in normal circumstances the greater part of both the strategic and tactical (medium-range) transport forces were ready to mount contingency or emergency operations within 72 hours. Some of the force was held at a higher state of readiness.

An explanation of the change of name from Transport to Air Support Command appears in a history of Air Support Command, which says: 'Throughout the discussions on a new RAF Command structure it was accepted that the UK-based strategic and tactical transport aircraft, with their responsibilities to all three Services, must remain within one Command. It was also recognised that the vital offensive-support element, working closely with the tactical transport aircraft and with the Army in the battle area, should also be under the same Commander. The title "Air Support Command" (ASC) was chosen to describe more accurately than "Transport" these varied but closely linked activities and to emphasise their importance in the national strategy'.

The new Command retained the Transport Command motto, 'Ferio Feriendo' – 'I Strike by Carrying', and inherited an illustrious legacy of 24

---

3 Cmnd 2902.

years' transport, airborne support and ferrying operations, a tradition it was to continue until its own merger into Strike Command in 1972.

The change of name did not denote any change in policy or operations; long range and close-support-roles went on as before. If it was a shock to old stagers in Transport Command to realise that the famous name had gone for good, at least the title Air Support gave the new Command a clear identity and purpose. No 38 Group, the formation responsible for getting forces into a battle area and supporting them there, became a Group of the new Command.

Although tanker forces came under the description of 'Air Mobility Forces' in the 1966 Statement the tanker squadrons were still listed under Bomber Command – and, after 1968, in the Strike Command Holdings of Aircraft[4].

The change of name from 'Transport' to 'Air Support Command' seems to have had little or no effect at squadron level. Roles and tasks remained the same, but not so the Command name on the aircraft. On Monday, 31 July, a No 46 Sqn Andover was flown to RAF Odiham by Flt Lt B J Cheverton. The aircraft was the first one with the new marking 'Royal Air Force Air Support Command'. It formed the backdrop for the handover ceremony between Air Vice-Marshal P C Fletcher, the retiring AOC No 38 Group, and Air Vice-Marshal H B Martin DSO DFC AFC, the newly appointed AOC, famous as a wartime bomber pilot with No 617 Sqn.

What were the dimensions of the new Command? It inherited ten Andovers (eight in No 46 Sqn and two on loan to the OCU); ten Belfasts in No 53 Sqn; 20 Argosies in Nos 114 and 267 Sqns; ten Beverleys in No 47 Sqn; five Comet 4Cs in No 216 Sqn; 14 Hastings in No 24 Sqn; nine Hercules C.1s being used for conversions before going to No 36 Sqn; 24 Hunter GA.9s of Nos 1 and 54 Sqns; 14 VC10s in No 10 Sqn; 23 Britannias in Nos 99 and 511 Sqns; plus the helicopters – 20 Wessex in No 72 Sqn and ten Whirlwinds in No 225 Sqn.

This was a formidable line-up and it demonstrated that in the final years of its distinguished existence Transport Command had become a powerful and effective arm for the nation's mobile, ever-ready defence forces.

For Transport Command – forged in war in 1943, 1967 was the moment of 'Sic Transit Gloria'. The older operational Commands – Bomber, Fighter and Coastal, formed in the thirties, were also soon to lose their individual identities when they were merged into the new single Strike Command in 1968 where they became Groups. Transport Command had had a shorter history than its sister operational Commands, but nonetheless an illustrious one, in supporting the Royal Air Force and the other Services with reliability, distinction and heroism – as this history of its operations and achievements from 1943 to 1967 has done its best to record.

---

4 Stats 603.

Appendix A

Charts
showing Groups, Squadrons and aircraft, 1943–67 and locations of units,
1943 & 1945

TRANSPORT COMMAND
GROUPS 1943 - 1967

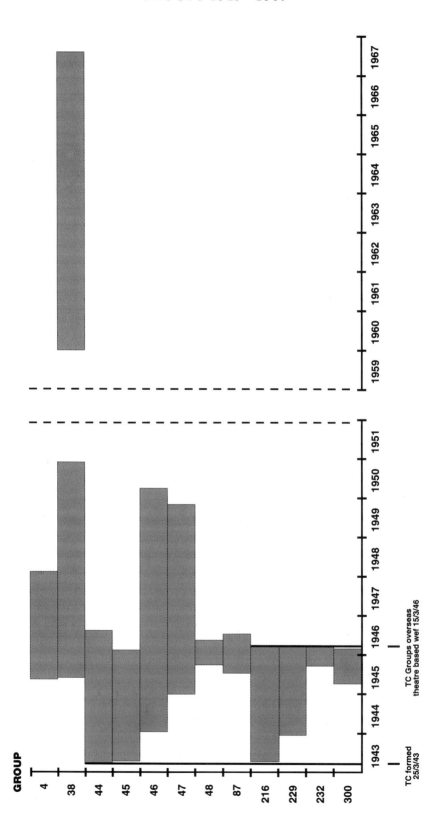

TRANSPORT COMMAND SQUADRONS

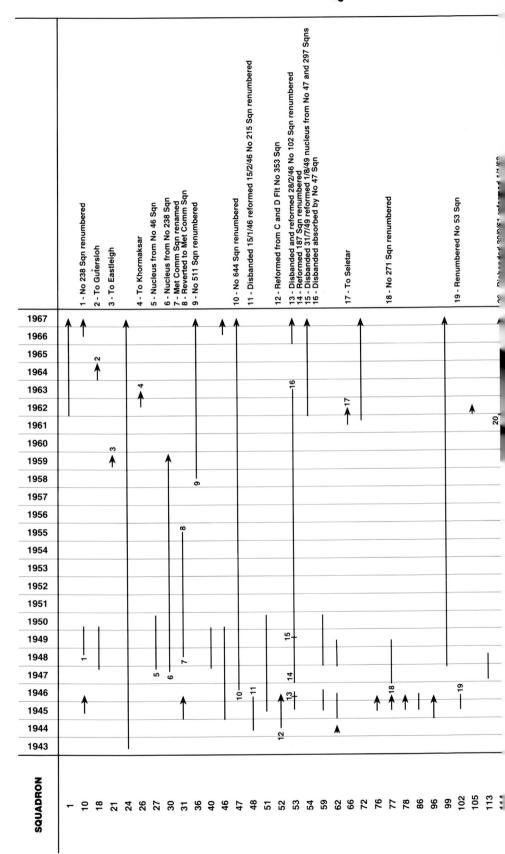

1 - No 238 Sqn renumbered
2 - To Gütersloh
3 - To Eastleigh
4 - To Khormaksar
5 - Nucleus from No 46 Sqn
6 - Nucleus from No 238 Sqn
7 - Met Comm Sqn renamed
8 - Reverted to Met Comm Sqn
9 - No 511 Sqn renumbered
10 - No 644 Sqn renumbered
11 - Disbanded 15/1/46 reformed 15/2/46 No 215 Sqn renumbered
12 - Reformed from C and D Flt No 353 Sqn
13 - Disbanded and reformed 28/2/46 No 102 Sqn renumbered
14 - Reformed 187 Sqn renumbered
15 - Disbanded 31/7/49 reformed 1/8/49 nucleus from No 47 and 297 Sqns
16 - Disbanded absorbed by No 47 Sqn
17 - To Seletar
18 - No 271 Sqn renumbered
19 - Renumbered No 53 Sqn

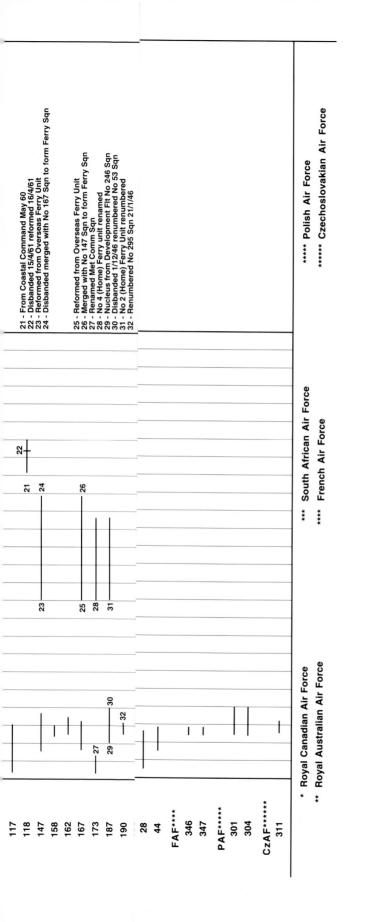

21 - From Coastal Command May 60
22 - Disbanded 15/4/61 reformed 16/4/61
23 - Reformed from Overseas Ferry Unit
24 - Disbanded merged with No 167 Sqn to form Ferry Sqn

25 - Reformed from Overseas Ferry Unit
26 - Merged with No 147 Sqn to form Ferry Sqn
27 - Renamed Met Comm Sqn
28 - No 4 (Home) Ferry unit renamed
29 - Nucleus from Development Flt No 246 Sqn
30 - Disbanded 1/12/46 renumbered No 53 Sqn
31 - No 2 (Home) Ferry Unit renumbered
32 - Renumbered No 295 Sqn 21/1/46

117
118
147
158
162
167
173
187
190

28
44

FAF****
346
347

PAF*****
301
304

CzAF******
311

* Royal Canadian Air Force
** Royal Australian Air Force
*** South African Air Force
**** French Air Force
***** Polish Air Force
****** Czechoslovakian Air Force

Hunter

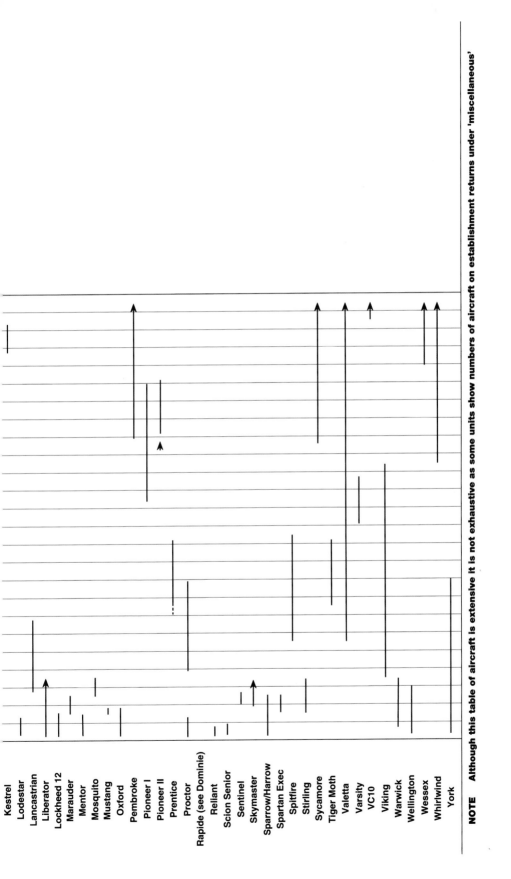

Kestrel
Lodestar
Lancastrian
Liberator
Lockheed 12
Marauder
Mentor
Mosquito
Mustang
Oxford
Pembroke
Pioneer I
Pioneer II
Prentice
Proctor
Rapide (see Dominie)
Reliant
Scion Senior
Sentinel
Skymaster
Sparrow/Harrow
Spartan Exec
Spitfire
Stirling
Sycamore
Tiger Moth
Valetta
Varsity
VC10
Viking
Warwick
Wellington
Wessex
Whirlwind
York

NOTE Although this table of aircraft is extensive it is not exhaustive as some units show numbers of aircraft on establishment returns under 'miscellaneous'

TRANSPORT COMMAND
LOCATION OF UNITS - OCTOBER 1943

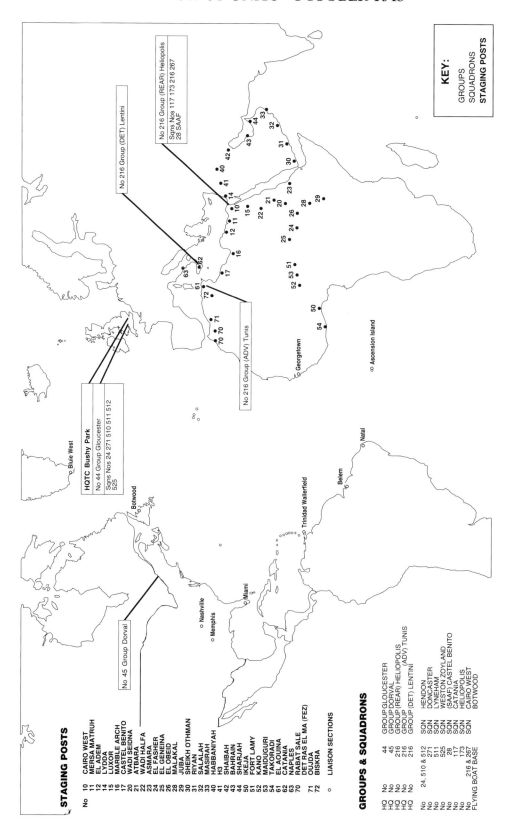

No 216 Group (REAR) Heliopolis
Sqns Nos 117 173 216 267
28 SAAF

No 216 Group (DET) Lentini

No 216 Group (ADV) Tunis

HQTC Bushy Park
No 44 Group Gloucester
Sqns Nos 24 271 510 511 512
525

No 45 Group Dorval

KEY:
GROUPS
SQUADRONS
STAGING POSTS

Bluie West

Botwood

Nashville
Memphis
Miami

Trinidad Wallerfield

Belem

Natal

Georgetown

Ascension Island

STAGING POSTS

No	10	CAIRO WEST
	11	MERSA MATRUH
	12	EL ADEM
	13	LYDDA
	15	LUXOR
	16	MARBLE ARCH
	17	CASTEL BENITO
	20	WADI SEIDNA
	21	ATBARA
	22	WADI HALFA
	23	ASMARA
	24	EL FASHER
	25	EL GENEINA
	26	EL OBEID
	28	MALAKAL
	29	JUBA
	30	SHEIKH OTHMAN
	31	RIYAN
	32	SALALAH
	33	MASIRAH
	40	HABBANIYAH
	41	H3
	42	SHAIBAH
	43	BAHRAIN
	44	SHARJAH
	50	IKEJA
	51	FORT LAMY
	52	KANO
	53	MAIDUGURI
	54	TAKORADI
	61	EL AOUINA
	62	CATANIA
	63	NAPLES
	70	RABAT SALE
		DET RAS EL MA (FEZ)
	71	OUJDA
	72	BISKRA
	o	LIAISON SECTIONS

GROUPS & SQUADRONS

HQ	No	44	GROUP	GLOUCESTER
HQ	No	45	GROUP	DORVAL
HQ	No	216	GROUP (REAR)	HELIOPOLIS
HQ	No	216	GROUP (ADV)	TUNIS
HQ	No	216	GROUP (DET)	LENTINI
No	24, 510 & 512		SQN	HENDON
No	271		SQN	DONCASTER
No	511		SQN	LYNEHAM
No	525		SQN	WESTON ZOYLAND
No	28		SQN	(SAAF) CASTEL BENITO
No	117		SQN	CATANIA
No	173		SQN	HELIOPOLIS
No	216 & 267		SQN	CAIRO WEST
FLYING BOAT BASE				BOTWOOD

Appendix B

AOsC-in-C
Transport Command, 1943–67

1943–45   Air Chief Marshal Sir Frederick W Bowhill GBE KCB CMG
          DSO
1945–47   Air Marshal the Hon Sir Ralph A Cochrane KBE CB AFC
1947–50   Air Marshal Sir Brian Baker KBE CB DSO MC AFC
1950–52   Air Marshal Sir Aubrey B Ellwood KCB DSO
1952   Air Vice-Marshal R S Blucke CB CBE DSO AFC
1952–54   Air Vice-Marshal C E N Guest CB CBE
1954–55   Air Vice-Marshal G R Beamish CB CBE
1955–59   Air Vice-Marshal (later Air Marshal Sir) Andrew McKee
          KCB CBE DSO DFC AFC
1959–62   Air Marshal Sir Denis H F Barnett KCB CBE DFC MA
1962–63   Air Chief Marshal Sir Edmund Hudleston GCB CBE ADC
1963–67   Air Marshal Sir Kenneth Cross KCB CBE DSO DFC
1967   Air Marshal Sir Thomas O Prickett KCB DSO DFC

Appendix C

Chronology

1943

25 March	Transport Command formed.
2 April	HQ transferred to Harrow.
11 April	No 45 (Transport) Group formed.
3 May	Avro York introduced as VIP aircraft.
9/10 July	Operation Husky mounted.
Sep–Nov	Operation Accolade.
	Operation Microbe.
16 Dec	No 179 Wing becomes No 229 (Transport) Group.
31 Dec	No 113 (South Atlantic) Wing despatched 1,000th aircraft

1944

4 Feb	No 46 Group HQ staff took up appointments.
10 Feb	First York (MW 104) taken on charge by No 511 Sqn.
4 Jun	15,000th crossing of Atlantic by RAF and US ATC.
6 Jun	D-day – Operation Overlord.
17 Sep	Operation Market – Arnhem.
14 Nov	York MW 126, carrying ACM Sir T Leigh-Mallory to take up his new appointment as Air Commander, South-East Asia Command, disappears en route Northolt–Naples. Wreckage not discovered until 4 June 1945 in mountains east of Grenoble. There were no survivors.

1945

15 Feb	ACM Sir F Bowhill retires – succeeded by AM Sir R Cochrane.
23 Mar	Operation Varsity – Rhine crossing.
7 May	VE day.
15 May	Air Ministry authority given for transfer of No 4 Group sqns to Transport Command.
6 & 9 Aug	Atomic bombs dropped on Hiroshima and Nagasaki.
15 Aug	VJ day.

158

| Oct | Large scale UK–India trooping began. |
| 15 Dec | Trooping lift of Dakotas increased. |

1946

2 Jan	UK–India trooping programme to be reduced.
15 Feb	No 45 Group to 'roll up' by this date: reduced to Wing status.
5 Mar	Air Ministry Directive issued delegating Transport Command responsibilities to individual Commands.
16 Mar	No 229 Group ceased to be a Transport Command Group; came under the direct control of AHQ India.
1 Aug	No 44 Group closed down.

1947

Jan	Re-organisation of Transport Command discussed.
22 Sep	Exercise Longstop – first airborne manoeuvres in UK since the end of the war.
Oct	Four Yorks of No 511 Sqn engaged in the transport of refugees from India to Pakistan and from Pakistan to India.

1948

| 28 Jun | Operation Plainfare – Berlin Airlift – begins. |
| Sep | Hastings C.1 enters service with No 47 Sqn. |

1949

| 12 May | Operation Plainfare ends. |
| May | Valetta enters squadron service with No 204 Sqn, Kabrit. |

1950

| Apr | Transport Command Headquarters moved to Upavon. |
| 21 Oct | Last flight in UK–Japan airlift of 600 British troops to Korea. |

1951

| Mar | No 47 Sqn Hastings detachment to Singapore for Japan shuttle begins. Transport Command aircrew detached to Fayid to stand by for operations resulting from threat to nationalise the Abadan refineries. |

1952 Troops flown to Kenya during Mau Mau campaign.

1953 In East coast flood disasters, sandbags flown in from Milan and Zurich. Supplies flown to Ionian Islands earthquake victims.

1954	Air Council considered long-range transport force requirements.
1955	Air Council discussed the future role and policy of Transport Command.

1956

12 March	First Blackburn Beverley C.1 left Brough on delivery flight to No 47 Sqn, Abingdon.
Apr	Beverley made first overseas proving flight.
23 June	First operational RAF Comet flight, by C.2 XK 670 to Moscow.
Oct	Suez 'Operation Musketeer': Transport Command transported men and materiel, evacuated casualties and operated in paratroop and leaflet-dropping roles.

1957	Support for Operation Grapple nuclear tests: weekly Comet service to Christmas Island inaugurated. Uplift of troops to Cyprus during EOKA troubles.
17 Sep	Comet 2 makes first direct Atlantic crossing by an aircraft of this type.

1958	Flights to Jordan and Lebanon during crises there.

1959

29 May	Hastings crash near Khartoum, en route from Aden to the UK.
9 Jun	First military Britannia (XL636) handed-over to No 99 Sqn.

1960

1 Jan	No 38 Group re-formed at Odiham.
Feb–Mar	Exercise Starlight, based on El Adem.
21 Dec	Minister of Aviation announced in House of Commons that contract had been placed with Shorts for ten Belfasts.

1961

4 Mar	First Argosy C.1 for Transport Command made first flight.
12 Mar	Beverley completed five years in operational service.
Apr	Two Britannias of Nos 99 and 511 Sqns carried out an airlift of Indian troops from Dar-es-Salaam to Kamina in the Congo at the request of the UN.
Apr–May	Exercise Fabulist – Cyprus.
20 Jun	No 216 Sqn adopted by the Worshipful Company of Coachmakers and Coach Harness Makers.

15 Sep	First Belvedere squadron (No 66) formed.
Oct–Dec	First Argosies received at RAF Benson.

1962

Jan	First Comet 4Cs arrive at Lyneham.
Feb	Argosy C.1s introduced into squadron service (No 114 Sqn).
26–28 Sep	Exercise Falltrap – Greece.

1963

26–29 Aug	No 38 Group G/A Wing (Nos 1 and 54 Sqns) moved to West Raynham.

1964

Oct	General Election – Labour Government elected.

1965

Apr	Cuts in Defence programme announced – HS681 cancelled.
20 Dec	Zambian oil airlift begins.

1966

20 Jan	First Belfast received by No 53 Sqn at Brize Norton.
7 Jul	First VC10 handed-over at Wisley.
1 Sept	No 46 Sqn reformed as first Andover squadron.
31 Oct	Zambian oil airlift ended.
16 Dec	First of 66 C-130s for RAF handed-over at Lockheed– Georgia.

1967

20 Jan	No 10 Sqn flew first VC10 operational sortie – to Changi.
1 Aug	Transport Command became 'Air Support Command'. First C-130K Hercules for No 36 Sqn delivered to RAF Lyneham.

Appendix D

Glossary

A&AEE	Aircraft and Armament Experimental Establishment
AASF	Advanced Air Striking Force
AC	Aircraftman
AC	Air Council
ACAS(P)	Assistant Chief of Air Staff (Policy)
ACM	Air Chief Marshal
ACSEA	Air Command South East Asia
ADLS	Air Despatch Letter Service
ADO(F)	Assistant Directorate of Organisation (Ferrying)
ADU	Aircraft Delivery Unit
AFC	Air Force Cross
AFB	Air Force Board/Air Force Base
AGS	Aircraft Ground Support
AHB	Air Historical Branch (RAF)
AHQ	Air Headquarters
Air Cdre	Air Commodore
AM	Air Marshal
AMC BAFSEA	Air Marshal Commanding Base Air Forces South East Asia
AMSO	Air Member for Supply and Organisation
AOG	Aircraft on Ground
AOC	Air Officer Commanding
AOC-in-C	Air Officer Commanding-in-Chief
AQM	Air Quartermaster
ARB	Air Registration Board
ASC	Air Support Command
ATA	Air Transport Auxiliary
ATAF	Allied Tactical Air Force
ATC	Air Traffic Control
ATFERO	Atlantic Ferry Organisation

auw	All-Up Weight
AVM	Air Vice-Marshal
AW	Armstrong Whitworth
AWRE	Atomic Weapons Research Establishment
BABS	Blind Approach Beacon System (Navigation/Airfield Approach Aid)
BAC	British Aircraft Corporation
BAFSEA	British Air Forces South East Asia
BOAC	British Overseas Airways Corporation
BPC	British Purchasing Commission
CA	Controller of Aircraft
CAS	Chief of the Air Staff
CB	Companion, Order of the Bath
CBE	Commander, Order of the British Empire
C-in-C	Commander-in-Chief
CIGS	Chief of the Imperial General Staff
CMG	Companion of the Order of St Michael and St George
CO	Commanding Officer
C of A	Certificate of Airworthiness
COM BRITZAM	Commander, British Forces Zambia
CoS	Chiefs of Staff
Comms	Communications (Aircraft)
Cpl	Corporal
DCAS	Deputy Chief of Air Staff
DFC	Distinguished Flying Cross
DFM	Distinguished Flying Medal
DGO	Director General of Organisation
DH	De Havilland
DP	Displaced Person
DSO	Distinguished Service Order
DZ	Dropping Zone
ELDO	European Launcher Development Organisation
EOKA	Ethniki Organosis Kyprion Agoniston
FC	Ferry Control
FEAF	Far East Air Force
FGA	Fighter/Ground Attack
Fg Off	Flying Officer

Flt Lt	Flight Lieutenant
Flt Sgt	Flight Sergeant
FR	Fighter Reconnaissance
GA	Ground Attack
GBE	Knight Grand Cross, Order of the British Empire
GCB	Knight Grand Cross, Order of the Bath
Gp Capt	Group Captain
HS	Hawker Siddeley
IG	Inspector General
JEHU	Joint Experimental Helicopter Unit
KBE	Knight Commander, Order of the British Empire
KCB	Knight Commander, Order of the Bath
LCN	Load Classification Number
LG	Landing Ground
Lt	Lieutenant
Lt-Col	Lieutenant Colonel
LTB LTH LTD	Code letters for the 1945 Large-scale Trooping Operation to India. The third letter indicated the squadron: e.g. LTD referred to Nos 187 and 525 (Dakota) Sqns, LTH to No 246 (York) Sqn and LTB to Nos 271 and 575 (Dakota) Sqns
Maj	Major
MAM	Mobile Air Movements
MAP	Ministry of Aircraft Production
MBE	Member, Order of the British Empire
MC	Military Cross
ME	Middle East
MEAF	Middle East Air Force
MEDME	Mediterranean/Middle East
MF	Medium-range Freighter
MRAF	Marshal of the Royal Air Force
MT	Motor Transport
MTCA	Ministry of Transport and Civil Aviation
MU	Maintenance Unit
MVO	Member of the Victorian Order
NATAF	North African Tactical Air Force

164

NATO	North Atlantic Treaty Organisation
NCO	Non-commissioned Officer
nm	nautical miles
OAMCU	Overseas Air Movements Control Unit
OC	Officer Commanding
OCU	Operational Conversion Unit
OR	Operational Requirement
ORB	Operations Record Book
ORBAT	Order of Battle
PAA	Pan American Airways
Plt Off	Pilot Officer
PR	Photographic Reconnaissance
PoW	Prisoner of War
PRO	Public Record Office
PUS	Permanent Under Secretary
QRA	Quick Reaction Alert
R&D	Research and Development
RAAF	Royal Australian Air Force
RAuxAF	Royal Auxiliary Air Force
RAE	Royal Aeronautical Establishment
RCAF	Royal Canadian Air Force
RFC	Royal Flying Corps
RNAS	Royal Naval Air Service
RNZAF	Royal New Zealand Air Force
RSP	Route Staging Post
RSU	Repair and Salvage Unit
SAAF	South African Air Force
SAC	Strategic Air Command (USAF)
SAM	Surface to Air Missile
SASO	Senior Air Staff Officer
SBAC	Society of British Aerospace Companies
SEA	South-east Asia
SFTS	Service Flying Training School
Sgt	Sergeant
SHAPE	Supreme Headquarters, Allied Powers Europe
SOA	Senior Officer Administration
S of S	Secretary of State

SP	Staging Post
Sqn	Squadron
Sqn Ldr	Squadron Leader
SS	Steamship
st	static thrust
st mi	statute miles
ST	Small-scale Trooping
STOL	Short Take-off and Landing
TAC	Transit Atlantic Control
TSR	Tactical/strike reconnaissance
UDI	Unilateral Declaration of Independence (Rhodesia)
UE	Unit Establishment
UKT	Code designation for Transport Command schedule flights from Lyneham to Allahabad and return; flown by Dakotas in June 1945 and Stirlings in September 1945
UM	Code designation for Transport Command schedule flights from Lyneham to Cairo West, returning to either Lyneham or Hendon; flown by Dakotas in June 1945 and Stirlings in September 1945
USAAC	United States Army Air Corps
USAAF	United States Army Air Force
USAF	United States Air Force
US of S	Under-Secretary of State
VC	Victoria Cross
VCAS	Vice Chief of Air Staff
VHF	Very High Frequency (Radio)
VIP	Very Important Person
V/STOL	Vertical/Short take-off and landing
VVIP	Very Very Important Person
Wg Cdr	Wing Commander
WO	Warrant Officer
WOp/AG	Wireless Operator/Air gunner
WT	Wireless Telegraphy

Appendix E

Selective Bibliography

Michael J F Bowyer *Aircraft for the Few The RAF's Fighters and Bombers in 1940*; Patrick Stephens Ltd, 1991

Alan Bramson *Master Airman A Biography of Air Vice-Marshal D C T Bennett CB CBE DSO*; Airlife, 1985

J Burtt-Smith *One of the Many on the Move*; Merlin Books, 1992

Carl A Christie *Ocean Bridge The History of RAF Ferry Command*; University of Toronto Press/Midland Publishing Ltd, 1995

Winston Churchill *The Second World War, Vol II Their Finest Hour*; Cassell & Co, 1949

Air Chief Marshal Sir Kenneth Cross KCB CBE DSO DFC *Straight and Level*; Grub Street, 1993

Air Vice-Marshal Tony Dudgeon CBE DFC *Wings over North Africa*; Airlife, 1987

Group Captain Patrick Foss *Climbing Turns*; Linden Hall, 1990

Don McVicar *Ferry Command*; Airlife, 1981

John Stroud *Annals of British and Commonwealth Air Transport*; Putnam, 1962

Owen Thetford *Aircraft of the Royal Air Force since 1918*; Putnam, 1988

Index

PRINCIPAL ROUTES TRANSPORT COMMAND 1957
AND THE MIDDLE EAST AIR BARRIER 1957

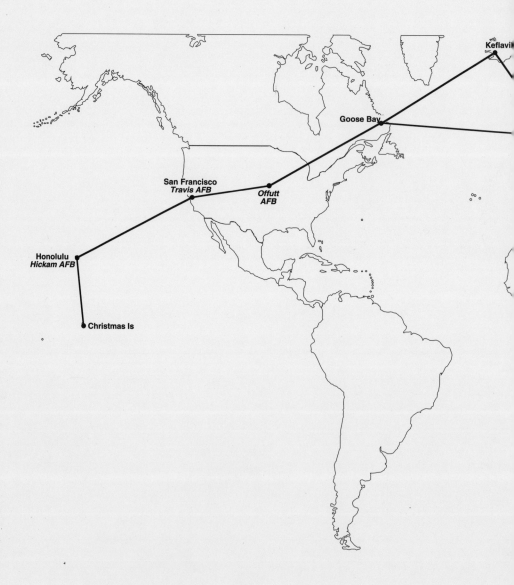

Keflavi[k]

Goose Bay

San Francisco
Travis AFB

*Offutt
AFB*

Honolulu
Hickam AFB

Christmas Is

NOTE: Precise route depended on
type of aircraft, payload, weather,
diplomatic clearance.